每天聊点美国文化

美国文化

一本书读懂美国

金利 主 编

肖严艳 杨云云 副主编

化学工业出版社

·北京·

前言

　　我们从小受到东方文化的熏陶，即使学了很多年英语，一般只是应试性的"背单词、学语法"。当我们读国外文章或看美剧的时候，有时会无法理解美国人的思考方式，觉得他们的笑话很"冷"，行为也非常"怪诞"。美国文化对我们来说仿佛是罩着一层神秘的面纱，让大家不了解真正的美国。

　　学习英语很多年，对美国人嘴里的口头禅，美国的特色俚语表达只是懂其"中文意思"，却不知道它们真正的来源以及地道准确的用法；很多时候背诵的单词都缺乏语言环境，导致大家记忆都不够深刻。不用担心！这本书将填补各位读者在学习英语过程中的缺憾，带你追根溯源，让你在一边浏览美国景色、品读趣闻的同时，一边记下难以消化的单词和特色表达、"夸夸其谈"美国文化！

【近距离看美国】

　　通过这本书，那些具有神秘感的自由女神、对世界经济举足轻重的金融华尔街、高端科技聚集的硅谷等美国文化标志在你面前通通"现身"，让你近距离了解它们。此外，我们还会揭秘美国人为何不选择公共交通、美国孩子为何如此独立、美国老人为何这么不服老？为你"捅破"美国文化这层窗户纸，让你对美国文化了如指掌。

【地毯式涵盖美国文化】

　　本书围绕11大分类，近79个主题，对美国的历史趣闻、体育音乐、影视娱乐、风土人情、民间习俗等方方面面进行地毯式涵盖，此外还会在每个主题里就相关内容进行延展，形式丰富，增强本书的可读性和趣味性；拓展形式有对主题下相关的名人轶事、特色景点、特色表达、历史事件的讲解。

【边品美国文化边学英语】

　　我们会针对每个主题，从国外网站选取地道的英文素材，语言地道，且附有中文翻译和生词讲解，让读者在品读美国文化的同时也学到英语知识。在对美国文化背景进行中英双讲之后，对相关主题里的特色俚语和特色表达进行深度讲解，让你知道它们的"来源"。此外，我们还会拓展与主题相关的特色英语句子，最后会与你一起用地道的英语侃谈美国文化。

　　这本书精心制作给对美国文化有浓厚兴趣的爱好者以及想提高口语能力的英语学习者。衷心希望此书能给你带来更精彩、更美好的生活！

编者

目录

Part 7 为何美国没有"北漂"现象

Part 8 不可不看的美国特色地标

Part 9 音乐和体育

Part 10 教育

Part 11 穿越回去看看美国历史

Part 1

美国人原来这样想

美国人的笑点在哪里

美式幽默有哪些

American humor usually *concerns* aspects of American culture, and depends on the historical and current development of the country's culture. The extent to which an *individual* will personally find something humorous obviously depends on a host of *absolute* and relative *variables*, including, but not limited to *geographical location*, culture, *maturity*, level of education, and context.

American humor might also be *distinguished* by its most common type of humor, for example, more *slapstick* and *physical* comedy. There is less emphasis on understatement, and so the humor tends to be more open; rather than *satirizing* the social system through *exaggeration*.

Candidate for the "founding father" of American humor is Mark Twain, the man Ernest Hemingway credits with the invention of American literature. Humor began to emerge in the United States soon after the American Revolution in written and spoken form, and delivery methods have continued to *evolve* since then.

美式幽默通常涉及美国文化的方方面面，它取决于美国的历史文化与当下文化的发展。美国人觉得事情是否幽默明显取决于许多绝对或相对的变量，包括地理位置、文化、听者是否成熟、教育程度、上下语境。

美式幽默也能通过其最常见的幽默类型区分开来，比如闹剧、肢体喜剧。不再注重含蓄陈述的方式，所以幽默变得更开放，而非通过夸张的手法对社会体系进行讽刺。

欧内斯特·海明威把美国文学归功于美国式幽默创始人的候选人马克·吐温。书写式和口头式幽默在美国独立战争后开始浮现。流传的方法也从那时起发展起来。

单词释义

concern 关注	individual 个人的	absolute 绝对的
variable 变量	geographical 地理的	location 位置
maturity 成熟	distinguished 著名的	slapstick 闹剧
physical 生理的	satirize 讽刺	exaggeration 夸张

千万不要拿美国文化开玩笑

Americans cannot laugh at their own culture. That *deficiency*, in fact, is the *defining trait* of American culture.

To be precise, the problem is not that Americans do not like to laugh at their own culture, but that they cannot, whether they wish to or not. At first *glance* that seems out of character. As individuals, Americans will laugh at themselves all day long. So much do they love self-deprecating humor that few politicians *attain* high office without a *knack* for it. "I sure hope you guys are Republicans," Reagan told the surgeons as they wheeled him into the operating room after John Hinckley shot him.

Nevertheless, they cannot laugh at their culture. Consider American humor in general: a tell-tale trait of it is the absence of "American" jokes, that is, jokes about Americans as such. Americans tell *ethnic* jokes, *regional* jokes, or *generic* jokes. But there are no characteristically American jokes, for the simple reason that there are no American characteristics.

美国人不能拿自己的文化开玩笑，事实上，这个缺点正是美国文化最典型的特点。

确切来讲，问题并不是美国人不喜欢拿他们自己的文化开玩笑，而是他们办不到，无论他们希望与否。乍一看觉得出乎意料。作为个体，美国人整天都拿自己开玩笑。他们非常喜爱自嘲的笑话，所以很少有不自嘲就登上要职的政客。里根总统在被约翰·辛克利枪击之后，对推他进入手术室的一群医生开玩笑道："我多么希望你们这些家伙是共和党人啊！"

然而他们不能开他们国家文化的玩笑。细想一下美式幽默大体上都有一种不可言喻的特质，缺乏"美国味"的笑话，也就是关于美国人的笑话，比如：宗教笑话、地方笑话、通用笑话。但是却没有典型性的美式笑话，原因很简单，因为美国没有特色。

单词释义

deficiency 缺点	defining 最典型的	trait 特点
glance 一瞥	attain 获得	knack 诀窍
ethnic 种族的	regional 区域的	generic 一般的

 美国特色文化

特色表达One

在美国，朋友间表示我理解你或者我懂你的意思时常用到I got you. 那么I got you.就只有这个意思吗？其实它还有其他用法，比如恶作剧的时候吓到了小伙伴，可以假装安慰一句Got you! 意思是"吓到你了吧！"或者是"上当了吧！"若你没被吓着就对他说：Haha... You didn't get me.

☆ 实景链接

A：Did you see the results? 你看了考试结果了吗？

B：Yeah, you failed again. I am so sorry. 看了，很遗憾，你又没过。

A：What? Why? I tried so hard. Wait, what are you laughing at? 什么？为什么？我那么努力。等等，你笑什么呢？

B：Haha... **got you**! 哈，你上当了！

特色表达Two

美国人爱笑，他们有各种各样的笑法，最痛快的莫过于belly laugh。belly是肚子，那么belly laugh就是捧着肚子笑，指极其好笑到肚子都"笑"了。美国人喜欢看comedian（喜剧演员）演的comedies（喜剧），因为他们觉得They are so full of belly laughs.（有好多地方让人感到非常好笑。）

☆ 实景链接

A：Hey, did you watch Johnny Carson last night? 嘿，你昨晚看约翰·卡森的节目了吗？

B：Of course. How can I miss that? 当然了，我怎么能错过呢？

A：I think last night was one of his best shows in a long time. 我觉得昨晚是他这么长时间以来最棒的一期。

B: Yeah, he got some great **belly laughs** trading jokes with his guest star. 是啊，他和嘉宾明星开的玩笑让很多人捧腹大笑呢。

拓展特色句

1. Where can I dump these white elephants? 这些无用的垃圾我要丢到哪里？

2. We have a female shortage here. 我们这里闹女人荒。

3. He told a story full of humor before the speech. 他在演讲前讲了一个非常幽默的故事。

"聊" 美国特色文化

A: Jack, I really can't understand your humor.

B: It's true that every culture's funny bone is tickled a different way. It's hard for you non-Americans to see why our jokes are funny.

A: Then how can I do it?

B: Humor is based on shared experiences and background knowledge. If you know what to look for, you can learn to appreciate American humor.

A: What are the basic parts of American humor?

B: The pun, or the play on words. Some people consider the pun a low form of humor, but many Americans still enjoy punishing each other.

A: Moreover, I found you like enjoy the kind of question-and-answer humor.

B: That's it.

A: 杰克，我真的无法理解你们的幽默。

B: 确实是每种文化的"笑点"都不尽相同。不是美国人就很难了解美式笑话的好笑之处。

A: 那我如何才能理解呢？

B: 幽默是建立在共有的经历和背景知识之上的。如果你能掌握诀窍，你就可以欣赏美式幽默了。

A: 美式幽默有哪些基本的组成部分呢？

B: 双关语，或称作文字游戏。有些人觉得双关语是一种比较低级的幽默方式，但是很多美国人仍然喜欢以双关语彼此开玩笑。

A: 此外，我发现你们很喜欢问答式的幽默。

B: 是这样的。

 美国特色文化

在美国，你能笑口常开？

在美国，各种幽默搞笑总能博你一笑。比如说，在洛杉矶至圣地亚哥的高速公路上，你也许会看见一辆德国产甲壳虫轿车在车流中显得娇小可爱，然而，后车窗却俏皮地写着：长大以后，我就变成卡迪拉克啦！或者是洛杉矶一家大型超市在报上刊登了这样一条广告词：你可以在这儿买到所有需要的一切，除了你的家人之外。这就是让人忍俊不禁的美式幽默。

阅读笔记

TOP 2 美国人的"洁癖"，你是否能够忍受

在美国，气味和整洁很重要

Americans are known for having very *sensitive* noses. In America, "B.O." (body *odor*) is socially unacceptable. For that reason, Americans consider the use of *deodorant* or *anti-perspirant* a must. Ladies often add a touch of perfume for an extra fresh scent. Men may *splash* on after-shave *lotion* or manly-smelling cologne. Another cultural no-no in America is bad breath. Americans don't like to smell what other people ate for lunch—especially onions or garlic. Their solution? Mouthwash, breath mints and even brushing their teeth after meals.

Grooming and personal *hygiene* have been around for ages. It's hard to imagine a time when people weren't concerned with taking care of their appearance and their bodies. Perhaps these *practices* started when Adam first took a bath and combed his hair before going on a date with Eve. Or maybe they began when Eve put on some *herbal* makeup to make herself more beautiful. No matter where they started, grooming and personal hygiene have become an important part of everyone's daily routine.

众所周知，美国人的鼻子非常灵敏。在美国，体臭在社交上是无法令人接受的。正是因为这个原因，美国人会认为使用除臭剂或止汗剂是必需的。女士们通常会再抹点香水以增加清香；男士则涂抹一些刮胡润肤膏或是男性古龙香水在脸上。美国的另一项禁忌是口臭。美国人不喜欢闻别人午餐后留在口中的味道——尤其是洋葱或大蒜。那他们是如何解决的呢？他们通过漱口、吃薄荷糖，甚至饭后刷牙来解决。

仪容整洁和个人卫生的讲究已经存在数年了。很难想象会有人们对打理外表和身体漠不关心的时代。或许这些卫生习惯始于亚当第一次洗澡梳头去和夏娃约会；也可能始于夏娃第一次涂抹青草制成的化妆品使自己更美丽。无论是从何时开始的，仪容与个人卫生已经成为每个人生活例行事务中重要的一部分。

单词释义

sensitive 敏感的   odor 气味   deodorant 除臭剂
anti-perspirant 防汗剂   splash 飞溅   lotion 洗液
hygiene 卫生   practice 惯例   herbal 草药的

美国奇葩的卫生习惯

You might think that all modern societies would have the same *grooming* and personal hygiene practices. After all, doesn't everybody take baths? Most people do recognize the need for hygiene, which is the *basis* for *cleanliness* and health—and a good way to keep one's friends. Grooming practices include all the little things people do to make themselves look their best, such as combing their hair and putting on makeup. However, while most modern people agree that these things are important, people in different cultures *take care of* themselves in different ways.

There *used to* be an old joke in America that people should take a bath once a week, whether they need one or not. In fact, though, Americans generally take a bath—or more commonly, a shower—every day. But in contrast to some cultures, most Americans get their *shower* in the morning, so they can start the day fresh. And *instead of* going to a beauty *parlor* for a *shampoo*,

你可能会认为所有现代社会中的仪容整洁与卫生习惯都是一样的。因为毕竟，每个人都是会洗澡的，这毋庸置疑。大部分人的确肯定卫生的必要性，它是清洁与健康的基础，也是维持友谊的好办法。仪容习惯涵盖了所有可以使人看起来体面的琐碎小事，像是梳头和化妆。虽然大多数的现代人都同意这些事很重要，但不同文化背景的人打理自己的方法也不一样。

以前在美国有一个老笑话，说不管人们需不需要，他们每个礼拜都必须洗一次澡。不过事实上，美国人每天会洗一次澡，或者更普遍的做法是每天淋浴一次。但是不同于某些文化习惯的是，美国人在清晨淋浴，以使

many Americans prefer to wash and style their own hair. So if Americans have a "bad hair day," they have no one to blame but themselves. But most people in America do *head for* the beauty parlor or *barber* shop occasionally for a haircut, a *perm* or just some friendly conversation.

他们展开清新的一天。而且美国人不上美容院去洗头，他们更愿意自己洗头和整理发型。所以美国人如果有一天头发很丑，除了怪自己之外就没什么可责怪的了。但是大部分的美国人偶尔还是会到美容院或理发厅去剪头发、烫头发，或是去跟人聊聊天。

单词释义

groom 打扮	basis 基础	cleanliness 清洁
shower 淋浴	parlor 客厅	shampoo 洗发
barber 理发师	perm 烫(发)	head for 前往
take care of 照顾	used to 过去……	instead of 而不是……

  美国特色文化

特色表达One

美国人很爱干净，看到好友房间乱得一团糟会毫不犹豫地指责"This room is an absolute armpit!"其实armpit本意是腋窝，对有洁癖的美国人而言，腋窝就是堆满污垢的汗水之地，所以俚语里用armpit来形容很脏、令人难以忍受的地方。另外，美国的女孩子流行刮掉腋毛，她们认为留着腋毛是很恶心且没有礼貌的事。

☆ 实景链接

A：Hey, I was just looking for you. 嘿，我正要找你呢。

B：What's up? 什么事？

A：Do you know where does Noah live? I am gonna return him some books. 你知道诺亚住哪儿吗？还他几本书。

B：Oh god, **his room is an absolute armpit**. You'll never wanna go there again. 天哪，他的房间真是脏得不像话。你再也不会想去那儿的。

💬 特色表达Two

在美国，很多人认为有洁癖的人一定be beaut。注意这里是beaut而不是beauty，但这个词语却与beauty有关，因为beaut是beauty的缩写，在19世纪中期的时候，人们常用beaut表示"漂亮的，吸引人的"。

☆ 实景链接

A： You are real **beaut**. 你真美。

B： I am flattered. I just do beauty on a regular basis. 过奖了，我只是定期做美容罢了。

A： No wonder does your spirit soar. 难怪你看起来这么精神焕发。

B： You can join in the beauty club. 你可以加入美容俱乐部。

拓展特色句

1. Don't left a mess in the kitchen. 别把厨房弄得一团糟。

2. Take out the food garbage. It stinks. 把垃圾拿出去，太臭了。

3. Roll your underwear and cram them in the second drawer. 把你的内衣卷起来塞进第二个抽屉里。

💬 "聊" 美国特色文化

A： Uhh, the kitchen is a pigsty.

B： Well, these days I am preparing for an examination. I can't put my attention on such things.

A： I really can't stand it. It's really gross here. I have to clean it.

B： Don't be. I will clean it after the examination tomorrow.

A： How can you study in such a disgusting environment? I thought you Americans are neat freaks.

B： I guess it really depends. I would like to consider myself a clean freak, but

A： 天啦，厨房像猪圈一样。

B： 好吧，这些天我都在准备考试，我无法把我的注意力放在这些事情上面。

A： 我真的无法忍受了。这里真的很脏乱。我得打扫一下。

B： 不用了，我明天考完试之后就会清理它的。

A： 你是如何能在这样的环境下学习的呢？我还以为你们美国人很爱卫生呢？

B： 我觉得这要视情况而定，我觉得自己是很爱干净的人，但是当我很忙的时候，我最后才会考虑清洁的问题。

it means if I am really busy, cleaning is the last priority.

A: Is that true? I begin to suspect it's due to your lack of hygiene.

B: Hey, hold up. We are outta here!

A: 是这样的吗？我开始怀疑这是因为你不爱卫生。

B: 别瞎猜了，我们要走了！

 美国特色文化

美国人洁癖到何种地步了？

如今的美国市场上随处可见各种各样的抗菌消毒产品。各大商家似乎给消费者一种难以抗拒的印象：别人碰过的地方你就不要碰了。而近几年来，多次公共卫生引起的恐慌也让各式各样的抗菌产品应运而生。如用消毒干雾杀死厕所门把手细菌；用"清洁购物贴"盖住购物车把手；用塑料袋套住电视机遥控器；用"城市手套"对付地铁扶手。

阅读笔记

打喷嚏能赢得祝福吗

打喷嚏的神话色彩

In America, people say "bless you" when someone sneezes. It is not sure how the tradition comes, but there are two possible stories about this.

The first one is related to the Pope Gregory I. In 590, the bubonic plague was reaching Rome. At the time, sneezing was considered to be an early *symptom* of the *plague*. The blessing became a common effort to *halt* the disease. It was also supposed the phrase could heal the disease.

Another version says that people believed that the soul can be thrown from the body when someone sneezing. Because sneezing opened the person's body so that the devil or evil spirits could *invade* the body or that sneezing was the body's effort to force out an invading evil spirit. Thus, "bless you" or "God bless you" is thought to be a sort of *shield* against evil.

Some people also believed that the heart stops when you sneeze, and the phrase "bless you" is a charm/blessing/prayer which is meant to ensure the return of life or to encourage your heart to continue beating. A similar version says that

在美国，如果有人打喷嚏，周围人就会说"保佑你"。有关这个习俗的来源并不清楚，但有两个可能与之相关的故事。

第一个故事与格里高利一世教皇有关。公元590年，罗马出现黑死病。在当时，打喷嚏被看作是患黑死病的前兆。所以，人们想通过说保佑的话来抑制疾病。另外，人们也相信这个短语能够治病。

另一种说法是，打喷嚏时人们会将灵魂从身体里甩出去。因为打喷嚏时人体的大门敞开，魔鬼和妖物很容易乘虚而入，或者说打喷嚏是身体试图把已入侵的妖物逼出体外。所以，"保佑你"或"上帝保佑你"就被视为是帮助打喷嚏的人对抗邪恶的一种保护。

还有人认为当人打鼾的时候，心脏会停止，短语"保佑你"被认为有一种魔力，可以祷告祈祷，可用来保证生命的轮回或激起心脏继续跳动。

your soul can be thrown out from your body when you sneeze, hence, a prayer or blessing in the form of "Bless You".

还有一个类似的版本认为人体的灵魂在打喷嚏的时候会抽离身体，所以"祝福你"这样形式的祈祷和祝福也就应运而生了。

单词释义

symptom 症状　　　plague 瘟疫　　　halt 制止
invade 进攻　　　shield 保护

打喷嚏的"百科全说"

Sneezing is still slightly mysterious, even for scientists. Most people no longer believe that a sneeze represents a soul leaving the body as some people in the past thought, but there are still a few *puzzles* left.

Sneezing is an interesting *phenomenon*, especially since most of us can't control it and we're *temporarily* helpless while it happens. The medical term for sneezing is "sternutation", and a sternutation is a *substance* that causes sneezing. Many different factors can *stimulate* a sneeze, including *infections* and *allergies*, inhaled *irritants*, a sudden *exposure to* bright sunlight or a cold temperature, and a stomach that is very full of food.

Humans aren't the only creatures that sneeze. Other mammals sneeze as well, and so do birds and some

打喷嚏到现在为止还是具有些许神秘色彩的，即使对科学家而言也同样如此。过去有人认为打喷嚏代表着人的灵魂离开身体，但是这个说法现今无法让大多数人信服，人们仍然存有很多疑惑。

打喷嚏是一个非常有趣的现象，尤其是因为我们中的大多数人都无法控制它，通常当它发生的时候，我们都会短暂性地感觉到无助。打喷嚏的医学术语是"sternutation"，它是一种引起喷嚏的物质。很多不同的原因都会引发打喷嚏，包括感染和过敏，吸入刺激物、突然受到刺眼的阳光或者低温的刺激，甚至吃得过饱等因素。

人类不是唯一会打喷嚏的生物。其

reptiles. Sneezing is a very common **occurrence** and has **given rise to** many myths and questions.

他哺乳动物也会打喷嚏，鸟类和爬行动物也能做到。打喷嚏是一件司空见惯的事情，却引发了很多的疑问和迷思。

单词释义

puzzle 疑问	phenomenon 现象	temporarily 暂时地
substance 物质	stimulate 刺激	infections 感染的
allergy 过敏症	irritant 刺激物	reptile 爬行动物
occurrence 事件	exposure to 曝光于	given rise to 引起

"品" 美国特色文化

特色表达One

在美国你连着打喷嚏的时候，周围的人会不断地告诉你God Bless You，若你不明白他们为什么说God Bless You，可以问一下，而不是随便地jump the gun。jump the gun原指比赛时不等鸣枪起跑就先抢跑，后引申作不清楚情况就乱发脾气，如Hey! Don't jump the gun. What's up?（喂，不急着生气，到底发生了什么事？）

☆实景链接

A：Why do you look so depressed? 你怎么看着不开心？

B：I **jumped the gun** by building the garage before permission had been given. 我还未得到允许就抢先盖了车库。

A：So have you got to pull it down? 那你现在是要把它拆倒吗？

B：I am not sure about it. 我还不确定。

特色表达Two

朋友要是感冒了，睡前问候一下sleep tight会让她满足地入眠。19世纪时，美国小孩睡前最爱听父母说：Sleep tight and don't let the bedbugs bite.（睡个好觉，别让臭虫咬。）tight的意思是"(睡得)很香，很甜"。后来sleep tight在亲朋好友间流传开来。

☆ **实景链接**

A： I felt a little tired. Let's make the bed. 我觉得有点儿累了，咱们铺床睡吧。

B： Well, I am wide awake. You go first. 我一点也不困呢，你先睡吧。

A： All right. Remember to turn off the TV when you go to bed. Good night then. 好吧，你睡的时候别忘了把电视关了。晚安了。

B： OK. **Sleep tight**. 好的，你好好睡。

拓展特色句

1. Please put a handkerchief over your mouth when you sneeze. 打喷嚏时请用手帕捂住嘴。

2. They usually say god bless you to the people sneeze. 他们通常会对打喷嚏的人说"上帝保佑你"。

3. Be careful not to catch a cold. 当心不要感冒了。

"聊" 美国特色文化

A： I am sneezing all the morning. People around me said bless you in response. I am really at loss about it.

B： That's normal. They did so to scare the devils around you.

A： It's weird. Is that a tradition in your nation?

B： Actually, we have been using this expression since at least 77 AD.

A： Do you know where did the tradition come from?

B： There is no sure answer about it, but there are two stories about this.

A： Wow, it arouses my curiosity, but I have to leave now. Tell me the stories next time. By the way, how should I reply to others' "bless you"?

B： All you have to say is thank you.

A： 我今天一上午都在不停地打喷嚏。我周围的人都会回应我"保佑你"，我不知道为什么他们会这样。

B： 这很正常，他们这么做是为了驱赶走你身边的恶魔。

A： 这太奇怪了，这是你们国家的传统吗?

B： 事实上，我们早在公元77年的时候，就开始用这个表达了。

A： 你知道这个习俗来源于哪里吗?

B： 关于这个并没有确切的答案，但是有两个关于这个的故事。

A： 哇，这引起了我的好奇心，但是我现在得走了，你下次再告诉我。对了，如果别人对我说"保佑你"的时候，我需要怎么回应?

B： 你需要说的就是谢谢。

 美国特色文化

为什么要说"God bless you"而不是"Are you OK?"

美国人相信一个人打喷嚏的时候，说明他离感冒不远了，所以他们会对打喷嚏的人说"God bless you"，即"请多保重"的意思。所以一旦身边的人打喷嚏，就能听到各种声音的"Bless you"。那么打喷嚏的人也要礼貌地说一句"Thank you"。如果不知道这种习惯，没有在别人打喷嚏的时候说Bless you，那不知者不怪；但要是别人跟你说Bless you时，你却没有回应一句Thank you，那可就丢人了。

阅读笔记

美国人为何很少选择国际旅行

美国竟然只有30%的人有护照

The numbers tell the story: Of the 308 million-plus citizens in the United States, 30% have passports. That's just too low for such an *affluent* country, said Bruce Bommarito, *executive* vice president and chief operating officer for the U.S. Travel Association.

"Americans are comfortable in their own environment," Bommarito said.

The percentage of Americans with passports has *spiked* since the Western Hemisphere Travel Initiative was *adopted*. It requires American and Canadian travelers to present documents showing *citizenship* when entering the United States.

Despite the climbing number of American passports in *circulation*, 30% is still low compared to Canada's 60% and the United Kingdom's 75%.

数字说明一切：全美国3亿8百万以上的公民，只有30%的人拥有护照。美国旅游协会的执行副总裁、首席运营商布鲁斯·勃马瑞多表示，这个比率对于这样一个富足的国家而言太低了。

勃马瑞多说："美国人能从自己的国家环境中获得满足感。"

自从西半球旅行计划被采用之后，美国人拥有护照的比例就有所上升。这个计划要求美国和加拿大的游客在到达美国边境的时候出示能够证明自己公民身份的相关证件。

尽管在流通中的美国护照数量正在增长，但是30%跟加拿大60%和英国75%的比率比起来，还是太低了。

单词释义

affluent 富足的　　　　executive 行政的　　　　spike 增加

adopt 采用　　　　　　citizenship 公民身份　　circulation 流通

美国人不愿出国旅行原因大解析

Tourism experts and *avid* travelers *attribute* Americans' lack of interest in international travel *to* a few key factors, including: the United States' own rich cultural and geographic *diversity*, an American *skepticism* and/or *ignorance* about international destinations, a work culture that prevents Americans from taking long vacations abroad and the *prohibitive* cost and logistics of going overseas.

America has it all: "From the mountains, to the *prairies*, to the oceans, white with foam," as "God Bless America" *proclaims*. Major cities offer visitors a *multitude* of urban *delights*. The *convenience* of modern freeways, railways and airplanes makes travel in America as easy as pie.

There are pockets of regional culture—the South has an attitude that New Yorker's don't have, but you don't have the cultural differences that you would get if you went to Asia, Paris or London. Even with Chinatown in Los Angeles and Little Italy in New York City, it's just not the same as walking the streets of Beijing or riding a gondola in Venice.

Many Americans follow the same pattern: work hard in high

旅行专家和狂热旅行者把美国人对国际旅行缺乏兴趣的原因归结为几点：美国人自身丰富的文化和地理多元性、美国人对国际景点持有的怀疑态度抑或是愚昧无知以及让美国人无法进行长时间出国度假的工作文化，此外，还有高额的费用和出国的物流。

美国什么都有：就像《天佑美国》歌颂道的："秀丽山川、北美大草原、泛起白色泡沫的海洋。"大城市提供给游客们很多都市形态的娱乐。现代高速公路、便利的铁路和飞机使得在美国旅行很容易。

美国这里拥有"区域文化"——南方拥有纽约人没有的态度，但是如果你去亚洲、巴黎或者伦敦，你无法感受到文化差异。即便是洛杉矶的唐人街也和走在北京街道上的感觉不同，纽约的小意大利也感受不到在威尼斯泛小舟的感觉。

很多美国人都遵从同样的模式：

school, go to college, *accrue* a load of debt and get a job right away to work it off. The United States doesn't promote taking a year off between major life phases like New Zealand or the United Kingdom.

在高中的时候努力学习，然后上大学背负一笔债务，最后工作需要偿还这些债务。新西兰和英国都会在主要的人生阶段花一年时间放松，但是美国却没有推行这样的做法。

单词释义

avid 热心的
ignorance 愚昧无知
proclaim 宣布
convenience 方便

diversity 多样化
prohibitive (费用的)过高
multitude 群众
accrue 积累

skepticism 怀疑论
prairie 大草原
delight 高兴

 美国特色文化

特色表达One

多数美国人喜欢一个人出国旅行，但也有人喜欢组团旅行，他们会约好集合时间，希望团内的每一个人都是a man of his word。word常指"信用、保证"，所以这里的意思是守信用的人，或说话算话的人。

☆ 实景链接

A：When will you give my money back? 你什么时候还我钱？

B：I promise to return them on next Friday. 我保证下星期五还给你。

C：You should **be a man of your word**. 你一定要说话算话。

A：Well then. Let's meet at 6 p.m. 那好，我们就下午6点见面。

特色表达Two

出门在外靠朋友这是人人都懂的道理，美国人亦如此，在外旅行时乐意play ball。play ball在这里指打球吗?美国人旅行途中要打球似乎说得过去，但这里play ball的意思是合作、相互帮助。一般提到相互帮助，大家都会想到help, cooperate，而play ball所表达的"相互帮助"有更深层的含义，它含有口头约定的意味，即这次我帮了你，下次你务必要和我合作的意思。

✿ 实景链接

A：I think I can help you with that suitcase. 我来帮你提那个手提箱吧。

B：I really appreciate that. You **play ball** with me and I'll play ball with you. 真是太感谢了，你这次帮我，我下次帮你。

A：Right. By the way, I am Jack, from California. 是啊。顺便说一下，我叫杰克，来自加利福尼亚。

B：I am Mason, from New Jersey. 我是梅森，来自新泽西。

拓展特色句

1. How long are you staying in Europe? 你要在欧洲待多久？

2. What do I need to apply for a passport? 申请护照需要哪些资料？

3. Why do Americans lack of interest in international travel? 美国人为什么对国际旅行不感兴趣呢？

"聊" 美国特色文化

A：I am planning to travel during the holidays. I really need to relax myself now.

B：Fabulous, so where are you heading for?

A：I plan to take a trip in Las Vegas with my girlfriend.

B：What? In America? Why don't choose to travel abroad?

A：There are no international destinations that arouse my interest. Beside I prefer to go on a low-budget excursion.

B：I found it's not only you, most of Americans prefer to travel within your nation's borders. Why?

A：For one thing, it's cheaper and there is no language problem; for another thing, there are numerous tourist attractions in America.

B：Then it makes sense.

A：我准备假期出去旅行。我真的需要放松一下自己了。

B：太好了，你准确去哪里度假呢？

A：我准备和我的女朋友去拉斯维加斯度假。

B：什么？在美国？你为什么不选择出国旅行呢？

A：国外没有什么地方让我特别感兴趣，并且我比较倾向于选择低预算的短途旅行。

B：我发现不只是你，很多美国人都喜欢境内游，这是为什么呢？

A：一方面，国内旅游更加便宜，不用遭遇语言问题；另一方面，国内也有很多的旅游景点。

B：那就说得通了。

"问" 美国特色文化

美国人喜欢去墨西哥和加拿大旅行吗?

美国人喜欢到墨西哥旅行倒不是因为该国有什么特殊吸引人之处,而是美国的外来移民来自墨西哥的人数最多,很多在美国工作的墨西哥移民,一到节假日就拖家带口回到"老家",和居住在墨西哥的家人团聚一番。同时由于美墨边境接壤,再加上很多年以来,往返墨西哥的美国人不需要护照,只要有驾驶执照证明身份就

可以,人们到墨西哥就像在美国国内一样方便。美国人喜欢到加拿大旅行也自有其原因,总体上是出入方便,多年来美国人到加拿大也是不需要护照的,加上边境接壤,驾车去加拿大旅行很符合美国人的口味。加拿大自然风光不错,可游玩的景点较多,这也比较对美国人的胃口。

阅读笔记

美式交友 "三观"

Americans are often very friendly and *helpful* to people that they do not know well, and they may also be more open in what they talk about than people from many other countries. This can be *confusing* to someone who comes from a country where people are *initially* more *reserved*. An international student may also feel that Americans are *superficial* or are not good friends when this initial friendliness does not continue as friendship.

Two important American values are *privacy* and *independence*. Thus, Americans may prefer to do something themselves rather than asking for help, as they do not want to impose on the other person's privacy. They may also expect others to do the same. This can create misunderstandings with people from societies with more *interdependent* relationships, who *assume* more *obligation* to friends.

In addition, Americans tend to use the word "friend" where people in some countries might use the word "*acquaintance*;" and they often have different types of friends: friends just to do activities with, close friends,

美国人通常对他们不认识的人很友好并乐于帮助他们,他们在谈话时也可能比其他国家的人更加开放。这对于初次见面比较保守的外国人来说有点难以理解。留学生也会觉得美国人浮于浅表,如果最初的友好没有发展成为持续的友谊,那他们就不是好朋友了。

在美国,两个重要的美国价值是隐私和独立。所以,美国人宁愿自己完成某事也不愿意求助,因为他们不愿意侵占别人的隐私。同样,他们也希望自己不受别人的打扰,这样会让那些来自依附关系强烈的社会的人们产生误会,因为他们对朋友会承担更多的义务。

此外,美国人更常用的词语是"朋友",而有些国家的人则会使用"熟人"这个词,并且他们朋友的种类也不同:只是一起活动的朋友、亲密的朋友、最好的朋友。有些国家,

and best friends. In some countries, people reserve the word "friend" for a few people who are very close.

"朋友"这个词只会用来指代那些非常亲近的人。

helpful 有益的
reserved 冷淡的
independence 独立
obligation 任务

confusing 令人迷惑的
superficial 肤浅的
interdependent 相互依赖的
acquaintance 熟人

initially 最初地
privacy 隐私
assume 认为

美式交友话题

When speaking to someone they do not know well, Americans tend to talk about *fairly neutral* topics and to look for *similarities*. Conversation generally begins with "small talk": people may discuss the weather, or the immediate situation (the class, professor, party, host, decorations, etc.) It might continue with questions or comments about common acquaintances, sports, movies, work or school. As they get to know someone better, Americans will gradually talk about increasingly personal topics.

Americans frequently use "self-disclosure" about personal *preferences* or activities, and they often ask questions about someone's background or interests. They usually avoid *potentially* controversial topics, such as politics, religion, or opinions about certain social issues. Debate about politics tends to be

但凡和不是很熟悉的人交谈的时候，美国人都会谈论一些比较中立的话题，以寻求相似点。通常情况下，交谈都只是由简单的寒暄开始的，人们会谈论天气，或间接的场景（教室、教授、派对、主人、装扮等）。通常都会问到或者评论双方熟悉的人、运动、电影、工作或者学校来继续聊天。当美国人跟某人的关系越来越亲密的时候，他们也会逐渐与其谈论一些私密的话题。

美国人在谈到个人偏好或者活动的时候，会经常用到"自我表露"这个表达，他们经常会问到某人背景或者兴趣的问题。通常他们会避免那些容易引起争论的话题，比如政治、宗教或者某些特定的社会问题。在很多国家，人们都会习惯性地和朋友以及熟人谈论和分析政治或宗教方面的问题，而美国这样的现象就会比较少。当在谈论时事的时候，美国人会经常

less common in the US than in many countries, where people may be much more accustomed to analyzing and debating about politics or religion with both friends and acquaintances. When discussing current events, Americans may often begin with questions, rather than with strong opinions. Even between good friends, *vigorous* debate about *controversial* topics is uncommon: Americans often choose to focus on their similarities instead of their differences.

以提问的方式开始，而不是一开始就陈述自己强烈的观点。即使在好朋友之间，激烈地争论有争议性问题的情况也非常少见：美国人经常会选择关注共同点而非差异点。

单词释义

fairly 相对地
preference 偏爱
controversial 饱受争议的

neutral 中立的
potentially 潜在地

similarity 共同点
vigorous 精力充沛的

 美国特色文化

特色表达One

　　美国人喜欢交朋友，有些酒肉朋友之间少不了curry favor。可得注意了，这里的curry favor与咖喱可没有关系，curry favor是"讨好某人，拍马屁"的意思。curry原意为梳理马的皮毛，源于14世纪法国诗人维特里的政治寓言《褐马传奇》。故事中的褐色老马Fauvel聪明狡猾，有人为谋利常梳理Fauvel的皮毛来讨好他，渐渐地to curry Fauvel就变成了奉承的意思，后演变成了to curry favor。

⭐ 实景链接

A：He tried to **curry favor** with the director. 他试图拍董事的马屁。

B：Yeah, everyone in this office can tell that. 是，办公室里的人都看得出来。

A：I don't think the director will buy his story. 我觉得董事不会吃那一套。

B：That is hard to say. 那可不好说。

特色表达Two

有些美国人不喜欢交一些会对自己get a Roland for an Oliver的朋友，这类朋友自尊心、报复欲都很强。a Roland for an Oliver这个短语来自中世纪，当时查理曼大帝有两位得力大将，一位是Roland，另一位是Oliver，他俩实力相当，即使交战5天都难分胜负。后来人们常用这个短语形容"针锋相对，势均力敌"，或者"以牙还牙"。

☆ 实景链接

A：I hate Michelle to my bones. 我恨米歇尔到骨子里了。

B：What happened to you? 你们怎么了？

A：She beguiled me of all my savings. 她把我的全部存款都骗走了。

B：You should **get a Roland for an Oliver**. 你应该以牙还牙。

拓展特色句

1. Jack is such a great guy. 杰克这个人很不错。

2. I'm so lucky to have a friend like you. 有你这样的朋友真是幸运。

3. We're very close. 我们的关系非常亲密。

"聊" 美国特色文化

A：Have you made any good friends when you go abroad?

B：Not really. I think it's due to culture difference, I don't know how to make friends with them.

A：I heard Americans are very friendly and helpful. It may be easier to make friends with them.

B：Yeah, however they are so open in what they talk about that I can't get along with them well.

A：It is especially true for someone who

A：你出国的时候有交到一些好朋友吗？

B：没有交到什么好朋友，我觉得可能是因为文化差异，我不知道如何跟他们交朋友。

A：我听说美国人都很友善并且乐于助人。跟他们交朋友应该更容易啊。

B：是这样的，但是他们谈论的话题比较开放，以至于我不知道如何跟他们做朋友。

A：尤其是对那些比较保守的外国人来说。

B：那你和国外朋友都谈论些什么？

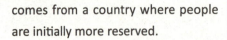

comes from a country where people are initially more reserved.

B: So what do you talk about with foreign friends?

A: Just some small talks. Americans stress privacy and independence. What we do is to try to avoid making judgments about the people of that country.

B: Well, I got something about Americans.

A: 就是闲聊。美国人比较注重隐私和独立性。我们所做的就是尽力避免去评论该国的人。

B: 好吧，我有点了解美国人了。

 ## 美国特色文化

如何与美国人交朋友？

其实和美国人做朋友可以投其所好，勇敢地主动地伸出友谊之手，约他们去教堂做礼拜、去公园遛狗、去俱乐部健身或者去酒吧小酌一杯，都能让他们对你产生好感，这就完成了建立友谊的第一步。在与美国人交谈时要注意，不要觉得多谈几句话就熟悉彼此了，要避免谈论对方的年龄、婚姻以及薪水等。

阅读笔记

原来迟到美国人看得这么重

切忌在美国迟到

In American culture, the *commitment* to spend time with someone is more important than anything else that might happen. Americans go *to great lengths* to keep their commitments. Even if their mother called them on the phone, they would say, "Oh, Mom, I can only talk a few minutes, because I'm meeting a friend for lunch. Can I call you back when I get home?" Their mother would not *take offense* at this, because their pre-existing plans *take precedence* over all others.

Americans place a high value on *punctuality*. If you make plans with someone, you should be there when you say you will. Three to five minutes early is even better, because it shows that you are really *looking forward to* spending time with the other person. Most people will allow five or maybe ten minutes late, but more than that is considered bad form. Not showing up at all—called "*standing someone up*"—is considered very rude and, unless you have a very good reason, the other person may never want to make plans with you again.

在美国文化中，按时赴约比其他任何可能发生的事情更重要。美国人会竭尽全力信守他们的承诺。即使他们的妈妈在家中打电话给他们，他们会说，"妈妈，我只能说几分钟，因为我跟朋友一起吃午饭。我回家的时候再给你回电话，可以吗？"他们的妈妈不会因此而生气，因为他们有优先于所有其他事情的安排。

美国人非常看重守时。当你在和某人安排约会的时候，一旦你同意了时间，你就得按时赶到那里。提前3~5分钟就更好了，因为这表明你真心期待与那个人共度时光。大多数人允许迟到5~10分钟，但迟到超过10分钟就会被视为是不礼貌的。爽约人不见——叫作"放人鸽子"——被认为是非常粗鲁的行为，除非你有非常好的理由，否则对方可能不会再想和你约会。

单词释义

- commitment 承诺
- take offense 生气
- stand someone up 爽约
- punctuality 准时
- take precedence 优先
- to great lengths 竭尽全力
- look forward to 希望

迟到理由很重要

Not showing up for a date is considered the height of *rudeness*, so you'd better have a good reason for it. *Valid* reasons include: death or serious illness of a close family member, being in a car accident, being sick, or not having child care due to a situation you could not have *foreseen* (for example, the babysitter didn't *show up*). If you must miss a date, call the other person immediately, explain what happened, and *apologize* repeatedly (about five times should do). "I'm so sorry, I feel just awful about it, I hope you can forgive me, but here is what happened…" Is a good way to start this conversation?

Valid excuses for being late generally involve *transportation* problems, such as: being stuck in traffic, your car *breaking down*, *unavoidably* missing your bus or train, or not being able to get a cab. Being late because you didn't want to miss the end of a TV show or because another friend called you on the phone is not acceptable. If you realize

约会不露面被认为是最粗鲁的，所以你最好找一个充分的理由。有用的理由包括：亲密的家庭成员去世或重病、遭遇车祸、生病，以及没有预料到某些情况而无法照顾孩子（如保姆没来）。如果必须错过约会，则要立即给对方打电话，解释发生的情况并多次道歉（大约5次就好了）。"很抱歉，我对此感到非常难受，我希望你能原谅我，我这里发生了情况……"这样开始道歉，不是很好吗？

有用的迟到借口通常涉及交通问题，比如：堵车、自己的车抛锚了、没赶上公共汽车或火车，或无法打到出租车。因不想错过电视节目或接另一个朋友的电话而迟到是不能被接

you are going to be late, you should call the other person immediately, explain the situation, apologize, and ask if they would like to meet later or do something else another time.

受的。如果发觉自己要迟到了，你应该立即给对方打电话，说明情况，道歉，询问他们是否愿意晚点再见或下次再出来。

单词释义

rudeness 粗鲁　　　　valid 有效的　　　　foresee 预见

show up 出现　　　　apologize 道歉　　　transportation 交通

unavoidably 无可避免地　break down 抛锚；崩溃；失败

美国特色文化

特色表达One

美国人认为不守时是没素质的表现，有时迟到的人会令他们想wring their neck。可见美国人对迟到的对方该有多生气才会想扭断人家的脖子。在俚语里常用wring one's neck表示某人很生气的意思。

☆实景链接

A：I am sorry, I am late again. 对不起，我又迟到了。

B：I really want to **wring your neck**. I have to wait for you every time. 我真快要气死了，每次我都要等你。

A：I apologize to you. I have something to say. 我要向你道歉，我有话要说。

B：There is no necessity. Don't make any excuse any more. 不用了，不要再编理由了。

特色表达Two

美国人心甘情愿做时间的奴隶，他们认为守时的人才有资格与他们打交道，对待守时的合作伙伴会发自内心地赞赏He is very clockwork. 这是暗讽他像钟表发条一样刻板吗？恰恰相反，美国人喜欢作风clockwork的人，因为这类人就像钟表一样认真对待时间，所以这句说的是他很守时。

☆ 实景链接

A： What do you think about John? 你觉得约翰这个人怎么样？

B： He is reliable and responsible. 他很可靠也很负责。

A： Why do you say that? 为什么这样说？

B： Because he is very **clockwork** whenever we make appointment. 因为每次和他约会的时候，他都非常守时。

拓展特色句

1. You have been one hour late! 你都迟到1小时了！

2. Several times have I told you not to be late. 我不知跟你说过多少次不要迟到。

3. Traffic is probably holding him up. 他可能在路上耽搁了。

"聊" 美国特色文化

A： Hi, Betty. I am sincerely sorry for keeping you waiting so long.

B： It's okay. Can you tell me what happened?

A： The babysitter called suddenly that she couldn't come to attend to Lizzy.

B： So how about her now? Who is taking care of her?

A： I called my mother-in-law and turned to her for help. I waited at home until she arrived. So I am late. Please forgive me.

B： No trouble at all. I read some magazines when waiting for you. It's interesting. So what would you like to drink?

A： Black coffee without milk. How about you?

B： I'd like to order a cup of tea.

A： 你好，贝蒂，抱歉让你等了这么久。

B： 没关系，你能告诉我是发生了什么事情吗？

A： 保姆突然跟我打电话说她不能来照顾丽琪了。

B： 她现在怎么样？谁在照顾她呢？

A： 我给婆婆打电话了，向她求助。我一直在家等着她来，所以我迟到了。请你原谅我。

B： 没事。我在等你的时候看了下杂志，也挺有意思的。对了，你喝点什么？

A： 不加奶的黑咖啡。你喝点什么？

B： 我就来一杯茶。

"问" 美国特色文化

在美国，守时是有素养的表现吗?

美国社会充满了激烈的竞争，处处都充满变化，这样的美国人始终处于奔忙之中，渐渐也就养成了对待时间的谨慎态度。美国人认为时间是一种切实的事物，是需要认真对待的，而且他们觉得因为时间的紧迫和缺乏更需要珍视。美国人相信，从一个人对待时间的态度上可以看出一个人的自身素质修养，以及他对同事或合作公司的尊重与否。

阅读笔记

美国老人年

在美国变老怎么样

Growing old is not exactly pleasant for people in youth-oriented American culture. Most Americans like to look young, act young and feel young. As the old saying goes, "You're as young as you feel." Older people *joke about* how many years young they are, *rather than* how many years old. People in some countries value the aged as a source of experience and *wisdom*. But Americans seem to *favor* those that are young, or at least "young at heart."

Many older Americans find the "golden years" to be anything but golden. Economically, "senior citizens" often struggle just to *get by*. Retirement—typically at age 65—brings a sharp decrease in personal income. Social *Security* benefits usually cannot *make up* the difference. Older people may suffer from poor *nutrition*, medical care and housing. Some even experience age *discrimination*. In 1987, American sociologist Pat Moore dressed up like an older person and *wandered* city streets. She was often treated rudely—even cheated and robbed. However, dressed as a young person, she received much more respect. Of

变老在美国这样以年轻人为中心的社会并非是一件令人愉悦的事情，大部分的美国人都希望自己看起来年轻、行动年轻，并且感觉年轻，就像一句老话说的："你感觉自己有多年轻，你就有多年轻。"年长的人在谈到自己的年龄时常开玩笑都会用years young，而不说years old。有些国家认为老年人集阅历与智慧于一身，但是美国人似乎更加青睐那些年轻人，或者至少是那些"心理年轻"的人。

许多美国的老年人觉得他们的"黄金年代"一点都不"黄金"。经济上，"年长的公民"常是艰难度日。退休——通常在65岁的时候——使个人收入骤减，而社会保障制度的福利并不能补足差额，老年人常遭遇营养不良、医疗照顾和住房供给的问题。有些人甚至碰到过年龄歧视的问题，1987年，美国社会学家派特·摩尔装扮成老人在街上游荡。人们多半对她很粗鲁——甚至骗她或抢她的东西，可是当她穿着年轻时，人们就对她尊重多了。当然，并非

course, not all elderly Americans have such negative experiences. But old age does present unique challenges.

所有的美国老人都会有如此不堪的经历，但是年纪大确实会让人遭遇一些特别的挑战。

wisdom 智慧
nutrition 营养
joke about 对……开玩笑
make up 补偿

favor 支持
discrimination 歧视
rather than 而不是

security 保障
wander 漫游
get by 过得去

美国老人怎么过

A common *stereotype* of older Americans is that they are usually "*put away*" in *nursing* homes and forgotten about. Actually, only about 5 percent live in some type of institution. More than half of those 65 or older live with or near at least one of their children. The vast *majority of* the elderly live alone and *take care of* themselves. According to the U.S. Census Bureau, 75 percent own their own homes. Over a million senior adults live in retirement *communities*. These provide *residents* with meals, recreation, *companionship*, medical care and a safe environment.

Despite the challenges they face, Americans in their "twilight years" generally refuse to *give up on* life. They find a variety of ways to keep themselves active. To help stay in shape, they may join walkers clubs,

对美国老人家常有的刻板印象是他们经常被"遣送到"养老院，然后被人遗忘。然而事实上，只有5%的人住在此类机构中，超过半数的65岁或65岁以上老人，是与孩子同住或住在其中一个孩子的附近。绝大部分的老年人是自己独居并自己照顾自己的，根据美国户口调查局的统计，他们中75%的人都拥有自己的房子。超过100万的老年人住在退休者的社区中，这些社区为其居民提供餐饮、娱乐、陪伴、医疗照顾以及安全的环境。

纵然他们面临挑战，处在"迟暮之年"的美国老年人通常还是不愿意随波逐流，他们寻求各种不同的方法让自己保持活力。为了保持身体强健，他们会参加竞走俱乐部、健身课程，甚至"老人奥林匹克运动会"。他们可以在老人中心和成人公园里玩乐几个小时，许多人报名参加延伸制教育以维持他们的心智技能。

fitness programs and even the "Senior Olympics." They can enjoy hours of entertainment at senior centers and adult amusement parks. Many enroll in continuing education programs to maintain their mental skills.

单词释义

stereotype 类型

resident 居民

majority of 大部分

nursing 看护

companionship 陪伴

take care of 照顾

community 社区

put away 抛弃

give up on 放弃

美国特色文化

特色表达One

美国老人大多是离开子女、独自生活的，有的老人孤零零一人，有的还好有老伴wait on sb. hand and foot。这个短语直译则是等着某人的手和脚，那什么情况才需要等着别人的手脚呢？当然是行动不便或者是有专人伺候的时候，所以，这里的意思是有人照顾。

☆ 实景链接

A: I am really worried about your agedness. 我担心你老了之后怎么办？

B: Sorry, I don't know what your implicit meaning. 对不起，我不知道你是什么意思。

A: I am afraid that no one **waits on you hand and foot** when you become old. 我怕你老了之后没人照顾你。

B: Fear is often greater than the danger. 不要杞人忧天。

特色表达Two

在美国，一般老夫老妻会和和睦睦地过日子，双方都会告诉自己water under the bridge，而不是三天一大吵，两天一小吵。water under the bridge字面意思是桥下的水，指桥下水流过后什么都不会留下，在俚语里指过去就过去吧，不要再纠结了。

☆ **实景链接**

A: I've known it was my fault. Please forgive me. 我知道这都是我的错。请原谅我。

B: It is **water under the bridge**, so just forget about it. 事已至此，就这样过去吧。

A: How can I make up for it? 我该怎么弥补？

B: Let's just start from the scratch again. 咱们就重新再来吧。

拓展特色句

1. What my grandmother wears is always quite fashionable. 我奶奶穿衣服总是很时髦。

2. He lived a happy life in his old age. 他的晚年生活过得很好。

3. How do you want to spend your old age? 你想怎么过你的晚年生活呢？

"聊" 美国特色文化

A: Do your parents adapt to the life in America?

B: Our attitude towards the elderly is very different from that of Americans.

A: What do you mean by that?

B: Our Chinese pay respect to the elderly but the old in America may experience age discrimination.

A: I guess their life must be miserable. Then what can they do?

B: Not that bad, they live in the nursing homes, where can offer them food, recreation, medical care and a safe environment.

A: What will they do after retirement?

B: They won't give up on themselves but continue to maintain their mental skills.

A: 你们家人适应美国人的生活吗？

B: 我们对于老人的态度与美国人大有不同。

A: 这是什么意思？

B: 我们中国人非常尊敬老人，但是在美国他们可能会受到年龄歧视。

A: 那我想他们的生活肯定很悲惨，那他们怎么办？

B: 也没有那么差，他们住在养老院，那里为他们提供了食物、娱乐、医疗照顾以及安全的环境。

A: 他们退休之后会做些什么？

B: 他们不会放弃自己而是继续保持他们自己的心智技能。

美国特色文化

为什么中美两国对待老年人的态度不同

首先，中国文化趋于依赖子女，美
国文化崇尚"个人主义"，赞同独立。中
国文化尊老爱幼，美国文化则提倡平等，
无论老人小孩都是待遇平等。其次，中
国文化讲究"孝道"，强调"责任""义
务"，而美国文化的"孝道"侧重的是自
由与尊敬，很多美国人认为即使人老了还

是有能力的，若是因此轻待他们是不尊敬的表现。所以中美两国对待老年人的态
度截然不同。

阅读笔记

Part 2

美国文化到底什么味儿

美国的做客之道

做客需要带礼物吗

An American friend has invited you to visit his family. You've never been to an American's home before, and you're not sure what to do. Should you take a gift? How should you dress? What time should you arrive? What should you do when you get there? Glad you asked. When you're the guest, you should just *make yourself at home*. That's what *hospitality* is all about: making people feel at home when they're not.

The question of whether or not to bring a gift often makes guests *squirm*. Giving your host a gift is not just a social *nicety* in some cultures—it's expected. But in American culture, a guest is not *obligated* to bring a present. Of course, some people do bring a small *token* of appreciation to their host. Appropriate gifts for general occasions might be flowers, candy or—if the family has small children—toys. If you choose not to bring a gift, don't worry. No one will even notice.

一位美国朋友邀请你去他家。你以前从未去过美国人的家，你不确定该怎么做。需要带一份礼物吗？怎么穿比较得体？什么时间到比较好？到了那里该做什么？很高兴你发问。你若是客人，只要使自己感到自在就好了。待客之道就是这样：虽然不是在家里，却也让人感到在家般的自在。

是否带礼物的问题常使客人纠结不安。在某些文化中，送主人礼物不只是社交礼节——还是大家期待的。但是在美国文化中，客人并不一定要带礼物。当然，有些人的确会带个表示感谢的小礼物给东道主。在一般情况下，比较合适的礼物是花或是糖果，如果这家人有小孩，玩具应当是恰当的礼物。如果你选择不带礼物，也不用担心，甚至都不会有人留意到这一点。

单词释义

hospitality 好客   squirm 羞愧   nicety 美好

obligated 有义务的   token 象征

make yourself at home 舒适自在

做客需要做些什么

American hospitality begins at home—especially when it involves food. Most Americans agree that good home cooking beats restaurant food any day. When invited for a meal, you might ask, "Can I bring anything?" Unless it's a *potluck*, where everyone brings a dish, the host will probably *respond*, "No, just yourself." For most *informal* dinners, you should wear comfortable, casual clothes. Plan to arrive on time, or else call to inform your hosts of the delay. During the dinner conversation, it's *customary* to *compliment* the hostess on the wonderful meal. Of course, the biggest compliment is to eat lots of food!

When you've had plenty, you might offer to clear the table or wash the dishes. But since you're the guest, your hosts may not let you. Instead, they may invite everyone to move to the living room for dessert with tea or coffee. After an hour or so of general chit-chat, it's probably time to *head for* the door. You don't want to *wear out* your welcome. And

美国人的待客之道都是从家里开始的——尤其是在和食物扯上关系的时候。大多数美国人都同意，无论怎样，好的家常菜都胜过餐馆的菜。受邀吃饭时，你或许可以问："我需要带些什么吗？"除非是每人自带一个菜的家庭聚会，否则东道主很可能会这样回答："不用，你自己来就可以了。"大多数非正式的聚餐，你应该穿舒适、轻便的衣服。设法准时到，否则打电话告诉主人你会晚点到。茶余饭后，习惯上，人们会称赞女主人烹调的美食。当然，对主人最大的赞美就是多吃！

当你吃得差不多时，可以主动表示要帮忙清理桌子或洗碗盘。但由于你是客人，你的主人可能不会让你这样做。他们或许会邀请大家到客厅吃点心、喝茶或咖啡。聊大约1小时或许

above all, don't go *snooping around* the house. It's more polite to wait for the host to offer you a guided tour. But except for *housewarmings*, guests often don't get past the living room.

就该走了。你可不希望变得不受欢迎吧。还有最重要的是不要在屋子里四处窥探，等主人主动邀请你的时候，再去参观，这样会比较有礼貌。可是除了乔迁喜宴之外，客人通常都只待在客厅里。

单词释义

potluck 家常便饭　　　　respond 回馈　　　　informal 非正式的
customary 习惯的　　　　compliment 恭维　　　housewarming 乔迁之喜
head for 前往　　　　　　snoop 探查　　　　　　wear out 耗尽

 美国特色文化

特色表达One

　　美国人一般会准时参加朋友的聚会，有时大家会谈起晚到的人，这时那个人突然就出现了，在中国，这种情况叫"说曹操，曹操到。"那么在美国俚语里是如何说的呢？美国人常用speaking of the devil来说这种情况，这里的devil可不是魔鬼的意思，devil在这里不特指某个人。

实景链接

A： Where is Sarah? 萨拉在哪里？

B： Tim told me, he is going with her daughter to zoo. 提姆说她陪女儿去公园了。

A： Look , who's here! 看，那是谁！

B： Well, **speaking of the devil.** 说曹操，曹操到。

特色表达Two

　　去朋友家聚会是挺欢乐的，但可别贪吃或贪杯，小心The Hong Kong dog。难道吃多了，朋友家的爱犬，某只香港狗狗还能对你狂吠？这里的The Hong Kong dog不是指某一种狗，而是某人吃多或吃坏了拉肚子的意思，你可以理解为Hong Kong来的狗狗水土不服坏肚子了。

实景链接

A：Joe, what's wrong with you? 乔，你怎么了？

B：I have a touch of **the Hong Kong dog**. 我坏肚子了。

A：Oh, I am sorry to hear that. 哦，真为你感到难过。

B：I must have eaten something unhygienic. 我肯定是吃了一些不干净的食物。

拓展特色句

1. Drop by sometime. 有空再来串门吧。

2. I feel awful I haven't come to visit sooner. 没有及早来拜访，我觉得很过意不去。

3. Please feel free to make yourself at home. 别客气，像在自己家一样。

"聊" 美国特色文化

A：Do you have time to hang out with me? I want to take something to Mr. Smith's family.

B：Do you have anything in mind?

A：Not yet, I am totally at sea for the presents. I asked him what I need take, but he said nothing.

B：In general occasions, it might be flowers or candy.

A：Well, I will choose a bouquet of flowers.

B：By the way, you can buy something for his five-year old son.

A：Thanks for your caution. When do you think it's appropriate for me to arrive at his house?

B：Just before ten minutes or five before the appointed time.

A：Thanks very much. You know so much about hospitality in America.

A：你有时间跟我出去逛逛吗？我想带点东西去史密斯家。

B：你想好买什么了吗？

A：还没有，我现在完全不知道该买什么礼物。我问过他我需要带什么，但是他说什么都不用。

B：一般情况下，送花或者糖果就可以。

A：那我还是选择一束花吧。

B：对了，你可以给他5岁的儿子买些东西。

A：谢谢你的提醒，你觉得我们什么时候去他家比较好？

B：就在约定时间的前10分钟或者5分钟就可以。

A：非常感谢，你对美国的做客之道还挺了解的。

"问" 美国特色文化

美国人去做客前如何准备礼物？

美国人给朋友送礼一点也不复杂。到别人家里串门吃饭，美国人常常会先问好主人需要带什么东西，一瓶葡萄酒还是一束鲜花。有朋友办喜事的时候，他们会按照朋友公开的礼单来准备要送的礼物。这种礼单里列举的是价钱不等但主人家正缺的东西，这样不仅可以避免浪费，还考虑到了客人的经济实力，而且送的礼物也不会重复，也保证都是主人需要和喜爱的东西。

阅读笔记

舌尖上的美国

美国的饮食为何如此多种多样

Culture is defined as the knowledge, beliefs, customs, and habits a group of people share. These are not *inherited* behaviors, but learned. Culture is passed on from generation to generation. Each ethnic group has its own culturally based foods and food habits. These traditions have been influenced and *adapted* through contact with the *mainstream* culture.

Conversely, the foods of mainstream culture have been influenced by the presence of these *ethnic* cultures. Fast-food restaurants and other *take-out* restaurants now offer such *wide-ranging* selections as pizza, tacos, falafel, egg rolls, and hamburgers. Thus, the American diet is a combination of many cultures and *cuisines*. To understand it, one must not only study the traditional foods and food habits of the many minority groups, but also the *interaction* between the majority culture and the cultures of these smaller groups.

文化定义为是一群人共享的知识、信仰、习俗以及习惯，而这些并非都是先天遗传下来的行为，而是通过后天习得的。文化是代代相传的。每个民族都有由自身文化衍生出的食物以及饮食习惯。这些传统习俗是在跟主流文化交流过后，受其影响而发生改变之后才形成的。

相反地，食物的主流文化也会受到现下民族文化的影响。快餐店以及其他外卖店都会提供各种各样的选择，比如比萨、炸玉米饼、沙拉三明治、蛋卷以及汉堡包。所以，美国饮食是很多不同国家的文化和各地烹饪综合而形成的。要想真地理解它，不仅要学习研究各地传统食物以及少数民族的饮食习惯，而且要了解大众文化和这些小众文化之间的关联。

单词释义

inherit 遗传　　　　　adapt 改变　　　　　mainstream 主流
conversely 相反地　　　ethnic 民族的　　　　take-out 外卖
wide-ranging 广泛的　　cuisine 烹饪　　　　　interaction 交流

美国人最爱吃什么

The United States is a country of immigrants. So Americans eat food from many different countries. When people move to America, they bring their cooking styles with them at the same time. In some cases, Americans have adopted foods from other countries as *favorites*. Americans love Italian pizza, Mexican tacos and Chinese spring rolls. But the American *version* doesn't taste quite *original*.

Americans who living at a fast pace often just *grab* a quick *bite*. Fast food restaurants offer people on the run everything from fried chicken to fried rice. Microwave dinners and *instant* foods make cooking at home a *snap*. Of course, one of the most common quick American meals is sandwich. Americans probably make a sandwich out of anything as long as it can fit between two *slices* of bread. Peanut butter and jelly is an all-time American favorite.

美国是移民国家，所以美国人吃的食物来自许多不同的国家。人们在移居美国的同时，也将自己的烹饪风格带了过去。在某些情况，美国人把外国的食物视为最爱。美国人喜爱意大利比萨、墨西哥玉米饼和中国春卷，但是这些东西的美国版味道却不很正宗。

生活在快节奏下的美国人通常只能很快地吃几口。快餐店为赶时间的人提供各种食物，从炸鸡到炒饭，应有尽有。微波炉晚餐和速食材料使得在家烧饭是件很容易的事。当然，最平常的美式快餐之一就是三明治。美国人可以把任何能夹在两片吐司中间的东西作成一份三明治。花生酱和果酱更是一直受到美国人的喜爱。

单词释义

favorite 喜爱	version 版本	original 原始的
grab 抓住	bite 咬	instant 立即的
snap 仓促	slice 片	

"品" 美国特色文化

特色表达One

美国人喜欢美食，各有各的喜好，有的人对别人钟情的美食不屑一顾，又不想明确表示时常说no skin off my nose.注意不要把skin off one's nose理解成滑下某人的鼻子，这个短语在俚语里常指"与某人有关"，所以no skin off my nose.就是与我无关。

☆ 实景链接

A：I like chocolate, it tastes delicious. 我喜欢巧克力，吃起来很美味。

B：**No skin off my nose.** 这与我无关。

C：Why? Are we still good friends? 为什么，我们难道不是好朋友吗？

B：Go to buy some of you wish, but I prefer candies. 你要喜欢就去买，只是我喜欢糖果。

特色表达Two

要是你在美国午餐时间，有人对你说"Dead meat."你会不会拍案而起，听不见任何话，抡起胳膊先干一架再说？其实"Dead meat."可不是字面上的"死亡之宴"，在俚语里指"某人有麻烦了"，是一种调皮话，一般是熟悉的人之间相互开玩笑。

☆ 实景链接

A：Hi, Sam, could you do me a favor? 山姆，能帮我个忙吗？

B：What's up? 什么事？

C：I wanna go shopping now with you. 我现在想去逛街。

B：You're still working. **Dead meat.** 你还在上班呢，看我不给你颜色瞧瞧。

拓展特色句

1. I grilled sausages for you. 我给你烤了香肠。

2. I have a weakness for strawberry cake. 我偏爱草莓蛋糕。

3. I like food with strong taste. 我口重。

 "聊" 美国特色文化

A: It's supper time. Let's get something to eat.

B: All right.

A: What would you like to eat?

B: I didn't have appetite. I am not into local food here.

A: Haven't you adapted to food here?

B: I think American food is a little bit lousy. It's all beef and potatoes and pizza. I am a little sick of it.

A: Then how about trying Chinese dishes?

B: But they don't have the original flavor. I am not interested in it.

A: Then how about other types of restaurants? We have different kinds of ethnic restaurants. How about Japanese cuisine? I know a famous one not far from here.

B: That sounds good. Let's head there. I am almost hungry to death.

A: 到晚饭时间了，我们吃点东西吧！

B: 好。

A: 你想吃点什么？

B: 我没有胃口。我不是很喜欢吃本土的食物。

A: 你还没有适应这里的食物吗？

B: 我觉得美国食物有点难吃，都是牛肉、土豆和比萨，我有点吃厌了。

A: 那我们去吃中国菜怎么样？

B: 它们没有中国本身的风味。我不是很感兴趣。

A: 其他类型的餐厅怎么样？我们有不同类型的民族风味的餐厅。日本料理怎么样？我知道附近有一家很出名的餐厅。

B: 这听起来不错，那我们去那里吧。我快饿死了。

"问" 美国特色文化

美国人也吃肯德基等快餐吗？

美国人习惯快节奏的生活，他们也喜欢吃快餐。在美国有麦当劳、汉堡王、肯德基和塔可钟这几个最大的连锁快餐品牌，另外还有一些口碑相当好的"进和出"汉堡店和菲尔基连锁餐厅。美国人虽然也常吃肯德基，但是他们也常不满肯德基的食物质量与服务态度，大部分的美国人都认为这些快餐店的食物有待改善。所以，也有很多美国人宁愿自己动手下厨，或者去高级餐厅消费。

车文化中的美国味

汽车对于美国人的重要性无可取代

"The American", William Faulkner *lamented* in 1948, "really loves nothing but his automobile." His *sardonic* observation retains its force over a half-century later. There are now more than 200 million cars in the United States. In Los Angeles there evidently are more *registered* cars than people. Some families spend more on their monthly car payments than on their home *mortgage*.

Americans have always cherished personal freedom and *mobility*, *rugged* individualism and *masculine* force. The *advent* of the *horseless* carriage combined all these qualities and more. The automobile traveled faster than the speed of reason; it promised to make everyone a pathfinder to a better life. It was the vehicle of personal *democracy*, acting as a social leveling force, granting more and more people a wide range of personal choices—where to travel, where to work and live, where to seek personal pleasure and social recreation.

1948年，威廉·福克纳哀叹道，"美国人真的只爱自己的汽车。"他这种讽刺的言论在超过半个世纪后仍意义不减。美国目前拥有超过2亿辆汽车。在洛杉矶，显然注册的汽车比人还要多。一些家庭每月在车上的消费比住房抵押还多。

美国人一直珍视个人的自由和灵活性、顽强的个人主义和男性的力量。老式汽车结合了所有这些品质，甚至包含更多。汽车行驶的速度比思考的速度还要快，它让每个人感到自己就是通向更好生活的探索者。汽车是体现个人民主的工具，充当衡量社会水平的角色，给予越来越多的人可以广泛进行个人选择的权利——去哪里旅行、去哪里工作和生活、去哪里寻求个人快乐和社会娱乐。

单词释义

- sardonic 讽刺的
- mortgage 抵押
- masculine 男性的
- democracy 民主
- retain 保持
- mobility 移动性
- advent 到来
- register 注册
- rugged 崎岖的
- pathfinder 探路者

美国人对汽车"至死不渝"

A century ago, automobiles were viewed as friends of the environment; they were much cleaner than horses. The car also offered a *quantum leap* in power. But it was one thing to *rhapsodize* about the individual freedom offered by the horseless carriage when there were a few thousand of them spread across the nation; it is quite another matter when there are 200 million of them. In 1911 a horse and *buggy* paced through Los Angeles at 11 miles per hour. In 2000, an automobile makes the rush hour trip averaging four miles per hour. American drivers are stuck in traffic for eight billion hours a year. Yet despite *congested* traffic, polluted air, and rising gas prices, Americans have not changed their driving or car ownership patterns.

Suburban commuters have *resolutely* stayed in their vehicles rather than join car pools or use public transportation. Teens continue to fill high-school parking lots with

一个世纪以前，汽车被视为环境的朋友；他们比马更清洁。汽车也带来了力量上的飞跃。人们痴迷于老式汽车带来的个人自由，这是一回事，当时全国的汽车数量仅有几千辆；当全国有2亿辆汽车的时候完全是另一回事、另一番景象。1911年的马和马车以每小时11英里的速度穿过洛杉矶。2000年的时候，汽车在交通高峰时段平均每小时行进4英里。美国司机每年堵车80亿小时。尽管交通拥挤、空气污染以及天然气价格上涨，美国人并没有改变他们的开车或买车的习惯。

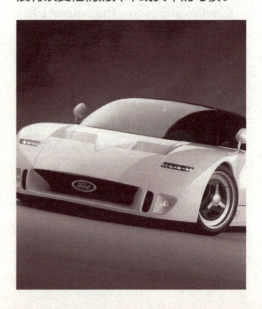

automobiles. America's love affair with the car has matured into a marriage—and an *addiction*. The automobile retains its firm hold over Americans' psyche because it continues to represent a *metaphor* for what Americans have always prized: these ideal of private freedom, personal mobility, and *empowered spontaneity*.

郊区的通勤者坚决待在他们的汽车里，而不是拼车或使用公共交通工具。年轻人们继续在高中学校的停车场里停车。美国对汽车的爱恋已发展为成熟的婚姻那种程度——非常痴迷。汽车牢牢地占据着美国人的心灵，因为它一直隐喻着美国人一直珍视的事物：理想的私人自由、个人的灵活性以及被授予的自发性。

单词释义

quantum 突飞猛进	leap 跳跃	rhapsodize 狂热地说
buggy 马车	congested 堵塞的	suburban 城区的
commuter 通勤者	resolutely 坚决地	addiction 沉溺
metaphor 比喻	empowered 被授予的	spontaneity 自发性

"品" 美国特色文化

特色表达One

美国这个国家，不仅车多，汽车出故障的机会也多，有时在郊区常听有人远远吆喝"My car went on the blink！"你可别听成"我的车开了车灯。"对方的意思是他的车坏了，想向你寻求帮助。blink可指眨眼睛，也可指闪闪发光，但on the blink指的是东西发生了故障，所以这里指汽车坏掉了，不灵了。

☆ 实景链接

A：Auto service center, how can I help you? 您好，汽车服务中心，有什么能帮您的？

B：My car is **on the blink**. Can you send somebody to tow it away? 我的车出故障了。请你派人来拖车好吗？

A：OK, your address please? 好的，请把您的地址告诉我。

B：It is at 23 Madison Avenue. 麦迪逊大街23号。

💬 特色表达Two

美国人常常形容某辆车是一个white elephant，这是在嘲笑某人新买的车是白色的大象吗？是笨重的意思吗？其实white elephant源自泰国故事，指的是当时国王喜欢拿白象做礼物赏给在朝堂上过度活跃的臣子，这样食欲巨大的白象就能把那位臣子拖累得身无分文，使他没有精力与国王作对。

☆ 实景链接

A: What are you doing recently? 最近在忙什么？

B: My wife and I are planning to buy a car. Well, what about the one you bought last year? 我老婆和我计划买辆车，你们去年买的那辆怎么样？

A: That is such a **white elephant**; it burns lots of petrol and breaks down again and again. 那辆车真是个累赘，费油，还经常出故障。

B: Oh, that really sucks. 哦，那可太糟糕了。

拓展特色句

1. I prefer full-size sedan, because it's spacious. 我喜欢大型轿车，因为够宽敞。

2. The latest convertible is very cool. 这个最新款敞篷车很拉风。

3. This model is a gas log. 这款车很耗油。

🗨 "聊"美国特色文化

A: Good morning, what can I do for you, sir?

B: I'd like to buy a new or second car and I don't care about its looking.

A: How about this one? It's a perfect buy, which was driven by an old man. It was really the cream of the crop.

B: But I don't want a sports car or a four-wheel drive. Just a Ford or Honda will be more suitable to me.

A: 早上好，先生，请问有什么需要的吗?

B: 我想买一辆新车或者二手车，我不太在意样子。

A: 那这辆车怎么样？他以前的车主是一位老人，这辆车无可挑剔，简直是百里挑一。

B: 但是我不想要一辆跑车或是四驱车，我觉得一辆福特车或本田就很适合我了。

A：Then I will recommend this Ford for you. It barely had any mileage and it's in perfect condition.

B：Wow, cool. How long is the warranty? How much is it.

A：It comes with a 3-year warranty and the sticker price is 3000 dollars.

B：The price looks to be close to my budget and I will take it.

A：那我推荐你用这款福特。它的行驶里数很少并且状况很好。

B：哇，看起来不错。保修期是多久？多少钱？

A：它的保修期是3年，标价是3000美元。

B：价格很符合我的预算，我买了。

 **美国特色文化**

美国为什么被称为"轮子上的国家"？

美国被称作"轮子上的国家"，因为在美国没有汽车简直寸步难行。美国地大物博，人们居住分散，习惯上班或购物都开着车去几十千米甚至几百千米以外的地方。美国人一旦上车，就不在乎所谓的距离远近了。有的人说在曼哈顿不用开车，因为那里人多，服务设施多，出门步行几分钟即可解决生活所需。但即使在曼哈顿也离不开轮子，只是人们会选择使用地铁、公共汽车或出租车。

阅读笔记

美国酒文化

酒在美国亦敌亦友

A champagne toast is a tradition at every wedding. Poured wine is served during the Christian Communion and represents the blood of Christ. Alcohol is not only part of most social activities; it has become a tradition over the centuries. Alcohol is accepted by society and often associated with a "good time".

With all its negative effects on society, alcohol must be strictly *regulated*. Unfortunately there is only so much that can be done. Alcohol is controlled by the Government's specific laws, regulations, and taxes. In the year 1920 the government attempted to ban alcohol through what we know today to be the *prohibition*.

The 18th Amendment stated that alcohol could not be *manufactured*, sold, imported, exported, or transported in the United States. The prohibition failed miserably extending crime to "organized crime" and increasing government spending. Alcohol consumers then *turned to* more dangerous drugs that may have been more readily available. Although the prohibition had a negative effect on society, a valuable lesson remains. Although it has many negative effects, alcohol is and will always be a part of the American economy and culture.

喝香槟是所有婚礼都会采用的传统。基督教圣餐上倒的酒代表基督的血。酒不仅是大多数社会活动不可或缺的一部分，它成为传统已经有几个世纪了。喝酒已被社会接受，并常与"好时机"联系起来。

酒精对社会有负面影响，必须严格监管。不幸的是，目前只能做到这些。酒精由政府特定的法律、法规和税收来管理。1920年，政府试图通过颁布我们今天熟知的禁酒令来禁止饮酒。

第18条修正案规定，不得在美国制造、销售、进口、出口或运输酒精。禁酒令后来惨遭失败，将犯罪延伸到"有组织犯罪"，政府开支也随之增加了。酒精消费者于是转向更危险和更容易获得的毒品上。尽管禁酒令对社会产生了负面影响，它仍然带来了有价值的教训。尽管有很多负面影响，酒精仍然是并将一直是美国经济和文化的一部分。

美国酒文化让美国人如此沉溺于品酒

The *consumption* and *appreciation* of wine among Americans has gradually given rise to a *distinctively* Americans wine culture. American wine *enthusiasts employ* their own language, *advocate* their own *behavioral* codes and engage in ceremonies or festivals that celebrate the fine things in life.

Various terms and phrases have emerged to *denote* the typical *sensory* experiences that are basic to the induction into American wine culture. For example, when wine tasters *accentuate* their appreciation of the visual appearance of a wine, they use such words as "straw-coloured, cloudy, casting amber" etc. To describe the olfactory properties of a wine, they use "fig and dough *aromas*, cherry and courant bouquet, rich on the nose" etc. When they express the oral *sensations* of a wine, they say it is "very restrained but broad and soft on the palate; lean and citric but with depth to the flavors and subtle texture that carries the flavor through to an impressively long finish, smooth and harmonious

美国人饮酒和品酒的习俗已逐渐成为一种独特的美国酒文化。美国酒迷们使用他们自己的语言，提倡他们自己的行为准则，并且举行庆典或举办酒节来庆祝生活中美好的事情。

美国酒文化出现了许多术语和短语，用来作为美国酒文化入门知识的各种品酒体验。例如，品酒人在强调他们对酒色的评价时会使用诸如"稻草色的、哑色、琥珀色的"等词语。在描述一种酒的气味特点时，他们会使用"无花果香兼有生面团味、樱桃香兼花香、纯正醇厚"等。在描述酒的口感时，他们说"口感不太强，但上腭感觉宽广，柔软；淡里透酸，但味道有深度，且质地醇厚，饮后令人

with a crisp acidity and long on the finish," There are numerous other expressions of American wine culture. The "wine talk" has gained more and more popularity among the American people. And American wine culture has drawn more and more attention in America.

回味无穷；平滑适度，有清新的酸度和无穷的回味。"美国酒文化还有许多其他的说法。美国人"说酒"越来越时兴。美国酒文化在国内引起了越来越多的关注。

单词释义

consumption 消费	appreciation 欣赏	distinctively 特别地
enthusiast 狂热者	employ 使用	advocate 倡导
behavioral 行为上的	denote 表示	sensory 感觉的
induction 感应	accentuate 强调	aroma 芳香

美国特色文化

特色表达One

俗话说得好，小酒怡情大酒伤身，喝多了就是shot in the neck了，这个表达并不是"射中脖子"的意思，而是用来形容"喝醉酒"。

☆ 实景链接

A: Where have Tom been? I havn't seen him during the dinner. 汤姆到哪里去了？我晚饭时没见着他。

B: Well, he was **shot in the neck** this noon. 他中午喝多了。

C: What? Is that serious? 什么？那他严重吗？

B: Don't worry. He will recover after one good sleep. 别担心，他好好睡一觉就好了。

特色表达Two

在美国聚会上，小心喝醉会被人取笑She was as drunk as David's sow. 为什么喝醉了会被人说成是大卫家的母猪呢？这个俚语来自苏格兰传说，据说当时有个叫大卫的店老板，家里养了一头六只脚的母猪令参观者络绎不绝。一天他的老婆喝醉睡在猪圈里正逢大批人来参观，都直呼"她"是他们见过最厉害的"母猪"。之后"as drunk as David's sow"流传开来，形容醉得不省人事。

☆ **实景链接**

A：Did you go to the party last week? 上礼拜的聚会你参加了吗？

B：No. Anything interesting happened? 没，有什么有趣的事儿发生吗？

A：Yeah, Emma from class three was found lying on street by the police. **She was as drunk as David's sow**. 有啊，三班的那个艾玛，被警察发现躺在大街上。她当时醉得不省人事。

B：How dangerous! She shouldn't have drunk that much. 多危险啊！她不该喝那么多的。

拓展特色句

1. Do you like to have a drink with us? 要不要和我们去喝两杯啊？
2. I have a hangover. 我头天的酒还没醒。
3. I can drink like a fish. 我是海量。

"聊" 美国特色文化

A：What will you do after work?

B：I asked several friends out tonight for pub.

A：For drinks again? Last time you were as drunk as David's sow.

B：In our eyes, alcohol often associated with a "good time"

A：Nonsense, It makes me feel under the weather.

B：You even didn't understand our culture. In America, we relax and refresh ourselves in pubs. Drinking is part of our life.

A：Many people had a massive hangover

A：你下班之后准备去干什么？

B：我约了几个朋友去酒馆。

A：又去喝酒吗？你上次喝得不省人事。

B：在我们眼里，喝酒常与"好时机"联系起来。

A：胡说八道，喝酒让人感到很不舒服。

B：你都不了解我们的文化，在美国，我们去酒吧放松消除疲劳。喝酒是我们生活的一部分。

A：很多人在愉快的夜晚之后，出现了严重的宿醉。

B：即便如此，但是我还是热爱酒精。在美国，我们每年都有品酒节。

after great nights.

B：That's it, but I still love alcohol. In America, we hold festivals for the consumption and appreciation of wine every year.

A：That's another thing.

A：这又是另外一回事了。

美国特色文化

美国人喝酒也划拳吗？

　　美国人时常各自喝酒，绝无劝酒的情况。即使是体力劳动者小聚喝酒，无论多么尽兴，都不能互逼对方多喝。若你缠着不放，即使是最好的朋友也不会

有好脸色，甚至出手给你一拳。因为美国人的观点是，喝酒是自己随意的事，被强迫喝酒有什么意思？另外，虽然大多美国人觉得中国人在在酒桌上划拳好玩刺激，但也有少数美国人觉得划拳喝酒很疯狂，不太理解。

阅读笔记

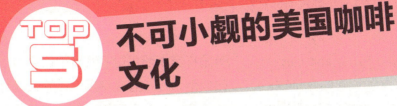
咖啡——美国的"饮料皇后"

Since the seventeenth century, Americans have *roasted*, *steamed*, and boiled coffee, causing its gradual *transformation* into our national *beverage* and a *potent patriotic* symbol. In his 1872 text, Coffee: Its History, Cultivation, and Use, Robert Hewitt Jr. captured the *historical prominence* of coffee in the United States, saying, "Since cotton has been proclaimed 'king' in the realm of commerce, coffee should be styled 'queen' among the beverages of domestic life".

More than just a *jolt* of energy in the morning or a caffeine kick to pull an all-nighter for finals, coffee is a real *obsession* in America. People drink coffee because it means something to them. Between the rich flavors and sense of lifestyle, it serves as a way to socialize and boost productivity in this constantly moving society.

Coffee has since risen from its status of queen of the domestic realm and emerged as a leading global commodity, second only to *petroleum* oil. The United States has led world coffee consumption for the past two hundred years. Coffee

早在17世纪，美国人就开始烤、蒸和煮咖啡，使其逐渐变成为国家级别的饮品以及强有力的爱国象征。1872年，罗伯特·休伊特在他的文章《咖啡：其历史、种植和使用》中抓住了咖啡在美国历史上的重要性，写道，"既然棉花已被称为商业领域之王，咖啡应被叫做国内饮品之后。"

咖啡不仅仅只是早上提神、增加能量的饮品，抑或让那些临近期末考试而准备通宵复习的人提神的兴奋剂，美国人对它是真正的迷恋。美国人喝咖啡是因为它对于他们而言很重要。介于其丰富的口味以及对生活的品味，咖啡为人们在这个时刻不停运转的社会里提供了一种社交和提高生产力的方式。

咖啡的地位现在已从国内饮品之后上升为全球领先的商品，仅次于石油。美国在过去的200年时间里都引领着世界的咖啡消费。咖啡作为饮料在

plays multiple social and cultural roles within American daily life as a beverage consumed upon waking, shared in social settings, enjoyed at the end of a meal, savored during the workday coffee break, and so on.

美国日常生活中扮演着多种社会和文化角色，可在醒来饮用，在社交场合中分享，在餐后享用，在工作小憩时细品，等等。

单词释义

roast 烘烤	steam 蒸	transformation 转换
beverage 饮料	potent 强有力的	patriotic 爱国的
historical 历史的	prominence 突出	jolt 晃荡
obsession 迷恋	petroleum 石油	

美国人为何每天必喝咖啡

Europeans on average drink more coffee than Americans, but its cultural importance and meaning to society lags far behind that of America. With a Starbucks on almost every street corner and chains such as Dunkin' Donuts now selling their coffee grounds in supermarkets, it is hard for any American to avoid the *craze*. The common phrase, "Wanna grab a cup of coffee?" is a go-to *pickup* line embedded in American culture that represents the transformation of coffee from just a morning pick-me-up to social *interaction*.

In addition, society "*normalizes*" behaviors associated with coffee through "ritualized *inebriation*". Alcohol consumption is very much part of the experience because the

虽然欧洲平均咖啡饮用量超过了美国，但是其咖啡文化的重要性以及对社会的意义远远落后于美国。几乎每个街角都会有一家星巴克，邓肯甜甜圈的连锁店也在各大超市售卖咖啡，美国人几乎难逃对咖啡的狂热。常见的短语："要来一杯咖啡吗？"是已经深入美国文化里的搭讪语，这

community sees everyone doing it, so they believe that specific behavior is expected. By drinking coffee as a means of performing tasks in the workplace, individuals believe they are achieving *optimal* levels of productivity. It is a *crutch* to get through the day even if it is not actually doing anything for the body. Much like the placebo effect, there is a sense that carrying coffee means that person is *productive* even if they are not actually working. Coffee then becomes a status symbol.

From the 1990's through the 2000's, a new Starbucks location opened every weekday, *conquering* every street corner across the globe. Fast-forward to today and coffee is now the second most traded commodity in the US with 400 million cups consumed daily.

也说明咖啡已不再是早上提神的饮品，而是一种社交手段。

此外，社会通过"仪式化的麻醉"让与咖啡相关的行为变得"正常"。酒精消费就是这个道理，因为当整个社会看到每个人都在饮酒的时候，他们就会觉得这个具体的行为是受瞩目的。在工作场合，通过喝咖啡这种方式来完成任务，人们会觉得自己达到了生产力最佳状态。即使一天并不做什么，咖啡也会是度过一天的支柱。这有点像安慰剂效应，人们会觉得拿着一杯咖啡意味着这个人很高效，即使他们其实并没有工作。咖啡就变成了一种身份象征。

从19世纪90年代到20世纪初，每个工作日都会有一家新的星巴克开张，征服了全球的每个街角。快速发展，直至今日，咖啡在美国是消费量第二的上市产品，每天消费量是4亿杯。

单词释义

craze 狂热	pickup 收集	interaction 相互作用
normalize 使正常化	inebriation 酒醉	optimal 最佳的
crutch 拐杖	productive 多产的	conquer 战胜

 美国特色文化

 特色表达One

在美国很多学校，尤其是在期末的时候，你会听到女生们常说Well，we'll give her a coffee. 你要是不熟悉美国文化就一定会不解，为什么要给某人一杯咖啡，似乎语气不好的样子。其实这里的coffee不仅仅指喝咖啡，还能指某位老师

要退休前，大家一起聚一下，相互送礼物，一起聊天。

☆ 实景链接

A： Mum, Mrs. Blair is going to retire so we are gonna **give her a coffee** after school today. 妈妈，布莱尔夫人要退休了，所以今天放学后我们会给她开一个小联谊会。

B： All right. Will you be home in time for dinner? 好的，那你能赶回家吃晚饭吗？

A： It depends. Don't wait for me. 得看情况，不用等我了。

B： OK. Have fun. 那好，玩得开心点。

特色表达Two

约三两好友喝杯咖啡，聊聊八卦是件极好的事，临走前可以赞美一下This coffee is good to the last drop. 这句话可以这样理解，既然最后一滴咖啡都好喝了，那么整杯咖啡肯定五星好评，所以This coffee is good to the last drop.的意思是滴滴香浓，意犹未尽。

☆ 实景链接

A： I want a refill. What about you? 我想续杯，你呢？

B： Me too. **This coffee is good to the last drop.** 我也想续，这咖啡真好喝。

A： Would you like to put some milk into the coffee? It will taste better. 你要往咖啡里加点儿奶吗？那样尝起来味道会更好的。

B： OK, thank you. 好啊，谢谢。

拓展特色句

1. We lazed the whole afternoon away at a cafe. 我们在一家咖啡馆消磨了整个下午。

2. Would you like some cream in your coffee? 你的咖啡要加点奶油吗？

3. A black coffee for me. 我要一杯不加奶的咖啡。

"聊" 美国特色文化

A: I really can't understand why you drink coffee everyday.

B: I drink it for refreshment and improve my productivity.

A: I just treat it as a caffeine kick to pull an all-nighter for finals

B: More than that, we drink coffee for socialization, such like business negotiation.

A: Why do you have such tradition?

B: It makes us look more professional in some degree.

A: So can you survive if you live without coffee?

B: Then it will be a nightmare to me. I can't imagine.

A: In fact, you can try some Chinese tea; it can also refresh you.

A: 我真的无法理解你们为什么每天都喝咖啡。

B: 我每天喝咖啡都是为了提神以及提高自己的效率。

A: 我只会在考试前突击的时候才喝咖啡。

B: 此外，我们还有在社交场合喝咖啡，比如商务谈判。

A: 你们为什么会有这样的传统呢？

B: 某种程序上这样让我们看起来更加职业。

A: 那么如果让你离开咖啡你可以生存下来吗？

B: 那对我将是一场噩梦，我无法想象。

A: 事实上，你可以试试喝茶，它也可以给你提神。

"问" 美国特色文化

美国人真的离不开咖啡吗？

　　美国人喜爱喝咖啡，而咖啡早已成为他们生活中的一部分，美国人一天无咖啡不欢。不论在家里、公司、娱乐场所还是路边自动贩卖机，似乎都弥漫着浓郁的咖啡香。于是美国人喝掉了世界咖啡产量的三分之一，是全球咖啡消耗量最大的国家。据说阿波罗十三号宇宙飞船在归航途中曾经发生生死攸关的故障，当时地面人员曾这样安慰——加油！香喷喷的热咖啡正等着你们归来。

宠物文化

孩子和宠物孰轻孰重

You might say Americans treat their pets like they treat their children-sometimes even better. There are more *households* with pets than those with children in America.

At least 43 percent of U.S. homes have pets of some sort *exotic* creatures, such as monkeys, snakes and even wolves, find a home with some Americans. More common pets include *tropical* fish, mice and birds. But the all-time favorites are cats and dogs, even at the White House. The Bushes dog, Spot, has replaced the Clinton's cat, Socks, as *reigning* First Pet. Americans sometimes have strong feelings about whether dogs or cats make better pets. "Dog people" and "cat people" often enjoy friendly *rivalries*.

可以这样说，美国人待他们的宠物就像待自己的孩子——有时有过之而无不及。

在美国，有宠物的家庭比有孩子的家庭还多。至少43%的美国家庭有宠物，有些美国家庭还会养一些外国品种的动物，例如猴子、蛇，甚至狼；比较常见的宠物有热带鱼、老鼠和鸟。不过，一直广受欢迎的是猫和狗，连白宫也不例外。克林顿总统的猫——袜子，已经取代了布什的狗——米利，作为当届的"第一宠物"。美国人有时候很在乎到底最好的宠物是猫还是狗，爱狗的人和爱猫的人喜欢开玩笑地彼此争辩。

在美国，宠物也是"人"

Americans love pets. And it's not just *puppy* love, either. Many pet owners treat their *furry* friends as part of the family. Sometimes they *spice* up their pets lives with *entertaining* videos and amusing toys. If they have an eye for fashion, pet owners can dress their pets in *stylish* clothes. For special occasions, they can use canine *perfume* to make their dogs smell well.

Beneath the furry luxuries, there lies a basic American belief: Pets have a right to be treated well. At least 75 animal welfare organizations exist in America. These provide care and *adoption* services for homeless and abused animals. Veterinarians can give animals an *incredible* level of medical care for an incredible price. To pay for the high-tech health care, people can buy health insurance for their pets. And when it s time to say good-bye, owners can *bury* their pets in a *respectable* pet *cemetery*.

Pets are as basic to American culture as hot dogs or apple pie. To Americans, pets are not just property, but a part of the family. After all, pets are people, too.

美国人很爱宠物，而且还不是一时的激情。很多宠物主人把这些毛茸茸的朋友视为家庭一员。有时候还为它们准备有趣的录像带和玩具，让它们过得有滋有味。如果主人追求时尚的话，他们还会给自己的宠物穿上时髦的衣服。在一些特殊场合，他们甚至为狗喷上犬用香水，让它们更好闻。

在舒适奢华的享受之下，反映了美国人的一种基本信念：宠物有受到妥善对待的权利。美国至少有75个动物福利组织，他们为流浪动物及被虐待动物提供照顾与领养的服务。兽医能提供给动物极好的医疗照顾——价格也极昂贵，若为了负担先进的医疗保健，人们可以为他们的宠物买健康保险。如果宠物的时日不多了，主人会为宠物买一块体面的墓地。

宠物是美国文化中很基本的一部分，就如热狗和苹果派一样。对美国人而言，宠物不仅仅是私人财产，更是家庭的一部分。毕竟，宠物也是"人"啊！

单词释义

puppy 宠物	furry 毛皮的	spice 使……增加趣味
entertaining 令人愉快的	stylish 时髦的	perfume 香水
adoption 接受	incredible 难以置信的	bury 埋葬
respectable 值得尊敬的	cemetery 墓地	

 美国特色文化

特色表达One

　　美国人爱狗，但有时过度宠爱狗会被警察in the doghouse。这里的doghouse是狗窝，无论在美国还是中国，犯错的狗大多被关进狗窝反省(in the doghouse)，短时间内会被主人冷落，不再受宠。在美国，in the doghouse这个短语不仅用于形容狗还能形容人不受喜欢，不被欢迎，如The girl was in the doghouse with his teacher.（这个女孩不讨老师喜欢。）

☆ 实景链接

A：I was **in the doghouse** with my wife these days. 这几天我老婆对我很冷淡。

B：What happened? 发生什么事了？

A：I forgot our wedding anniversary last week. 上周我把我们的结婚纪念日给忘了。

B：How careless of you! That must break her heart. You really deserve this. 你太粗心了，她一定伤心死了，你真是活该啊。

特色表达Two

　　狗狗是美国人的好伙伴，他们喜欢在寂寞的时候与狗狗"无声地"对话，如模仿狗狗的声音说What's eating you? 这里可不是说什么东西在吃你，而是问你怎么了？或者你为什么不开心？然后他们又自言自语道各种伤心事。

☆ 实景链接

A：Hey, Bob, **what's eating you**? 嘿，鲍勃，你怎么了，那么不开心？

B：It is the final exam. Not very hard but I blew it. 是期末考试的事情，考试并不难，但是我考砸了。

A: It happens. Don't give it too much thought. By the way, I would hold a party tomorrow in my house. You should come and join us. 这种事很常见的，别多想了。顺便说一句，我明天会在家办一个聚会，你来参加吧。

B: Thanks for asking but I am really not in the mood. Next time maybe. 谢谢你的邀请，但我真的没心情，还是下次吧。

拓展特色句

1. I consider my dog as a part of the family. 我把我的狗当作家庭的一分子了。

2. I don't think raising a bird needs a lot of time. 我觉得养鸟不需要很多时间。

3. I often see you walking the dog. 我经常看见你遛狗。

"聊" 美国特色文化

A: Will you feel alone living by yourself?

B: Actually not. I am accompanied by two dog. They are my honest companions.

A: That's incredible. Then you will spend lots of time walking them. How could you spare time to do so everyday?

B: They bring much fun to me. However, dogs are energetic. I take them out everyday and they are not willing to come back.

A: Well, you get exercise as you walk them. One stone kills two birds.

B: You can say that again. My boys are always there no matter what.

A: Yeah, that's true. Ok, besides dogs and cats, what other animals will

A: 你一个人睡会感到孤单吗？

B: 实际上不会，我有两只狗陪我，它们是我忠诚的伴侣。

A: 那太不可思议了，你需要花费很多时间来遛它们。你怎么会每天都有这么多时间来做这些？

B: 它们给我带来了很多乐趣，然而，狗的精力都很好，我每天都会带它们出去，但是它们都不愿意回来了。

A: 好吧，你在遛狗的时候也得到了锻炼，一箭双雕。

B: 你说得太对了！无论什么事情，我的狗儿们总会在我身边陪伴我。

A: 确实如此，你们除了养狗和猫之外，还会养些其他什么动物呢？

B: 我身边的朋友会养各种各样的动

your people keep?

B: My friends around me raise various animals, such as snakes, turtles, tropical fishes, lizards and so on.

A: That's really cool. What are some costs associated with keeping your dogs?

B: I always buy dog food for them and take them to care center periodically. That consumes a great deal.

物，比如蛇、乌龟、热带鱼、蜥蜴等。

A: 真酷！你养宠物需要耗费多少钱?

B: 我会为它们买狗粮，还会定期带它们去做护理。这会花费一大笔。

"问" 美国特色文化

狗狗在美国居然有狗权?

　　美国人将狗狗视为家庭中的重要一员，对它们关怀备至。他们经常在公园、超市甚至机场大厅里遛狗、逗玩。在美国，狗狗是享有"狗权"的，比如有些公园里会设置专门的宠物乐园让小狗们尽情玩耍。当然，有权利就有义务，这个义务就得主人来承担了。为环境着想，美国人对养狗有严格规定，比如狗主人要随时准备清理狗狗的粪便。所以在美国养狗的人虽多，但却很少能看见狗狗或其他宠物的排泄物。

小费不是你想不给就不给

While tipping is NOT *mandatory* in most of the United States, it is expected in many *circumstances* for service, especially at almost all *sit-down* restaurants which offer table service.

Many visitors to the U.S. feel pressured to tip even when they do not feel it is fair or reasonable to do so. Customers cannot be forced to tip as a matter of law, but they are *legally* required to pay any charges that are clearly marked prior to service, and these may include mandatory *gratuities*. Mandatory gratuities are used by some restaurants with large numbers of foreign customers who may not be familiar with American tipping customs, often in tourist centers such as New York City. Mandatory gratuities also are charged by many restaurants when large groups are being served.

A very few restaurants and restaurant *chains* may *discourage* tipping. There are a few U.S. restaurant chains with limited table service that discourage tipping when customers receive table service. For those who prefer not to tip, but also don't want to deal with their own trays or the trays and drinks of children at fast food restaurants, these restaurants may offer an *alternative*.

尽管付小费在美国大部分地区并不是强制性的，但在许多情况下，服务业特别是提供餐桌服务的几乎所有非自助式的餐馆都希望得到小费。

许多游客到美国后感到自己是被迫付小费，尤其是当他们觉得这样做不公平或不合理的时候。顾客并不会受到相关的法律强迫而付小费，但法律规定顾客须承担服务前就明确指明的任何费用，这可能包括强制性酬劳费。强制性酬劳费出现在一些有大量可能不熟悉美国小费习惯的外国顾客为主的餐馆，通常是在旅游中心城市，如纽约。大型团体享受服务时也会要求支付强制性酬劳费。

只有很少的餐馆和连锁餐厅不收小费。有一些提供有限餐桌服务的美国连锁餐厅在服务顾客时不收小费。快餐店对于那些不愿意付小费，以及不需要点餐或儿童餐饮服务的人，是另外一种选择。

单词释义

mandatory 强制的	circumstances 情况	sit-down 非自助的
legally 合法地	gratuity 小费	chain 连锁
discourage 使气馁	tray 托盘	alternative 选择

没有小费，会有服务吗

Fast food restaurants do not have tipping, nor do they have table service.

Obviously at restaurants with no tipping policies or where gratuities are *automatically* added to customer checks, there is no need to tip unless there is a *desire* to *additionally* reward some exceptional service. Some coffee shops, *bakeries* and other *establishments* have tip jars on their check-out *counters*. These have become more *prevalent* in recent decades and there is some *confusion*, even *controversy* about them. Generally, those who feel a desire to reward good service will make a *contribution to* a tip jar. Others do not. Both are fine.

As explained below in greater detail, customers should understand that tips are often a major source of *compensation* for wait staff and other U.S. service providers. Customers may not be paying more for the service that they are receiving than if the cost of the services were built into prices as they are in many other countries.

快餐店不收小费，也不提供餐桌服务。

显然在不收小费或不将强制性酬劳费加入顾客账单的餐馆，没必要付小费，除非希望额外感谢部分特殊服务。有些咖啡店、面包店和其他店面会在结账柜台放置小费罐。这在近几十年更加普遍，但也会让人困惑，甚至为此争论。一般来说，那些希望感谢良好服务的人会在小费罐里投币。其他人就不会。二者都没有问题。

如以下更详细解释的那样，顾客应该明白，付小费是对服务人员或其他美国服务商表示感谢的主要来源。顾客并不会支付比他们享受服务更多的费用，而在许多国家这些服务的成本是计算在消费金额内的。

单词释义

automatically 自动地　　　desire 欲望　　　　additionally 额外地

bakery 面包店　　　　　　establishment 公司　　counter 收银台

prevalent 普遍的　　　　　confusion 迷惑　　　　controversy 辩论

contribution to 促成　　　compensation 补偿

 美国特色文化

特色表达One

　　在美国流行给小费，但服务员也别太得寸进尺，小心被give the hook。大家都知道hook是钩子，难道在美国要小费还会被给一钩子吗？100年前，美国各地盛行戏剧表演，时常有业余演员来舞台客串。要是观众们不满意这些业余演员的表演时就会往台上扔西红柿和鸡蛋，这时舞台经理会用一个长钩子将令人不满的演员拉下台，就是give the hook。如今，give the hook常指突然解雇某人，就是炒鱿鱼的意思。

☆ **实景链接**

A: How big of a tip did you get? 你拿到了多少小费？

B: I told the customer they should tip at least 15% of the cost of the meal. So I got 18%. 我告诉顾客他们至少要付15%的餐费作小费，所以，他们就给了我18%。

A: But the boss told us it was at least 12%. He will **give you the hook** if he finds out. 但老板说至少收12%的，他发现的话会把你解雇的。

B: He'll never know. 他永远不会知道的。

特色表达Two

　　在美国给小费是不需要大惊小怪的，就如It's just a storm in a teacup. 据说最早使用a storm in a teacup 这句话的是法国学者孟德斯鸠，当时用它来评论圣马力诺政治动乱。因为圣马力诺是欧洲最小国家，孟德斯鸠认为那里的动乱无伤大雅，就如同"茶杯里的风暴"，不值得注意，后引申为"小题大做"的意思。

☆ **实景链接**

A：They tipped that waiter. 他们给了那个服务员小费。

B：It's just a **storm in a teacup**. Just their culture. 没什么可大惊小怪的，只是他们的文化而已。

A：How much? Is there a standard? 那应该给多少呢？有标准吗？

B：10% of the cost of our meal is OK. 给我们餐费的10%就可以。

拓展特色句

1. We've left the tip on the table. 我们把小费放在餐桌上了。

2. How big of a tip are you leaving? 你给了多少小费？

3. This is for your service. 这是给你的小费，谢谢你的服务。

"聊" 美国特色文化

A：Why are you so fond of this restaurant?

B：I like dinning here because it's not a must to tip here.

A：Yeah, but in our custom, if you receive satisfactory service, the servicemen really expect tips.

B：I just can't figure out why I must do so. I really bother to do it.

A：In some parts of America, wait staff are paid below the minimum wage. They are expected to make up the difference, so to speak, in tips.

B：But how can I assure the tips are attained by them instead of the keepers?

A：Then it will be appreciated paying in cash rather than by card.

B：If someone is just phoning it in,

A：你为何如此钟情于这家餐厅呢？

B：我喜欢在这里吃饭是因为这里不一定要给小费。

A：好吧，但是按照我们的习惯，如果你受到了满意的服务，服务人员会很期待小费。

B：我真的无法理解为什么我们必须这样做，因为我真的很讨厌给小费。

A：在美国有的地方，服务人员的薪资低于最低水平，他们希望自己补足收入差异，也就是通过小费来补足。

B：那我如何保证小费是他们收了而不是老板？

A：所以他们更加青睐于收现金而不是刷卡。

B：如果有人只是敷衍了事，那我还需要同样地给小费吗？

should I tip anyway?

A: Of course not. You should inform the manager at once. Don't tip the poor service.

B: Thanks for telling me so much. I acquired a lot about tipping culture.

A: 当然不用, 你应该马上告知经理, 不要给差劲的服务小费。

B: 谢谢你告诉我这么多, 我对小费文化有一定的了解了。

美国特色文化

各国都有"小费"吗?

　　有的国家流行付小费, 有的则不认同这种小费行为。比如在中国是不允许付小费的, 因为中国人认为既然餐馆收了钱就该提供好的服务, 而不是另外再给小费。在日本也不给小费。在新加坡付小费会被人们认为服务质量差, 所以拒付小费。而在美国, 付小费算是一种生活习惯与衡量服务员服务质量的方式, 或者是一种礼节行为。在墨西哥, 人们将付小费与收小费视为一种感谢与感激的行为。

阅读笔记

美国为何对公共交通如此冷漠

Some large cities like New York, San Francisco and Los Angeles, the U.S. provide different methods of public transportation, such as buses, taxis or trains. However in most places, public *transportation* is poor. The *frequency* of stops is less and they are not well connected. You will have to *rely on* your private car for transportation in most cases.

The American love of the auto runs so deep it often *verges* on the *pathological*. And it will *abide* for at least one *practical* reason: the continent is too damn big. Public transportation can't cover it. For maximum *flexibility* and *convenience*, and to explore *rural* America and its wide-open spaces, you have to have a car. Even with the rising cost of gas, private cars still remain the most *prevalent* and economical mode of transportation, keeping in mind the *flexibility* and freedom you get with your car. You can travel whenever you want, whenever you want. You don't have to rely on the schedule of public transport.

There is no river or canal public transportation system in the USA, but there are many smaller, often state-run, coastal ferry services, which

在美国，像纽约、旧金山、洛杉矶这样的大都市，都配备有形形色色的公共交通，如公交车、出租车和火车。然而在大多数地方，公共交通现状却非常糟糕，公交车车站间隔太大，并且设置并不通畅。很多时候，你都需要依赖自己的私家车来进行交通活动。

美国人对于汽车的热爱之情几乎已经到了变态的地步，这都源于一个非常现实的理由：美国的州都太大了，公共交通根本就无法完全覆盖它。为了最大程度的灵活性和便利性、能够对美国乡村和其开放空间进行探索，你必须得有辆车！即使油价不断增长，但是只要你想到开车能够让你畅通无阻的时候，开车就仍然是交通的主导方式和最经济的方式。你可以随时随地去你想要去的地方，你不需要在乎公共交通的时间表。

美国没有河上公共交通，但是有很多小型的，通常是州立的、沿海渡

provide efficient, scenic links to the many islands off the US coasts.

船服务项目，让人们可以去美国海岸周围的许多岛屿观光。

美国的公共交通发达吗

Except in large cities, you will not find taxis waiting around the street corners. You will find taxis waiting at the airport, at some big hotels and at Las Vegas *casinos*. At other places you have to call a taxi company for a ride. Most of the taxis are in yellow color and very comfortable. When you enter the taxi, the *meter* will show a *flat* rate change. *Additionally*, there may be extra fees for more than one passenger, airport fees, and baggage fees.

To save money, travel by bus, particularly between major towns and cities. Gotta-go middle-class Americans prefer to fly or drive, but buses let you see the countryside and meet folks along the way. As a rule, buses are *reliable*, clean and comfortable, with air-conditioning, *reclining* seats, *onboard lavatories* and no smoking permitted. Most

除了大城市，你几乎在街角寻不到出租车的踪迹。你可以在机场、一些大型酒店和拉斯维加斯赌场打到出租车。然而这些地方以外的其他地方，你都需要给出租车公司打电话。大多数出租车都是黄色的，并且非常舒适。你一进入出租车，计价器就会平稳地变化。此外，如果乘客超过一人或是在机场打车或者有行李，都会额外再收费。

为了省钱，在主要乡镇和城市之间穿梭可以选择公交车。随即就走的中产阶级可能会选择坐飞机或者自驾，但是坐公交车可以让你欣赏沿途乡间的风景以及邂逅不同的人们。众所周知，公交车可靠、干净、舒适，还配有空调、可调节座椅、车载厕所等设备，并且车上不允许吸烟。很多城市和大的乡镇都有自己独立的公交系统，但是很多时候都只是为上下班通勤者设立，并且在夜间或者周末班

cities and larger towns have dependable local bus systems, though they are often designed for commuters and provide limited service in the evening and on weekends. Costs range from free to $1 to $2 per ride.

Commuter trains are meant for transporting people back and forth from the city to the *suburbs*. There are no *reservations* and there is no only one class of travel. Commuter trains run more frequently during rush hour. At most places, you have to buy tickets at the train station itself.

次很有限。公交车有时免费，有时是1美元或2美元。

通勤列车是为了让人们能在城市和郊区间往返而设立的。这些车都是无法预订座位的，也不分座位等级。通勤车在上下班高峰期间运营的次数会更多。在很多地方，你都需要在车站买好票。

单词释义

casino 赌场	meter 用表计量	flat 逐渐变平
additionally 额外地	reliable 可靠的	reclining 倾斜的
onboard 在船上	lavatory 厕所	commuter 通勤者
suburb 郊区	reservation 预定	

美国特色文化

特色表达One

在美国遇到乱闯马路、不遵守交通规则的人，我们怎么称呼他？美国有个特色的词语可以直接形容他，那就是jaywalk。这个词语的渊源具有一定的歧视性。jay是形容那些头脑呆傻、整天乱叫的鸟，后来用来形容"乡巴佬"，他们说话声音大，不懂交通规则，看到高楼大厦、汽车感到大惊小怪，缺乏素养而遭到城里人笑话。到20世纪，jaywalker用来指代那些不遵守交通规则擅闯红灯的人，而闯红灯的行为被称作jaywalking。

✪ 实景链接

A： Watch out! The light turns red. 小心！红灯。

B： Ash, I have just distracted. 天啦，我刚刚走神了。

A： That's ok. If we ran the red light, others must call us **jaywalker**. 没事。如果我们闯了红灯，其他人一定会说我们不守交规。

B： Well, it turns green. We can go now. 好吧，绿灯了，我们可以走了。

💬 特色表达Two

　　我们经常在看美国电影的时候，会看到美国人在车里引吭高歌，非常有激情、非常热闹的样子，我们可以说他们在车里Caraoke，这个词是指在车里大声唱歌，与Karaoke(卡拉OK)读音一样。还有人冒着生命危险，边开车边发短信，其实这种情况也可以归纳为一个词，intexticated, 就是边开车边发短信的特色表达。

✪ 实景链接

A： Don't be intexticated. It's so dangerous. 别边开车边发短信了，这很危险。

B： Ok, the last message. 好的，最后一条短信了。

A： The road trip is so long. Maybe we can do **Caraoke**. 这趟路程真漫长。或许我们可以唱唱歌轻松一下。

B： Good idea. I will choose a rock song. 好主意，让我选首摇滚的歌曲。

拓展特色句

1. Man, he is as slow as Christmas! 天啊，他开车真是够慢的！

2. Sit tight. I am gonna floor it. 坐好，我要加速了。

3. The car behind us really annoys me. I don't know why the driver keeps blowing. 我们后面的那辆车真是让我受不了了。我不知道司机为什么一直按喇叭。

 **美国特色文化**

A: How do you get to work every day?

B: I drive to work or join the car pool. What about you?

A: I take the train to work and home every day. I choose this way because I can read or listen to music.

B: Um, that's really nice.

A: Moreover, it saves me a lot of money by train.

B: It holds water. You don't have to pay for gas, car maintenance and things like that.

A: But every coin has two sides. The worst thing about taking trains is that they are very crowded.

B: Does that mean you have to stand sometimes?

A: Actually it is. Sometimes it smells a bit nasty. But overall I like trains.

 **美国特色文化**

A: 你每天怎么去上班呢?

B: 我每天开车去上班或者是跟别人拼车。你呢?

A: 我每天都是坐火车上下班。我之所以选择这样的交通方式是因为我可以在车上看书或者听音乐。

B: 嗯，这真的非常好。

A: 另外，坐火车为我省下了不少钱。

B: 确实是这样，你不需要花钱去加油、进行汽车维修等这样类似的事情。

A: 但是每件事情都是有利有弊，乘火车最坏的事情就是火车非常拥挤。

B: 意思是你有时候需要站着吗?

A: 事实上是的，有时候味道不好闻。但是总体上我还是喜欢火车。

美国出租车是"呼之则来，挥之则去"的吗?

美国的出租车可不像中国的出租车那般穿梭在城市各个地方，大多数出租车都潜伏在机场或者火车站附近，有时候与其为了图方便，在马路中间潇洒地挥一挥手，还不如打电话提前预约，这样成功打到车的概率可能会更高。说起出租车，可以谈谈各国有趣的打车习惯。在英国，打车价格昂贵，且的哥爱讲俚语，这让很多英语水平有待提高的国人深感苦恼；素有"狗的天堂"的法国，在打车这方面也可见一斑，出租车上专门设有宠物的座位。

Part 3

不可不知的美国经典名词

TOP 1 世界"大苹果"在哪里

纽约"大苹果"称谓是好还是坏

In the early 1920s, "apple" was used *in reference to* the many *racing* courses in and around New York City. Apple referred to the prizes being awarded for the races—as these were important races, the rewards were substantial.

According to the history, the city was not *officially* named the Big Apple until 1971. The *nickname* was first used in a book "The Wayfarer in New York" written by Edward Martinin in 1909. In the book, a tree is *employed* to *compare with* the national economy. And New York is the big apple on the tree, which "gets a *disproportionate* share of the national *sap*".

The purpose of the book was to criticize the disproportional amount of the nation's money New York City received annually. But the residents of New York City may have interpreted that living in the Big Apple meant enjoying the benefits of a *robust* economy.

早在20世纪20年代,"苹果"用来指代纽约城附近的那些赛车项目。苹果即是在比赛后会颁发的奖项——由于这些都是非常重要的比赛,因此奖项也非常殷实。

根据历史记载,纽约"大苹果"这一称呼直到1971年才被官方承认。这个绰号在1909年爱德华·马天尼写的一本名为《旅人在纽约》的书中最早出现。书中,作者用一棵树来比喻国家经济。而纽约就是树上的一个大苹果,它"吸取了国家经济这棵大树的大部分汁液"。

这本书是为了指责纽约每年从国家财政中得到的不相称的数额。但纽约市民却将之解释为生活在纽约就意味着享受繁荣经济带来的好处。

单词释义

racing 竞赛	officially 官方地	nickname 昵称
employ 使用	disproportionate 不成比例的	sap 汁液
robust 旺盛的	in reference to 关于;就……而言	
compare with 与……对比		

纽约"大苹果"被赋予积极意义

In the late 1920s and early 1930s, New York City's jazz musicians began referring to New York City as the "Big Apple." An old saying in show business was "There are many apples on the tree, but only one Big Apple." New York City being the *premier* place to perform was referred to as the Big Apple.

A 1971 campaign to increase tourism to New York City adopted the Big Apple as an officially recognized reference to New York City. The *campaign featured* red apples in an effort to *lure* visitors to New York City. It was hoped that the red apples would serve as a bright and *cheery* image of New York City, *in contrast to* the common belief that New York City was dark and dangerous. Since then, New York City has officially been The Big Apple.

19世纪20年代后期以及19世纪30年代初期,纽约城的爵士音乐家开始把纽约城比作是"大苹果"。娱乐行业有个古老的说法是"树上有很多苹果,但是只有一个大苹果",纽约作为演出的第一站也因此被称作是"大苹果"。

1971年的一场宣传活动为了推动纽约城市的旅游业,正式将纽约市命名为大苹果。这场宣传活动的主要特色是采用了红色苹果,为的就是吸引游客来纽约城。大家寄希望于红苹果身上,希望它能给纽约带来光鲜愉快的形象,与众人心目中黑暗危险的纽约城市形象形成对比。自那以后,纽约城在官方上有了"大苹果"的称号。

单词释义

premier 最初的
lure 诱惑

campaign 活动
cheery 愉快的

feature 以……为特征
in contrast to 与……对比

 美国特色文化

特色表达One

既然美国人喜欢大苹果赋予纽约的光亮形象，可想而知，很多美国人都是希望自己或身边的人能feel like a million dollar的。这句短语可不是说看起来就像钱一样，美国人常用它形容感到精神状态很棒。因为美国人崇尚金钱，所以往往用与dollars相关的短语表示"极好"的意思，这里的dollars还可以省略。

☆ 实景链接

A：How are you feeling now? 你现在感觉怎么样？

B：**I feel like a million dollar.** 我感觉很不错。

A：That couldn't be better. I am glad you say like that. 那太好了，真高兴你这么说。

B：You are so considerate. 你真体贴。

特色表达Two

纽约人遇到好久不见的人常说"Let me spring for dinner."这里的spring可不是春天或温泉，在俚语里是"结账"的意思，通常指某人准备请客吃饭了。所以这句话的意思是由我来请客吧。

☆ 实景链接

A：Mike, are you available this evening? 麦克，你今晚有空吗？

B：I don't have anything urgent to solve this evening. So do you have any plan? 我今晚没有什么紧急的事情需要处理。你有什么活动吗？

A：**Let me spring for dinner.** I have to thank you for your help last time. 我来请你吃饭吧，我需要感谢你上次的帮助。

B：It's just a piece of cake. Don't put it on your heart. 小事一桩，别把它放在心上。

拓展特色句

1. She has been honored with Apple Awards. 她荣获了"苹果奖"。

2. New York, perhaps is the most dynamic and prosperous city in America. 纽约或许是美国最有活力、最繁荣的城市。

3. He will give his acceptance speech at the awards ceremony. 他在颁奖典礼上会发表获奖感言。

"聊" 美国特色文化

A: What's the nickname of New York?

B: Usually when you mention "Big Apple", it refers to New York.

A: What does this term come from?

B: The New York City Visitor's Bureau says jazz musicians and other entertainers first called New York the Big Apple fifty years ago.

A: I heard this story, too. The city officials wanted to get more people to visit this city by using this nickname.

B: Yup, New York at that time had a bad reputation. The red apples would serve as a bright and cheery image.

A: Then it works. This nickname makes deep depression on people.

B: By the way, if you are available, I'd like to invite you to visit New York.

A: 纽约的昵称是什么？

B: 一般当我们提起"大苹果"，就会想起纽约。

A: 这个词语来源于哪里？

B: 纽约城市旅游局表示50多年前爵士音乐家以及其他演艺人员第一次称呼纽约为"大苹果"。

A: 我也听说过这个故事。城市官员为了吸引更多的人来纽约就用了这个昵称。

B: 是的，纽约当时名声不是很好，红色苹果可以给人鲜明快乐的印象。

A: 那还挺有作用的。这个昵称给人留下了深刻的印象。

B: 对了，如果你有时间，我想邀请你一起去纽约旅游。

"问" 美国特色文化

美国人爱吃苹果派吗？

众所周知，纽约市的别名是Apple Pie，那么美国人会喜欢吃苹果派吗？其实，很多美国人相当中意苹果派，他们认为那是可以代表国家的甜品。而且，苹果营养丰富、养颜护肤，人人爱吃，美国苹果产量也很多。很多美国人，尤其是纽约人常带几个苹果上班或上学。另外，苹果汁和苹果派是受人欢迎的食品。据说华盛顿的苹果产量可供全世界一人一个。

阅读笔记

"祖父条款"是祖父定的条款吗

"祖父条款"是什么

Grandfather clause is a legal term, which is used to describe a situation where an old rule continues to apply to some existed situations, while a new rule will apply to the rest and future situations. The term also can be used as a verb to *grant* an *exemption*. Normally, the exemption is limited to a period of time.

The Grandfather Clause was *enacted* by seven states in the southern America in the late-19th century. The clause is designed to *negate* the 15th Amendment to the U.S. Constitution. The *intend* of the clause aiming at reduced African American political *participation* by preventing black people from voting while allowing *unqualified* whites to vote.

祖父条款是法律用语，指在新法规出台后，旧法规仍旧适用于某些已经存在的情况，新旧法将适用于其他及未来的情况。这个短语也可表示豁免这一动作。通常情况下，豁免是有时间限制的。

在19世纪末期，祖父条款在美国南部的七个州推行起来。这项条款的提出是为了否定美国宪法中的第十五修正案。条款的目的是，通过阻止黑人投票而允许不符合投票资格的白人投票，从而削弱非裔美国人的政治参与。

单词释义

grant 授予　　　　　exemption 豁免　　　　　enact 颁布
negate 否定　　　　　intend 打算　　　　　participation 参与
unqualified 不合格的

"祖父条款"应运而生

Louisiana, looking to find a more *straightforward* method

美国路易斯安那州为了寻求一种更加直接的方式来豁免白人的权

to exempt whites, created the Grandfather Clause in 1898 which allowed those who were able to vote before 1867 and those whose father or grandfather could vote before 1867 to *skip* the tests and *taxes*. As no blacks could vote in Louisiana before 1867, the year in which the Reconstruction Act ordered *universal* male *suffrage*, the grandfather clause *excluded* blacks in an *inexplicit* manner, thus, in theory, avoiding the *ire* of the Supreme Court and Northern Congressmen. Additionally, the enactment of the grandfather clause avoided national scrutiny because the national media was *preoccupied* with the *coinciding* outbreak of the Spanish-American War.

The United States Supreme Court *deemed* grandfather clauses unconstitutional in Guinn v. United States (1915). The Court stated that Oklahoma's grandfather clause was "*repugnant* to the prohibitions of the Fifteenth Amendment" and that Oklahoma must remove its clause. The other states that had grandfather clauses were also forced to *dismantle* their versions. In practice, however, the Supreme Court's verdict had no impact on black suffrage. Each state affected by the ruling quickly enacted new policy to sidestep Guinn. In Oklahoma, for example, legislators

利，从而在1898年提出了祖父条款，让那些在1867年前有权投票的人以及那些在1867年前可以投票的人的父亲和祖父免受考验并且免交税收。由于在1867年之前，路易斯安那州的黑人是没有投票权的，但是在1867年那一年，重建法案下令实行普选权，祖父条款则用一种含糊的方式剥夺了黑人的选举权。此外，祖父条款的通过也没有经过美国的审核，因为当时整个国家都把注意力集中于同时爆发的美西战争上了。

1915年，通过吉恩诉美国案，美国最高法院认为祖父条款违反了宪法，法院指出美国俄克拉荷马州的祖父条款"与第十五修正案的禁例背道而驰"，并下令俄克拉荷马州废除祖父条款。其他实行祖父条款的州也被迫废除他们相关的法令。而实际上，最高法院的裁定对黑人选举并未产生任何帮助。受这项法令影响的各州颁布新的政策来规避它。比如，在俄克

passed a statute which extended the vote only to those who did vote or were eligible to vote prior to Guinn. Black voting remained suppressed in a number of Southern states until the civil rights campaigns of the 1960s.

拉荷马州，议员们通过了一项法令，仅让那些投票选举过的以及在吉恩诉美国案之前就有资格投票选举的人来投票。在20世纪70年代的公民权利运动之前，黑人还受到压制无权投票。

straightforward 直白的
universal 普遍的
inexplicit 含糊的
deem 认为

skip 跳过
suffrage 投票
preoccupied 全神贯注的
repugnant 矛盾的

tax 税金
exclude 排除
coinciding 同时发生的
dismantle 拆卸

  美国特色文化

特色表达One

在日常生活中，可没有什么"祖父条款"，有时遇事可得to bet one's bottom dollar。这句话是什么意思？难道遇上麻烦了还能用最底层的钱来赌上一把？大家都知道bet与赌有关，dollar是钱，而one's bottom dollar指的是某人把钱快花光就剩最后一张美币，所以to bet one's bottom dollar就是说某人即使只剩一点钱了还是要打赌，暗含这人自信能回本，有"愿赌服输"的意思。

☆ 实景链接

A: I **bet my bottom dollar** that Rose will not marry Jack. 我敢打赌罗斯是不会嫁给杰克的。

B: Enlighten me. 为什么？你跟我说说。

A: First, her parents would not consent to their marriage. Second, she was living a lavish life in her whole life and she couldn't bear the poverty with him. 首先，她父母是不会同意他们的婚事的。再者，她一直过着奢侈的生活，受不了跟他一起过苦日子的。

B: Well, that is hard to tell. True love wins all. 那可说不准。真爱能战胜一切的。

💬 特色表达Two

有一句话"上有政策，下有对策"是全球适用的，但是想要找出好的对策，就需要"Use your loaf"，这可不是让你用你的一块面包，虽然loaf是面包，但是loaf在俚语中通常指"脑袋"，这个释义源自20世纪20年代的海陆军谚语字典，之后广泛传播。所以这句的意思是"用你的脑袋想一想"。

⭐ 实景链接

A：Why is Lily indifferent to me these days? 为什么莉莉这段时间对我都这么冷漠呢？

B：Have you done anything wrong? **Just use your loaf.** 你是做错了什么事情吗？用你的脑袋想想。

A：I just humiliated her in the public, but I apologized to her later. 我在公众面前羞辱了她，但是我事后跟她道了歉。

B：I think that must be the reason. 我想原因就是这个了吧。

拓展特色句

1. Please comply with the agreement. Do not fool me. 请遵守你的约定，别骗我。

2. If you breach of contract, our company can terminate the contract immediately. 若你方违反合约规定，本公司有权立即终止合同。

3. They drafted a new contract. 他们起草了一份新合约。

"聊" 美国特色文化

A：Professor, I have a question about last class and I want to consult you.

B：Just bring it on. I welcome your questions.

A：Last class you mentioned the Grandfather clause, but I can't see my point.

B：It is used to describe the situation

A：教授，对于上堂课我有个疑问，我想问一下你。

B：说吧。我很欢迎你们的提问。

A：上节课您提到了祖父条款这个词，但是我不是很明白。

B：它是指一条旧规则适用于现有的某些情况，而新规则就适用于其他的或者未来的情况。

where an old rule continues to apply to some existed situations, while a new rule will apply to the rest and future situations.

A: In that way, is that new rule valid?

B: At that time, many states took steps to sidestep this rule.

A: How can they make it?

B: Specifically, the enactment of the grandfather clause avoided national scrutiny because the national media was **preoccupied** with the **coinciding** outbreak of the Spanish-American War.

A: 如果是这样的话，那这条新规则有效吗？

B: 那个时候，很多州都会采取措施来规避它。

A: 他们是如何做到的？

B: 实际上，祖父条款的通过也没有经过美国的审核，因为当时整个国家都把注意力集中于同时爆发的美西战争上了。

"问" 美国特色文化

Guinn v. United States是什么意思？

美利坚合众国宪法第十五修正案（Fifteenth Amendment to the Constitution of the United States of America），简写作 Guinn v. United States，禁止联邦或州政府根据公民的种族、肤色或以前曾是奴隶而限制其选举权。这条修正案于1870年2月3日通过，是三条重建修正案的最后一条。该修正案经过艰苦的批准战后得以幸存，于1870年3月30日正式生效，是美国南北战争后通过的三条宪法修正案之一，它赋予所有肤色的人选举权。

黄丝带

"黄丝带"扬起爱情信念

As a *reminder* that an absent loved one, either in the *military* or in *jail*, would be welcomed home on their return, the symbol of a yellow ribbon became widely known in *civilian* life in the 1970s.

In October 1971, newspaper *columnist* Pete Hamill wrote a piece for the New York Post called "Going Home". The story is about college students on a bus trip to the beaches of Fort Lauderdale make friends with an *ex-convict* who is watching for a yellow handkerchief on a roadside *oak*. Before coming through, the ex-convict wrote to his wife and told her if she want him back, she should put a yellow handkerchief on the tree, and he'd *get off* and come home. If she didn't want him, forget it—no handkerchief, and he'd go on through. He *turned out* to be very welcome: there were a hundred yellow ribbons.

早在20世纪70年代,黄丝带作为欢迎军队或监狱中归来的爱人的信物的这一象征意义早就家喻户晓了。

1971年10月,报纸专栏作家皮特·汉米尔在《纽约邮报》上发表了一篇名为《回家》的文章。这篇文章讲述的是大学生在乘坐去往劳德代尔堡海滩的公交车上结识了一位刚从监狱里放出来并期待其妻子在路边橡树上挂黄手帕的囚犯的故事。因为在这名囚犯被放出来前,他曾写信给其妻子,告诉她,如果她愿意他回去就在树上挂一条黄丝带,他看见了就下车回家。如果她不愿意就忘掉这件事,看不见手帕,他也就不下车了。故事的结局是他的归来得到了妻子的强烈欢迎,因为那棵橡树上挂了100条黄丝带。

单词释义

reminder 提醒	military 军队	jail 监狱
civilian 平民	columnist 记者	ex-convict 前科犯
oak 橡树	get off 下车	turn out 结果是

何时挂起"黄丝带"

In the United States, a yellow ribbon is used as a symbol of *solidarity* with someone who is far from home, and an expression of hope that he or she will return safely and soon. *Numerous* unrelated causes have adopted the yellow ribbon as a symbol, somewhat *blurring* the *symbolism* of the yellow ribbon, but after the *deployment* of American troops to the Middle East in 2001, most Americans came to associate the yellow ribbon specifically with active duty members of the military, and supporting American troops.

The history of the yellow ribbon is ancient. Several *folktales* and songs from England document the wearing of yellow ribbons by young women waiting for their lovers to come home, and the *association* of a yellow ribbon with waiting for a loved one appears to have been carried to North America with colonists. Several Civil War folksongs *referenced* the tradition, and a popular marching song from the First World War, "She Wore a Yellow Ribbon," included a yellow ribbon as a *prominent* symbol of a waiting lover at home.

在美国，黄丝带被用来当作和远离家乡的某人心心相印的标志，同时也表明希望他或她能够安全归来。关于拿黄丝带作为象征的原因众说纷纭，导致黄丝带真正的象征意义也让人迷惑不清，但是自从2001年美国军队部署在中东地区之后，大多数美国人都会不由自主地把黄丝带和现役军队的成员联系起来，支持美国军队。

关于黄丝带的历史很悠久。英国有些民间故事和歌谣记载着年轻女士带着黄丝带等待着她们的爱人回家，一看到黄丝带就会联想起等待心爱的人，最后这一习俗也由殖民者带到了北美洲。好几首关于南北战争的民谣都提到了这个习俗，还有一首著名的第一次世界大战游行歌曲《她带着黄丝带》，其中唱到了将黄丝带作为等待深爱的人回家的著名标志。

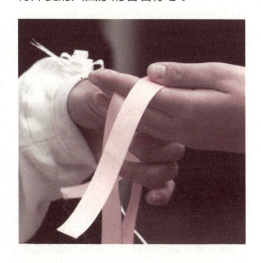

单词释义

solidarity 团结
symbolism 象征主义
association 联想

numerous 众多的
deployment 调度
reference 引用

blurring 模糊的
folktale 民间故事
prominent 显著的

美国特色文化

特色表达One

黄丝带是美国人相思的代言物，但可别随手拿着它去hit on某人。美国人常说Don't hit on my girlfriend!意思是"你省省吧，别对我女友献殷勤！"hit on在口语里常作"追求"的意思，而并不是其字面意思"打击"。

☆ 实景链接

A: I'd plan to give Bella a yellow ribbon. Hope she knows what I mean. 我打算送给贝拉一条黄丝带。希望她能懂得我的心意。

B: But Bella is Mike's dream girl. You'd better not **hit on** her. 但贝拉是麦克的梦中情人啊。你还是不要打她的主意。

A: Are they an item? No. So, I've got the chance. 他们是一对吗？不是。所以，我是有机会的。

B: You are really crazy. 你真是疯了。

特色表达Two

黄丝带寄语着思念，美国人期待久不归家的亲朋好友在远方能生活美好，在回归的那一天能the picture of health。这里不是说回归的亲人看起来像一幅健康的图片，在俚语里常用来形容一个人，表示某人"红光满面"。

☆ 实景链接

A: When will your husband be back from the troop? 你丈夫什么时候能从部队里回来？

B: I was informed of the date of next Friday. 通知我的时间是下个星期五。

A: No wonder do you look the **picture of health** recently. 难怪你这几天看起来红光满面的。

B: This news really excites me because I have waited for one year. 这个消息确实让我很激动，因为我已经等他有1年了。

拓展特色句

1. You are in my mind all the time. 我一直都在想你。

2. I miss my husband very much at this moment. 此时此刻，我非常想念我的丈夫。

3. She felt strong yearnings toward home. 她很思念家乡。

"聊" 美国特色文化

A: Melisa, the yellow ribbon on your hair looks really nice.

B: I am flattered. I bought it from a flea market.

A: So who is the guy on your heart?

B: I can't catch you. What's the relationship with the yellow ribbon and that?

A: Don't you know that? In our tradition, a yellow ribbon is a symbol of solidarity with someone and a hope that he will return safely and soon.

B: That's really cultural shock. This is my first time to hear about it. So at sight of this yellow ribbon, you will associate it with waiting for the beloved?

A: It also hints the girl with yellow ribbon has a favorite object of it.

B: It explains the matter. I'd better take off this ribbon in case of misunderstanding.

A: 玛丽莎，你头上的黄色丝带真好看。

B: 你过奖了，我从跳蚤市场买的。

A: 你心里记挂着谁呢？

B: 我不太明白你的意思。黄丝带和这个有什么关联呢？

A: 你不知道吗？在我们的文化中，黄丝带被用来当作和某人心心相印的标志，同时也表明希望他能够安全归来。

B: 这可真是文化震撼啊，我是第一次听到这个说法。所以你们看到黄丝带，就会联想起等待爱人吗？

A: 这也暗示系黄丝带的女孩有心仪的对象了。

B: 那就说通了，我还是别系这个丝带了，以免被别人误会。

"问" 美国特色文化

黄丝带的来历是什么？

黄丝带来自一个感人的爱情故事。在1971年的某一天，《纽约邮报》刊登了一篇小说：长途车上坐着一位沉默不语的男子，在同车的年轻游客的盘问下终于开了口。原来他刚从监狱出来，释放前曾写信给妻子：如果她已另有归宿，他也不责怪她；如果她还爱着他，愿意他回去，就在镇口的老橡树上系一根黄丝带；如果没有黄丝带，他就会随车而去，永远不会去打扰她……汽车快到目的地了，远远望去，镇口的老橡树上挂了上百条黄丝带，车上的乘客都欢呼起来。后来有人将这个动人的故事作成了歌曲，伴着歌声这个故事也传遍了全世界。于是黄丝带也成了美国"欢迎被囚禁的人重获自由"的标志。

阅读笔记

写给约翰的分手信

看到"dear John"你就惨了

Some American soldiers fighting during World War II discovered that months of *separation* from their hometown sweethearts could *lead to* unfortunate personal events. One such event involved receiving a formal and *terse break-up* message from home called a Dear John letter. Such a letter often began with a formal or perfunctory greeting, not the usual "My Dearest Sam" or "My Sweet Darling," which served to let the *recipient* brace himself for bad news.

The contents of a typical Dear John letter would also be direct and *detached*. "Dear John," the letter began. "I have found someone else whom I think the world of. I think the only way out is for us to get a divorce," it said. They usually began like that, those letters that told of *infidelity* on the part of the wives of *servicemen*... The men called them "Dear Johns".

有些参加第二次世界大战的美国士兵发现与家乡的爱人分别数月之后，可能会有一些不幸的事情发生在自己身上。这样的事情就包括收到一封从家里寄来的叫作"Dear John letter"的正式而又简洁的分手信。这样的一封信通常并非以常见的"我最亲爱的山姆"或者"我最亲爱的"开头，而是以非常正式敷衍的问候语开头，这样也能够让收信人做好接受坏消息的心理准备。

一封典型的"Dear John letter"的内容应该也是直接洒脱的。信的开头会说"Dear John"，"我已经找到我觉得世界上最爱的人了，我觉得对我们而言唯一的出路就是离婚。"她们通常都是这样开始，服役人员妻子都在信中告知自己的不忠……人们称呼这样的男人为"Dear Johns"。

单词释义

separation 分离	terse 简洁的	break-up 分开
perfunctory 敷衍的	recipient 收信人	detached 超然的
infidelity 不忠	servicemen 技工	lead to 导致

为何分手信如此"钟情"John

The origin of the name "John" in a Dear John letter is still a matter of *controversy*. Some sources believe the name John was chosen because of its *commonality* at the time, much like John Q. Public or John Doe is used today. Others say that the name was a reference to several popular songs which referred to foot soldiers as "Johnnies," as in When Johnnie Comes Marching Home Again. There is also a theory that a popular 1930s radio show began each *episode* with a female actress *intoning* Dear John as she began reading a letter to her unknown *paramour.*

The practice of sending these letters as a long distance break-up *tactic* became so common, in fact, that some women didn't even bother to *compose* more than the salutation. A soldier might only receive the message "Dear John" and nothing else. When *fellow* soldiers pressed the recipients for more details, many replied "That's all she wrote." This is said to be how the phrase that was all she wrote came into popular usage.

Dear John letter里面John这个名字的由来仍然饱受争议。有人认为之所以会选择John这个名字是因为在当时，叫这个名字的人很多。很像今天的张三或者李四。还有的人认为这个名字只是参考了几首有名的歌而来，比如像《当约翰尼游行归来》这首歌里就有"约翰尼"这样的步兵。还有一个说法是20世纪40年代的一个有名的广播节目中，每一期节目的开头都会有一个女演员以Dear John开始来吟咏她写给未知情人的信。

寄这样远距离的分手信的习俗变得非常普遍，实际上，有很多人甚至都不会费心来编写内容而只是写个开头的问候语。有的士兵甚至只会收到"Dear John"却没有其他内容的信件。当战友向收件人表达更多信息的时候，很多人会说"这就是她表达的所有意思。"这也是为什么这个短语最后能够表达所有意思而受到广泛使用了。

单词释义

controversy 争论	commonality 共性	episode 插曲
intone 吟咏	paramour 情人	tactic 策略
compose 编纂	fellow 同伙	

美国特色文化

特色表达One

很多女生喜欢有责任感的男生，觉得他们不会pass the buck，做事会顾全大局。Buck在美语中常指"美元"，在这里是刀柄，过去美国人玩纸牌时常用刀柄做记录，就是把刀柄传给发牌的人(pass the buck)，以防有人耍赖作弊。后来，这个短语常指"把责任推给别人"。

☆ 实景链接

A： That is not my fault. 那不是我的错。

B： Don't try to **pass the buck**. You should take the full blame. 别想推卸责任。你应该负全责。

A： Things were not like that. I can explain to you. 事情不是那样的，我可以跟你解释。

B： You always act like this. There is no need for explanation. I am done with you. 你总是这样。没必要解释了。我已经受够了。

特色表达Two

在分手之前，男女一方常会主动对另一方说"I expect you to be on the level with me."level常指"水平面"，那么在水平面上就能看得清晰，在俚语里常用来形容某人，所表达的意思是"某人是坦诚的、可以信任的"。

☆ 实景链接

A： Tom, I decide to break up with you after three months' living together. 汤姆，3个月的一起生活之后我还是决定跟你分手。

B： Why? Don't you love me anymore? 为什么？你不再爱我了吗？

A： Nope, I just find we don't fit each other. 不是的，我只是觉得我们不适合彼此。

B： All I need is the truth. **I expect you to be on the level with me.** 我只需要你说实话，希望你坦诚以对。

拓展特色句

1. We were on a break! 我们已经分手了。

2. I don't feel anything for you. 我对你没感觉。

3. I'm sensing a real distance between us. 我感觉我们之间有很大的隔阂。

 美国特色文化

A: Trent skips classes again. Lately he looks downhearted. Do you know what happened to him?

B: Last week he received a Dear John letter.

A: Who is John? What's the letter about?

B: John was just a general term, much like John Q. Public or John Doe is used today. This letter is about break-up.

A: Does that mean Beth broke up with him?

B: That's it. Beth just sent him a message "Dear John" and nothing else. But Trent will get everything.

A: How does this tradition derive from?

B: It derives from World War II. At that time, many soldiers separated from their hometown sweethearts, which lead to receiving a message from home called a Dear John letter.

A: 特伦特最近又逃课了。他最近看起来很消沉。你知道他发生了什么事情吗？

B: 上周他收到了一封"亲爱的约翰信"。

A: 约翰是谁啊？这封信讲的是什么？

B: 约翰只是个泛称，有点像今天的张三李四。这封信是关于分手的。

A: 你的意思是贝丝跟他分手了吗？

B: 是的，贝丝只是给他发了一封"亲爱的约翰"这样的短信，没发别的内容。但是特伦特就会明白一切。

A: 这个习俗来源于什么？

B: 它来源于第二次世界大战。那个时候，很多士兵都会与家里的爱人分离，也就导致收到从家里寄来的分手信。

"问" 美国特色文化

分手信是Dear John letter，John Doe又是谁？

John Doe最初来自英国，在当时《驱逐法案》的讨论中，虚构了两个人名，一个是John Doe，代表土地所有者；另一个是Richard Roe，是租地的人，他将租来的土地据为己有，而把John Doe赶走了。后来，John Doe和Richard Roe被广泛用于诉讼程序中对不知姓名当事人的假设称呼，在美国常用John Doe指在凶杀案现场身份不明的死者。

阅读笔记

山姆大叔

山姆大叔是何许人也

Uncle Sam is the *culmination* of a *tradition* of representative male icons in America which can be traced well back into colonial times. The actual figure of Uncle Sam, however, dates from the War of 1812. The setting was *ripe* for a *figure* such as Sam at that point. Previous icons had been *geographically* specific, *centering* most often on the New England area. The War of 1812 *sparked* a *renewed* interest in national *identity* which had faded since the revolutionary war.

In 1813, the United States gets its nickname, Uncle Sam. The name is linked to Samuel Wilson, a meat packer from Troy, New York, who supplied barrels of beef to the United States Army during the War of 1812. Wilson (1766—1854) stamped the barrels with "U.S." for United States, but soldiers began referring to the food as "Uncle Sam's", because the "U.S." stood for "Uncle Sam" as well. The local newspaper picked up on the story and Uncle Sam eventually gained widespread acceptance as the nickname for the U.S. federal government.

山姆大叔是所有传统美国男性代表图标中，最具典型性的一位，相关图标可以一直追溯到殖民时代。山姆大叔这个真实的人物则要一直追溯到1812年的英美战争。在当时的环境下，创造山姆这样一个人物的时机非常成熟。之前的图标都具有地理位置特殊性，大多都集中在英国的区域。自美国独立战争之后，大家对民族认同感的热情逐渐消退，1812年的英美战争又让这个热情再度"复燃"。

1813年，美国获"山姆大叔"这个绰号。这个名字的由来与塞缪尔·威尔逊有关系。塞缪尔·威尔逊是一名纽约特洛伊城的肉类包装员，在1812年战争期间他为美国军队供应牛肉罐头。塞缪尔·威尔逊在牛肉桶上刻上代表美国的U.S.，但士兵们逐渐将食物理解为"山姆大叔"的，因为U.S.也是Uncle Sam的缩写。当地报纸刊载了这个故事，于是山姆大叔最终被广泛接受，成为了美国联邦政府的绰号。

单词释义

culmination 顶点　　　　tradition 传统　　　　ripe 成熟

figure 形象　　　　　　geographically 地理上地　　center 集中

spark 鼓舞　　　　　　renew 更新　　　　　identity 身份

山姆大叔形象如何

By the early twentieth century, there was little physical *resemblance* left between Samuel Wilson and Uncle Sam. As a symbol of an *ever-changing* nation, Uncle Sam had *gone through* many *incarnations*. *Initially* cartoon versions of Sam were very familiar to those of Brother Jonathan. The Civil War saw a major *transition* in the development of Uncle Sam as his image was associated with that of Abraham Lincoln. It was during this period that Sam aged and *acquired* a beard.

The final *version* of Uncle Sam that we are most familiar with today, came about in 1917. The famous "I Want You" *recruiting poster* by James Montgomery Flagg set the image of Uncle Sam firmly into American consciousness.

Although there continue to be numerous *variations* on the image of Uncle Sam, the Flagg version can be considered the standard from which others *deviate*.

20世纪初，塞缪尔·威尔逊和山姆大叔的外形上没有多少共同点。作为一个历经变化的国家的标志，山姆大叔的形象也经历了很多变化。塞缪尔·威尔逊最初的卡通版对于那些了解乔纳森大哥的人会非常眼熟。美国内战对于山姆大叔的演变来说是一个重要的转折点，因为他的形象与林肯总统联系起来了。就在那段时间，山姆变老了，脸上也长起了胡子。

山姆大叔的最后一个版本也是今天最为大家所熟悉的版本，诞生于1917年。詹姆斯·蒙哥马利·弗拉格在山姆大叔的形象中加入了"I Want You"这行字来作为招募海报，这一形象也深深地印入了美国人的脑海。

尽管山姆大叔的形象仍然经历着无数次的改变，但是费拉格的版本却被认为是区别于其他人的标准版本。

单词释义

resemblance 相似处	ever-changing 千变万化的	go through 经历
incarnation 化身	initially 最初地	transition 转变
acquire 获得	version 版本	recruit 招募
poster 海报	variation 变化	deviate 脱离

 美国特色文化

特色表达One

山姆大叔是个白胡子、白发、高个的老头，你可别bark up the wrong tree以为他是个慈祥老头，其实他可厉害了呢！to bark up the wrong tree最早出自17世纪美国殖民地时期。当时西部大开发，拓荒者们靠猎狗打猎为生。有的猎狗会被浣熊糊弄，不停地对着空空的树洞狂吠不已(to bark up the wrong tree)。随着时间的推移，"to bark up the wrong tree"引申意义为"精力或目标集中在错误的地方"。

实景链接

A: Is this Uncle Sam in this picture? 这张照片上的人是山姆大叔吗？

B: You are really **barking up the wrong tree**. Let me search one picture for you. Here it is. This is the classic image of Uncle Sam. 那你可真是认错人了。我来给你搜一张，看这个，这才是山姆大叔的经典形象。

A: Well, he looks smart and sharp. I thought he would be an amiable old guy. 哦，他看起来很精明能干，我还以为他是个和蔼可亲的老头呢。

B: Now you know he isn't. 现在你知道他不是那样了吧。

特色表达Two

要像山姆大叔一样做一个有气度有分寸的美国人，而不是不合时宜地monkey with something。一般猴子喜欢爬高，玩耍，给人的印象就是蹦跳个不停，所以monkey做动词时，常表示"摆弄""干预"等意思。这里的"monkey with something！"就是"糊弄，累赘"的意思。

☆ **实景链接**

A：Jackie, how many times have I told you not to **monkey with your finger**? 杰克，我告诉过你多少次了，不要老是玩你的手指。

B：I can't help it. But what's wrong with it? 我也忍不住，但是这有什么错呢？

A：It makes you look childish, but you know you're an adult already. 这让你看起来很幼稚，但是你已经是个成年人了。

B：Well, I will try my best to get rid of it. 好吧，我尽全力改掉。

拓展特色句

1. Uncle Sam stands for the United States. 山姆大叔代表美国。

2. Uncle Sam is represented as a tall man with chin whiskers. 山姆大叔被描画成一个身材高挑、满脸胡茬的人。

3. People call the United States "Uncle Sam", don't you know that? 人们都称美国为"山姆大叔"，你不知道吗？

"耶" 美国特色文化

A：Fancy meeting you in the library. What are you reading?

A：很高兴在图书馆遇到你，你在看什么呢？

B：I read something about American culture. Before I read this book, I thought Uncle Sam was the uncle of a president or something.

B：我在读一本关于美国文化的书。在我读这本书之前，我还以为山姆大叔是总统或者某位名人的叔叔呢？

A：Many people have misunderstanding like that. He is a popular symbol of America. He has long white hair, a beard and very interesting clothing in cartoons.

A：很多人都有这样的误解。他是美国很有名的象征。漫画上他留着白色长发，蓄着胡子，穿着有趣的衣服。

B：Do you know where did his appearance come from?

B：你知道他的形象来源于哪里吗？

A：I know it. Brother Jonathan and Yankee Doodle.

A：我知道，来自乔纳森大哥和扬基曲。

B：但是我不知道它是从什么时候开始被采用的？

A：1961年，美国国会采用了山姆大叔作为美国的象征。

B: But I don't know when was it adopted?

A: In 1961 the American congress adopted Uncle Sam as the national symbol.

B: He is the true symbol of the American people.

B：他是美国人民的真实象征。

"问" 美国特色文化

美国有山姆大叔，英国有什么？

英国有位大叔叫约翰牛(John Bull)，是英国的拟人化形象，源于1727年由苏格兰作家约翰·阿布斯诺特所出版讽刺小说《约翰牛的生平》。这部书中的主人公约翰牛是一个稀罕戴高帽、拿雨伞的矮胖绅士，不仅为人愚笨而且性格粗暴，欺善怕恶。这个形象原为了讽刺辉格党内阁在西班牙王位继承战争中的政策所作，随着小说的流行，逐渐成为英国人自嘲的形象。

阅读笔记

"我来自密苏里"到底作何意思

读懂"我来自密苏里"的内涵

SHOW ME
I'M FROM MISSOURI

The phrase "I'm from Missouri" in a more **completed** form is "I'm from Missouri. Show me." It is known that Missourians **are proud of** being skeptical, not accepting an **assertion** without seeing the proof. So the phrase expresses the meaning of "I don't believe you. Show me proof."

Most people who have heard of the Show Me state will understand that the speaker is being **skeptical** while saying "I'm from Missouri," in the **appropriate** context. **On the other hand**, it is important to say "I'm" here **instead of** "I am", as I am from Missouri expresses the **literal** meaning.

短语"我来自密苏里"更加完整的表达方式是"我来自密苏里,给我证据看看。"密苏里人自豪于自己经常怀疑的态度,不轻易接受没有证据的言论。所以这个短语的意思是"我不相信你,给我证据看看。"

大部分听过密苏里名言的人都知道,有人说"我从密苏里来"时表达的是怀疑的态度。另一方面,在说这个短语的时候一定要用"I'm"这种形式而不是"I am"。因为"I am from Missouri"表达的就只是字面上的意思。

单词释义

completed 完整的　　　　assertion 断言　　　　skeptical 怀疑的
appropriate 合适的　　　literal 字面的　　　　be proud of 以……为骄傲
on the other hand 另一方面　instead of 相反

"密苏里"暗号获得公认

The phrase did not receive national attention until 1899, when Willard Vandiver used it in a speech before the Five O'Clock

1899年,威拉德·范迪弗在费城五点俱乐部发表演讲的时候用到了"我来自密苏里"这个表达,直到那个时候,这个表达才受到国民的关注。范

Club in Philadelphia. Vandiver, a *congressional* representative from Missouri and a member of the House Committee on Naval Affairs, was in Philadelphia to *inspect* that city's navy yard. Afterwards, *in honor of* the *inspection*, a dinner was held.

Even though Vandiver and Governor Hull of Iowa were the only invited guests without formal evening clothes, they agreed to attend the *banquet*. Hull, at the last minute, managed to *show up* wearing evening attire—but the suit had an *odd* look about it. After dinner, Hull gave a speech in which he jokingly explained why his suit did not fit. He then introduced Vandiver, who was also scheduled to speak.

Vandiver, *embarrassed* at being more informally dressed than his dinner *companions*, concluded it with a *playful jab* at Hull: "He tells you that the tailors, finding he was here without a dress suit, made one for him in 15 minutes. I have a different explanation. You heard him say he came over here without one, and you see him now with one that doesn't fit him. The explanation is that he stole mine, and that's the reason why you see him with one and me without any. This story from Iowa doesn't go at all with me; I'm from Missouri, you've got to show me."

迪弗是来自密苏里州的国会代表，同时也是海军军事委员会的一员，他当时去费城是为了视察当地的海军部队。随后，为了纪念这次视察，当地还举办了一场晚宴。

即使范迪弗和爱荷华州的州长赫尔是唯一两位没有正式晚宴服装而被邀请的嘉宾，他们也欣然同意去赴宴了。在最后一刻，赫尔终于搞到一件晚礼服出席晚宴，但是这件衣服看起来很不合身。晚宴结束后，赫尔发表演讲，开玩笑地解释为什么他的服装会不合身。然后他就介绍被安排发表讲话的范迪弗上台。

范迪弗因为自己的穿着比其他赴宴的人更加随意而感到非常尴尬，最后以开玩笑的口吻冷嘲热讽赫尔："赫尔告诉各位的是裁缝在发现他没有西装礼服之后，在15分钟之内给他做了一件。而我的解释却不同，你们都听到赫尔说过他来的时候没有一件礼服，但是现在大家看到的是他穿着一件不合身的衣服站在这里，我的解释是赫尔偷了我的衣服，这也是为什么大家现在能够看到他身穿晚礼服，而我却不没有任何晚礼服。这个来自爱荷华州的故事在我身上根本就行不通。我来自密苏里，你需要拿证据给我看。"

单词释义

congressional 国会的 inspect 视察 in honor of 纪念
inspection 视察   banquet 晚宴 odd 奇怪的
embarrassed 尴尬的 companion 同伴 playful 开玩笑的
jab 猛击   show up 出现

"品" 美国特色文化

特色表达One

为什么会有"我来自密苏里"这样的暗号呢？当然是为了默认一种规矩，形成一种文化认同，防着那些loose cannon。可是松散的大炮有什么要防备的呢？loose cannon源自百年前在海上大战的情景。当时，很多战船上都安置了大炮，但是大炮既是作战利器也是危险品，因为有时遇上暴风雨大炮又没拴紧时，反而会砸伤船上的士兵。所以loose cannon有"祸起萧墙"的意思，如今，美国人多用这个词指伤害自己的熟人或打破规矩的人。

☆ 实景链接

A： I'm from Missouri. You've got to show me. 我不相信你，你得拿证据给我看。

B： Why don't you trust me? Why do you always view me as a **loose cannon**? 你为什么不相信我？为什么总认为我会给你找麻烦呢？

A： Because of what you did before. 就因为你之前的所作所为。

B： Fine, wait here. I'll show you the document. 好，你在这儿等着，我去拿文件给你看。

特色表达Two

当时密苏里州流行说这句话，有很大原因是人们担心被人骗，害怕到头来是一场army game。这个词组的字面意思是"军队游戏"，有点"兵不厌诈"的意义，可引申作"骗局"。

☆ **实景链接**

A：If you make the small bet, you definitely win. 如果你下小赌注的话，你肯定能赢。

B：How can you be so convinced? 你怎么这么确信呢？

A：Just believe me. I will play some tricks. 就相信我吧，我会玩些小技巧的。

B：Sorry, I am outta here. I thought it is an **army game.** 对不起，我得走了，我觉得这是一场骗局。

拓展特色句

1. Do you have any evidence? 你有什么证据吗？

2. His idea is speculative. No evidence yet exists. 他的观点是推测出来的，还没任何证据。

3. What are the sources of your evidence? 你那些证据的来源是什么？

"聊" **美国特色文化**

A：Kitty, please stay a moment. I have to search your handbag.

B：How dare you say that? It's so rude.

A：My necklace was missing after you getting into the room.

B：It's sheer nonsense. Many people went into your room. Why did you just suspect of me?

A：Someone told me he saw you wear it.

B：It's beautiful. I can't help trying it on. But I put it back in place.

A：All in all, if you want to prove you are innocent, you'd better let me check your bag. I'm from Missouri.

B：Sorry, I can't make it. You have no right to do that.

A：基蒂，请稍等一会，我需要搜搜你的手提包。

B：你怎么敢说这种话？这很粗鲁。

A：你进房间之后，我的项链就不见了。

B：这简直是无稽之谈。很多人都进了你的房间。你为什么单单只怀疑我呢？

A：有人告诉我说你戴过它。

B：它很漂亮，所以我忍不住想试戴一下，但是我把它放回原位了。

A：总而言之，如果你想证明自己是清白的，你最好让我检查一下你的包。我来自密苏里。

B：对不起，我办不到，你也没有权利这样做。

"问" 美国特色文化

马克·吐温来自密苏里吗？

密苏里州为美国著名的作家马克·吐温(Mark Twain)的故乡，他的名著《汤姆历险记》(The Adventures of Tom Sawyer)就发生在这里。马克·吐温一生成就无数，写了大量作品，题材涉及小说、剧本、散文、诗歌等各方面，而"马克·吐温"是他的笔名，原是密西西比河水手使用的表示在航道上所测水的深度的术语。他的作品批判了不合理现象或人性的丑恶之处，专家们和一般读者都认为，幽默和讽刺是他的写作特点。马克·吐温是美国批判现实主义文学的奠基人，被誉为文学史上的"林肯"。

阅读笔记

星期五和13为何如此不吉利

星期五是好还是坏

Superstitions swirling around Friday as being lucky or unlucky have existed since ancient times, beginning with the northern nations. Ancient Romans *dedicated* the sixth day of the week to their beautiful, but *vain*, goddess Venus, so, when the Norsemen adopted the Roman method of naming days, they naturally adopted Venus as their name for the sixth day of the week. Their closest translation for Venus, Frigg, or Freya, eventually evolved into Friday, a day they considered to be the luckiest day of the week.

From a religious *standpoint*, legend has it that Adam and Eve ate the *forbidden* fruit, the apple, on a Friday, and later died on a Friday, and Christians consider Friday as the day on which Christ was *crucified* by the Romans.

围绕着星期五是吉利还是不吉利的迷信从古代起就一直存在，最初是从北方各国开始的。古罗马人每周都徒劳地把每周的第六天奉献给他们美丽的女神维纳斯，因此北欧人在采用罗马人的日期命名方式的时候，他们很自然地将维纳斯作为每周第六天的名称。他们把Venus、Frig或Frey最接近的翻译最终演绎成Friday（星期五），即他们认为一周中最吉利的日子。

从宗教的角度看，传说亚当和夏娃在星期五这一天偷吃了禁果，后来又在星期五这一天去世。基督教徒们认为星期五是耶稣被罗马人钉在十字架上的日子。

单词释义

superstition 迷信	swirl 盘旋	dedicate 致力
vain 徒劳的	standpoint 观点	forbidden 被禁止的
crucify 折磨		

星期五和13为何预言"不详"

The modern basis for the *aura* that surrounds Friday the 13th *stems from* Friday October the 13th, 1307. On this date, the Pope of the church in Rome in Conjunction with the King of France, *carried out* a secret death *warrant* Against "the Knights Templar". The Templars were *terminated* as *heretics*, never again to hold the power that they had held for so long. There Grand Master, Jacques DeMolay, was arrested and before he was killed, was *tortured* and crucified.

The Scandinavian belief that the number 13 *signified* bad luck sprang from their mythological 12 demigods, who were joined by a 13th demigod, Loki, an evil cruel one, who brought upon humans great misfortune. The number 13, in the Christian faith, is the number of parties at the Last Supper, with the 13th guest at the table being the *traitor*, Judas. When Christians combine this day and number, the combination can only hold special significance.

现代人认为星期五、13号成为不祥预兆是来源于1307年10月13日，星期五这一天。在这一天，罗马教廷的教皇和法国国王联合起来执行了一条对"圣殿骑士团"的秘密处决令。圣殿骑士们因为是异教徒而被判处死刑，从而也失去了他们长期以来所拥有的权利。基督教大长老雅克·德沐莱被捕，他死前受尽了折磨，最终被钉死在十字架上。

斯堪的纳维亚人认为数字13是厄运的意思，这来源于他们神话中的12个半神半人的神，后来一个叫洛奇的第13个半神半人的人加入了，他是一个残酷的魔鬼，它给人类带来了巨大的灾难。而根据基督教徒的信仰，数字13是最后的晚餐中聚会的人数，餐桌上第13位客人是叛徒犹大。当基督教徒们将数字13与日期联系起来的时候，这种结合就有了特殊的意义。

单词释义

aura 预兆	warrant 委任状	terminate 终止
heretic 异教徒	torture 折磨	signify 意味
traitor 叛徒	stem from 来自	carry out 执行

 美国特色文化

特色表达One

在美国要入乡随俗，既然美国人忌讳数字13，那你就要谨记小心说错话，可别成了backseat driver。在美国，backseat driver的字面意思是"坐在汽车后座的驾驶员"，常用来指坐在车上不信任司机而指挥这指挥那的"指挥家"，他们总是给开车的人提一些自以为很重要的指导和警告。可是有哪个司机愿意被这样"贴心指导"呢？所以backseat driver就是指瞎操心、乱提建议的人。

☆实景链接

A： Next Friday is OK for all of us, right? Let's choose that day to set sail. 下个星期五我们大家都没问题吧？我们就选那天起航吧。

B： Don't be such a **backseat driver**. It is 13th next Friday. 别瞎提议。下周五是13号。

A： So? 那怎么了？

B： You are in American, man. The number 13 signifies bad luck. 拜托，你现在是在美国。13代表厄运的。

特色表达Two

大部分美国人觉得数字13是相当不吉利的，在这样的统一文化认同之下，他们会觉得那些不在意13黑暗意义的人有点airs and graces。airs的意思是"高傲的样子"，而grace是"优雅"，这个短语在美国俚语里常指"装腔作势"。

☆实景链接

A： Why don't you guys play with John? 你们为什么不愿意和约翰玩？

B： He lost many friends including us because of his **airs and graces**. 他失去包括我们在内的朋友就是因为他的架子太大了。

A： It's hard to imagine he is such a person. 很难想象他是这样的一个人。

B： We saw him in his true colors after a long time. 我们也是在很久之后才发现他的真面目。

拓展特色句

1. I should restrain myself from shopping spree on Black Friday. 我要克制自己不要在黑色星期五疯狂购物。

2. They believe that Friday the 13th is bad luck. 他们认为13号的星期五代表厄运。

3. The fear of number 13 is called triskaidekaphobia. 这种对数字13的恐惧被称作恐数字13症。

"聊" 美国特色文化

A: So have you fixed the date for marriage?

B: Preliminary date is next Friday, May 13th. It's just the day we met first time three years ago.

A: Are you kidding? What a day you choose!

B: You react too much. What's wrong with that day?

A: Friday and 13 are treated as the aura of bad luck.

B: Can't think you Americans are so superstitious. I can't change my date just because of superstitions.

A: Our Americans really care about 13 especially. We nearly avoid this number for everything, for example, there is no room number of 13 in hotel.

B: It seems I should have the second thought about the date.

A: 你们确定好结婚的时间了吗？

B: 初步定的日期是下周五，5月13日。这正好是3年前我们第一次相遇的时间。

A: 你开玩笑的吗？你怎么选择这一天？

B: 你反应也太大了吧。那一天有什么问题吗？

A: 星期五和13号都被认为是会带来坏运气。

B: 真的是没有想到你们美国人这么迷信啊。我不可能因为这些迷信而改变日期。

A: 我们美国人尤其在意13这个数字。我们几乎避免一切跟这个数字有关的事情，比如，酒店里不会有13号房间。

B: 看来我真的得好好想想这个日期了。

"问"美国特色文化

数字13被人嫌弃到什么地步？

因为数字13是不吉利的象征，所以西方人想方设法避免和"13"接触。比如，在每月的13号，若非有什么极其重要的事情，他们都不会举行活动。你很难在荷兰找到13号楼和13号的门牌。因为他们用"12A"取代了13号。你要去英国的剧场或影院，也找不到第13排和13座。而法国

人就更灵活了，他们将剧场的12排和14排之间设置为人行通道。此外，西方人不愿在13号这一天出去旅游，更不乐意有13个人一起进餐，更别提吃饭时上13道菜了。另外，美国前总统罗斯福也忌讳13，据说每月13日罗斯福很少出门，尽管并非每个13日都赶上"星期五"。

阅读笔记

Yankee到底是指谁

在美国，我们称谁为Yankee

The term "Yankee" and its contracted form "Yank" have several *interrelated* meanings, all referring to people from at least the northern United States. Its various senses depend on the *scope* of context. Most broadly:

Within the United States, it usually refers to people from the north, largely those who fought for the regions in the Union side of the American Civil War, but also of those with New England cultural ties, such as *descendants* from colonial New England settlers, wherever they live. The speech dialect of New England is called "Yankee" or "Yankee dialect."

Within Southern American English, "Yankee" refers to Northerners.

Outside the United States, "Yank" is used informally to refer to any American, including Southerners.

"Yankee"这个词及其缩写形式"Yank"有几个相关的意思，但所有的意思都指"来自美国北部的人"。它的意思主要取决于上下文语境，最广泛的用法如下。

在美国，它经常用来指代来自北部的人，主要是指美国内战时支持美利坚合众国的人，以及那些沿袭新英格兰文化的人，比如新英格兰殖民定居者的后代，而他们住在哪里并不重要。新英格兰人的方言则被称作"扬基话"或者"扬基方言"。

在美国南部，"Yank"用来指代北方人。

在美国以外的其他国家，"Yank"在非正式情况下可以指代包括南方人在内的任何美国人。

单词释义

interrelated 相关的　　　　scope 范围　　　　descendant 后代

Yankee这个词有何恶意

The informal British English "Yank" is especially popular among Britons and Australians and sometimes carries *pejorative overtones*. The Southern American English "Yankee" is typically uncontracted and at least mildly pejorative, although less *vehemently* so as time passes from the American Civil War. The meaning of Yankee has varied over time. In the 18th century, it referred to residents of New England descended from the original English settlers of the region. Mark Twain, in the following century, used the word in this sense in his novel *A Connecticut Yankee in King Arthur's Court*, published in 1889. As early as the 1770s, British people applied the term to any person from what became the United States. In the 19th century, Americans in the southern United States employed the word in reference to Americans from the northern United States.

Perhaps the most *pervasive* influence on the use of the term throughout the years has been the song "Yankee Doodle", which was popular during the American Revolutionary War (1775—1783) as, following the battles of Lexington and Concord, Today, "Yankee Doodle" is the official "state song" of Connecticut.

在英式英语中，非正式的"Yank"在英国人和澳大利亚人之间广泛使用，有时带有轻蔑的意味。而美国南方则通常使用完整形式"Yankee"，即使在美国内战之后，这个词的语气已经没有以前那么恶劣，但口气中还是略带轻蔑。Yankee这个词的意思随着时间的流逝也在发生变化。在18世纪，它用来指代最初那批来到美国的新英格兰人移民的后代。在随后的19世纪，马克·吐温在他1889年发表的小说《误闯亚瑟王宫》中就用了这个词来表示此意。早在18世纪70年代，英国人用这个词来指代后来成为美国人的任何移民。19世纪的时候，美国南部的美国人用这个词来指代从美国北部来的美国人。

也许这些年这个词最具影响力的使用体现在《扬基曲》里，在列克星敦与康科德战役后爆发的美国独立战争(1775—1783)时期，这首歌非常有名。现在，《扬基曲》已经成为美国康涅狄格州的官方"州歌"。

单词释义

pejorative 轻蔑的　　　　overtone 寓意　　　　vehemently 激烈地

pervasive 普遍的

 美国特色文化

特色表达One

Yankee Doodle这首小曲不仅是美国康涅狄格州的官方"州歌"，甚至还是非官方的美国第二国歌，这可不是hot air哦。在俚语hot air中，hot的意思是"热"，air是"空气"，但hot air除了表示"热空气"，在美国俚语里还有"夸夸其谈，吹牛"的意思，你可以理解为吹牛吹得太厉害了，把空气都吹热了。

⭐ **实景链接**

A：I have learned painting for many years. 我学了很多年画画。

B：Really? Can you show us some of your works? 真的吗？你能给我们看看你的作品吗？

A：I threw them away. But I can paint very well. 我全都扔了。但我画得非常好。

B：Sounds like what you said is just **hot air**. 听起来你就是在吹牛。

特色表达Two

与中国相似，美国南北方的人们之间也有小摩擦，有时他们会觉得对方有点Jekyll and Hyde。Jekyll and Hyde是英国一部著名小说。书中的主角Jekyll很善良，有一天他将自己当作实验对象，结果变得人格分裂，一到夜晚就会爆发邪恶Hyde的属性，成了"双重人格"。

⭐ **实景链接**

A：Hey, what makes you so upset? 嘿，你怎么这么苦恼啊？

B：I'm afraid of giving speech in front of the public. 我害怕在人前讲话。

A：I get the impression that you are confident and outgoing. I can't imagine that you will get nervous. 我印象里你自信又外向。很难想象你会紧张。

B：I'm afraid of speaking to the strangers. I think I'm **Jekyll and Hyde**. 我害怕在陌生人面前说话。我觉得我是双重人格。

拓展特色句

1. Yankee candle is the best loved candle in America. 在美国，扬基蜡烛是最受欢迎的蜡烛。

2. During and after the American Civil War, Yankee was popularized as a derogatory term to Northern enemies by Confederates. 在美国内战期间以及结束之后，南部联邦开始广泛用起了扬基这个词表达来贬低北方的敌军。

3. The New York Yankees is a very popular professional baseball team, which is shortened as NYY. 纽约扬基队是一支非常有名的职业棒球队，它的缩写为NYY。

"聊" 美国特色文化

A：Have you heard the song of **Yankee Doodle**?

B：I am not sure. Do you refer to the official "state song" of Connecticut?

A：That's it. How do you think about it?

B：Actually, I don't know what the meaning of Yankee is. Can you illustrate it?

A：It has several interrelated meanings, all referring to people from at least the northern United States.

B：So does the word have any pejorative overtone?

A：Sometimes, especially when Britons and Australians call Americans.

B：I got it. Thank you.

A：你听过《扬基曲》这首歌吗？

B：你指的是康涅狄格州的官方"州歌"吗？

A：就是那首，你觉得怎么样？

B：事实上，我不知道"Yankee"是什么意思，你能解释一下吗？

A：它有几个相关的意思，但所有的意思都指"来自美国北部的人"。

B：那这个词有贬低的口吻吗？

A：有时候会，尤其是在英国人和澳大利亚人称呼美国人的时候。

B：知道了，谢谢。

"问" 美国特色文化

美国如今还有所谓的南方文化吗？

以前，南方学者强调黑人和白人要极其有礼地接触。随着种族矛盾的缓和，南方人仍然致力维持适当的礼仪举止，强调这是一项重要的文化标志。然而，自南北战争以来，南方的文明程度有所下降，很大程度上，他们将此归咎于北方人。此外，新移民的涌入也打破了原有的文化模式，使南部许多地区不再封闭，使在南方生

活的美国人不再是单纯的土生土长的一代。所以南方一些大城市失去文明的速度似乎比全国其他地区更快，如今美国南方的文化也逐渐演变成了多元文化。

阅读笔记

Part 4

美国为何不可复制

美国人的工作和休闲态度

美国人是否满意自己的工作

How satisfied are Americans with their jobs? What gives people the most satisfaction at work? And how much *leisure* time do they really have?

For at least half of Americans, work gives them their sense of *identity*, and a large number of workers believe that the job they do is essential to the success of their organization. They feel that their opinions matter and that they are treated with respect, and perhaps surprisingly, most believe they are fairly *compensated*. It is not difficult for most workers to *take* time *off* from work for personal matters. Some people are not so satisfied with their jobs. For example, although most *respondents* report little experience with *discrimination*, African Americans are more likely to believe that improvements are needed. People earning less also tend to say that their workplace needs improvement.

美国人对他们的工作满意吗？在工作中，什么最能让人感到满意？他们到底有多少休闲的时光？

大多数的美国人认为工作让他们获得自我认同感，大多数的工作人员认为整个公司的成功离不开他们所做的工作。他们认为自己的想法很重要，并且大家非常尊重他们，令人意外地或许是大多数人都觉得自己收入

还不错。对于大多数员工而言，因为私事而请假不会很难。还有的人对自己的工作不满意。比如：即使大多数调查对象说他们并非是受到了歧视，非裔美国人倾向于觉得自己需要提高的可能性更大。那些赚得越来越少的人可能也会反映他们工作的场所需要改善。

单词释义

leisure 休闲	identity 认同	compensate 补偿
respondent 应答者	discrimination 歧视	take off 请假

美国人如何度过休闲时光

As for leisure, large majorities of workers say they are satisfied with number of hours they work and the amount of leisure time they have. *Contrary to* popular belief, only a small percentage have long *commutes* or use laptops for taking work home.

Workers report enjoying their time off more than their time on the job, and they add that technology makes leisure time more enjoyable. Riehle's new poll found that when Americans' leisure time suffers, they experience increased levels of stress both on and off the job.

A comparison of recent polls with those from *mid-century* found that leisure time is being *redefined*. Vacations were once used for work of other kinds, such as for *charity* or housework, or to *recharge* for one's job. Now Americans are growing more comfortable with the idea of leisure for itself.

至于休闲，大多数工作人员会说他们对工作的时间以及休息的时间都感到很满意。与流传的说法完全不一样的是，只有很小部分的人通勤时间很长或者把工作带回家，用电脑办公。

工作人员认为他们在工作之外的时间更享乐，而并非是在工作的时候，他们补充道科技让休闲的时光更加愉悦。里德的新调查发现，那些连休闲的时光都觉得是折磨的美国人，无论在工作中还是在休闲的时候，他们所承受的压力也更大。

把最近的调查和那些在本世纪中叶就有的调查对比会发现休闲的时光的定义发生了变化。曾经利用休假来做其他的工作，比如参加公益或者做家务，或者为工作"充电"。美国人现在满足于休闲时光就是用来放松的这个想法。

单词释义

commute 通勤	mid-century 世纪中期	redefined 再定义
charity 慈善	recharge 充电	contrary to 与……相反

"品" 美国特色文化

特色表达One

没人会讨厌赞美的话，在美国亦如此。当美国人在外偶遇同事，发现他穿了一双新球鞋的时候，会大方地赞美一句Nice kicks！一般球鞋在美国的说法是basketball shoes，但美国人习惯用kicks指代球鞋，而赞美球鞋潮流就是Nice kicks！

☆ 实景链接

A：Woo, **nice kicks!** did you buy it during holiday? 哇，你的新球鞋好酷！休假时买的吗？

B：Well, my girlfriend bought them for me. 嗯，我女朋友送我的。

A：They're not just shoes, it's an art! 这双鞋简直是艺术品呀！

B：Yeah, I love it. 是啊，我相当喜欢。

特色表达Two

美国人对待工作的态度很谨慎，因为他们讨厌a can of worms。你可不要以为a can of worms是指一罐子的蠕虫，这个短语的本意是钓鱼的人用一罐子蠕虫当鱼饵，后来演变成让人毛骨悚然的"毛茸茸"的场面，在日常生活中常指"一大堆麻烦的事情，或者将某件事情搞得更糟糕"。

☆ 实景链接

A：Where is Tom? 汤姆在哪里？

B：I think he is taking his lunch? 我想他在吃午餐吧？

A：Call him back, his case has opened up **a real can of worms**. 叫他回来，他管理的项目又扯出一堆问题。

B：OK. 好的。

拓展特色句

1. Yeah, it's pay day again! 耶！又到了发薪日了！

2. I go to the gym every weekend. 我每周周末都去健身馆。

3. I want to have a complete relaxation this weekend. 这周末我想好好休息。

"聊" 美国特色文化

A: I am prepared for job-hopping.

B: You have just gotten promotion, why do you quit suddenly?

A: It's hard to explain.

B: Aren't you satisfied with the salary or the welfare?

A: Not really. I have to work overtime most of time. I have little time to accompany my family. My wife always quarrels with me about this.

B: Many workers quit because of lacking in leisure time. It makes sense.

A: So are you satisfied with your work now?

B: Yeah, my opinions are mostly adopted and I am treated with respect. I found my identity in the company.

A: 我准备跳槽呢？

B: 你刚刚才升职，为什么突然辞职呢？

A: 很难解释。

B: 你是不满意薪资还是福利呢？

A: 其实并不是的，而是因为大部分时间我都需要加班，我很少有时间来陪伴我的家人。我的妻子经常因为这个而跟我吵架。

B: 很多员工都因为没有多少休闲时间而辞职，这很好理解。

A: 你现在对你的工作还满意吗？

B: 很满意，我的意见很多都被采用，也很受人尊敬，我在公司里找到了认同感。

"问" 美国特色文化

美国人与日本人工作态度一样吗？

美国人工作习惯讲究效率的同时也要兼顾结果，他们不喜欢做无效率或者希望渺茫的工作，但也会调整好休息时间，尽量在规定时间完成所有的工作。而日本人大多注重过程，他们尤其崇尚朝着目标努力的过程，能否成功倒是次要的了。据说日本人自愿加班的时间和人数都是最多的，晚上加班的大有人在。

美国大熔炉

"大熔炉"从何而来

America has traditionally been *referred to* as a "melting pot," welcoming people from many different countries, races, and religions, all hoping to find freedom, new opportunities, and a better way of life.

A person's culture is the customs and beliefs that they hold. A person's culture is strongly tied to the country where they grew up. It is tied to their *relationship* with their family. Many people come to America from so many different places all over the world. For this reason, many people call America a "melting pot" of cultures.

The American *mosaic* is one of different cultures and regional *identities*, each with unique characteristics and *flavors*. Americans often think of themselves not only as coming from a particular ethnic *heritage*, but also of being part of a *geographical* region. Understanding these regional characteristics and flavors is an excellent way to get to know Americans.

习惯上，喜欢把美国比喻成"大熔炉"，来欢迎来自不同国家、种族和宗教的人，这些人都祈求获得自由、新的机遇以及更好的生活。

每个移民者必会带着的是他们国家的文化。这种文化是指国民们所怀有的信念以及他们的习俗，与他们成长的国家有紧密的联系，与他们和家人的关系有关。正是因为去美国的人都来自全世界形形色色的地方，这些人将美国称为文化"大熔炉"。

美国是一个由不同文化和区域特性构成的万花筒，每种文化都有自己的特色和偏好。美国人通常会觉得自己并不单单是一个来自特定地方民族的个体，而是这个地理区域里的一分子。了解了这些不同的地域特性和偏好是了解美国人的绝佳方式。

移民者构筑美国"万花筒"

The "melting pot" idea *compares* America *to* a giant soup pot. Each immigrant is an *ingredient* added to the pot. Each immigrant adds their own flavor. After each immigrant comes to America, they connect to other people. People learn about each others' culture. This is the beginning of the soup pot of America melting together.

American history began with waves of immigrants, bringing their own cultures and traditions to a vast new country. No other place in the world has such a *diverse* population. It is this *diversity* that makes America what it is and, at the same time, creates the challenges it faces.

American immigration began in 1607 with the *colony* of Jamestown. In 1620, another group of people left England to build a *settlement* in America. These people called themselves *Pilgrims*. They wanted to go to a place where they could practice their religion freely. They wanted to be *free of* the control of the English government. Both of these groups worked hard to build good settlements.

"大熔炉"这个概念是将美国比作成一个巨大的汤锅，而每个移民者则是加入这个汤锅里的配料。移民者来到美国之后，他们和其他人联系起来，开始了解彼此的文化。这也就是美国这个大熔炉汤锅最初的状态。

美国历史始于移民浪潮，这些移民者带着他们自己的文化习俗和文化传统来到这个庞大的新国家。世界上再没有一个这样的地方拥有这样多样化的人口组成。但是正是这个多样性特点让美国成为美国，与此同时，也为这个国家创造了它将面对的挑战。

美国移民者最开始出现在詹姆斯敦这个殖民地。1620年，另一群人离开英国在美国建立了自己的安置地。这些人称自己为清教徒。他们想找到一个能够自由追求他们宗教信仰的地方。他们不想受英国政府的约束。这两批移民者都非常努力地工作将自己的家园创建得更加美好。

单词释义

compare to 把……比作……	ingredient 成分	diverse 多种多样的
diversity 多样性	colony 殖民地	settlement 安置地
Pilgrims 清教徒	free of 免受……	

 美国特色文化

特色表达One

作为"大熔炉"的美国，有很多新移民来的人经济并不富裕，而是来美国求财谋生，他们常把"I don't have a bean."挂在嘴边。这回你或许会纳闷没豆子有什么好炫耀的？其实bean不仅指豆子，还指毫无价值的东西，因为美国人认为像豆子那样小的东西是微不足道的，所以当一个人叨念他连一颗豆子都没有的时候，就是自嘲一无所有了。

☆ 实景链接

A：Hey, can you lend me some money, buddy? I am hard up these days. 嘿，能借点钱吗？最近手头紧。

B：The funds I bought came down again yesterday. **I don't have a bean** now. 我买的基金昨天又跌了，我现在1分钱都没有。

A：Well then, it seems we both need to tight our belt this month. 看来这个月我们都得勒紧裤腰带过日子了。

B：You said it. 你说得没错。

特色表达Two

美国同世界其他国家一样，也有贫民窟，那里的人们lead a dog's life。这句话是说他们过着狗狗一样的生活吗？差不多就是这个意思，美国人常用与dog相关的短语来自嘲或讽刺生活中的方方面面。

☆ 实景链接

A：How is it going, David? 大卫，最近怎么样啊？

B：I have **led a dog's life**. 我过得挺悲惨的。

A：How come? Last time you told me that you got a well paid job. 怎么会呢？上次你告诉我你找到了一份薪水不错的工作啊。

B：I don't even know where to begin. Long story. 我都不知道从哪儿说起，说来话长了。

拓展特色句

1. He immigrated to the United States in 1985. 他1985年移民到了美国。

2. They usually have an Easter egg hunt on Easter. 他们在复活节通常会有彩蛋寻宝活动。

3. This custom originated in a legend. 该风俗源于一个传说。

 ## "聊" 美国特色文化

A: I can't judge which country Ella is from. Do you know about that?

B: I heard she said her mother is a Japanese and her father is a German. She was the descendant of the immigrants but she was born and grew up in America.

A: No wonder does she have no accent.

B: In America, such situation is very common. America is called melting pot in that way.

A: Then how did the immigrants earn a living initially? Were they all rich?

B: I had very little to say in reply to the first question. As to the second question, not everyone is rich. Many people had to lead a dog's life.

A: By the way, you had just referred to the melting pot. What do you mean by that?

B: Because many Americans come from different countries, races, and religions, America is compared to melting pot.

A: Got it. Then you are the ingredient in it.

A: 我不知道艾拉来自于哪个国家，你知道吗？

B: 我听她说过她妈妈是日本人，她爸爸是德国人。她是移民者的后代，但是她在美国出生和长大。

A: 难怪她没有任何口音。

B: 美国这样的情况非常普遍，美国也因此被称作大熔炉。

A: 那这些移民者最初靠什么谋生？他们都很富有吗？

B: 你说的第一个问题，我答不上来，第二个问题是，并不是所有的人都很富有。很多人都过得非常悲惨。

A: 对了，你刚刚提到了大熔炉这个概念，它是什么意思呢？

B: 因为很多美国人以前都是来自不同的国家、种族和宗教，美国就被比作大熔炉。

A: 知道了，那你就是这里面的成分。

 美国特色文化

美国这个大熔炉"熔"的是什么?

美国是一个各种各样的"大熔炉",例如,美国的音乐融合了黑人音乐、西方民间音乐和拉丁民间音乐;美国的料理不仅具有欧洲料理、墨西哥料理和亚洲料理的特色,同时又有自己的特点——如奶酪多;而风靡美国的牛仔文化,融合了美国劳工服装文化和法国服装文化。另外,美国的后现代主义文化既融合了来自欧洲的后现在主义风潮,又含有来自亚洲和非洲的美学素材。

阅读笔记

127

硅谷成功的秘诀是什么

硅谷能成功，文化是关键

Home to many of the biggest names in high-tech and with the highest *concentration* of high-tech *manufacturing* and workers, Silicon Valley has been a *hothouse* for creativity and *innovation* that's *notoriously* difficult to replicate elsewhere. What explains the uniqueness? Is it only the Valley's highly educated, diverse and *inventive* talent or, does the overall workplace culture play a key role? What are the components of that culture? What *fosters* these characteristics?

Arguably, the most important factor in its success has been the *formation* of a unique culture—one that allows people with diverse skills, who often don't know each other, to mix and match: *collaborating* and trusting in ways that people in other cultures don't. It is not simply creative destruction, as many observers say. More importantly, it is a process of creative reassembly, as people join forces on temporary projects and then *recirculate* and recombine for other projects later.

作为许多高科技"明星大腕"的发祥地，以及高密度的高科技生产和工人的聚集地，硅谷是开发和创新的"温床"，它的知名度让其无可替代。为什么硅谷是独一无二的呢？仅仅是因为这个地方聚集了高等学历、各种各样具有创造性的人才吗？还是因为整个工作场地的文化起了关键性作用呢？那这个文化又涵盖了些什么呢？这些特点又是由什么培养起来的呢？

可以说，硅谷成功最重要的因素在于其独特文化的形成——这使得掌握了多样化技能但互相并不认识的人们混合在一起合作：以其他文化背景下不可能有的方式取得合作与互信。这可不是简单的创造性破坏，许多观察家如是说。更重要的是，这是一次创造性重组的过程，因为人们会在临时项目上通力合作，然后寻求新的合作，再加入后来的其他项目。

💬 特色表达Two

既然在美国顾客是上帝，那上帝会被敲竹杠吗？这种情况是难以避免的，尤其是"女性上帝"，所以女顾客之间常常流传一句"the store was a clip joint."这里的clip joint在美国俚语里指商品价格昂贵、专门敲顾客竹杠的场所，而不能只看它字面的意思。

☆ 实景链接

A：Why did you stop? 你怎么不走了？

B：That store looks good. Why don't we go in there to buy a drink? 那家店看起来不错，我们进去买杯酒喝吧。

A：Better not. A bottle of local beer costs ten dollars at that store. 最好不要，当地啤酒在他们家卖10元一瓶。

B：What? It was such a **clip joint.** 什么？真是黑店。

拓展特色句

1. We offer good customer service. 我们提供优质的售后服务。

2. We have sent a professional to inspect it. 我们已经派了专业人员来检查。

3. Bring your receipt to the customer service, and they will refund you. 把你的收据拿给顾客服务部，他们会退钱给你的。

"聊" 美国特色文化

A：Why are you looking so depressed? What's wrong with you?

B：I bought a dress last month, but it faded. I regret over buying that.

A：You don't have to cry over such things. You can just refund it or change a new one.

B：Can I do this? But I have washed it for numerous times.

A：你怎么看起来这么闷闷不乐的？你怎么啦？

B：我上个月买了一条裙子，但是它褪色了。我很后悔买了这条裙子

A：你不需要为这种事情懊恼。你可以退款或者换一件新的。

B：可以吗？我都洗了无数次了。

A：即使这样，但是这条裙子褪色，那就是质量问题了，你可以有正当的

there in the future. *On the other hand*, customers often remain loyal to a business that has excellent service even if their prices are high. Customer service in America grows out of the belief that "the customer is always right." That may not always be true. But, as someone has said, the customer is always the customer.

单词释义

warranty 保质期   ensure 确保   trouble-free 可靠的

motto 座右铭   trivia 琐事   full refund 全部退费

on the other hand 另一方面

 美国特色文化

 特色表达One

　　无论在中国还是美国的超市里，总能看见商家在某个专柜搞促销活动，比如电饭煲现场煮食做饭。在美国俚语里，这样的展柜叫dog-and-pony show，本意是为促销或其他活动而安排的精彩表演。Dog-and-pony show最初在19世纪末，用来形容"马戏表演"。当时，马戏团里的主角儿多是狗和马。于是，人们就戏称这种马戏表演为dog-and-pony show。再后来dog-and-pony show开始用来比喻外表华丽、内容空洞的演讲。而如今，dog-and-pony不再指贬义，常做中性词使用。

☆ 实景链接

A：That place is like a zoo. What's going on? 那地方真热闹，发生什么事了？

B：Let's go check it out. 咱们去看看吧。

A：Oh, that's because there is a **dog-and-pony** show of that brand. 哦，是因为那个品牌在搞促销活动。

B：To be honest, I am not really into the style of their clothes. 说实话，我不太喜欢他家衣服的风格。

to help them find what they want. In most stores, the signs that label each department make shopping a *breeze*. Customers usually don't have to ask how much items cost, since prices are clearly marked.

并且协助寻找需要的东西。在大部分商店里，每个商品分类区清楚的标示使逛街成为一项轻松的乐事。由于价钱已清楚地标示出来了，顾客们通常不需要再问价钱。

单词释义

commercial 广告   courteous 有礼貌的   breeze 轻而易举的事
wait on 服侍   hand and foot 无微不至地

商家如何保住更多的顾客

In America, customer service continues long after the sale. Many products come with a money-back guarantee. Expensive items—like cars, computers or stereos—often have a *warranty* that *ensures trouble-free* use for a period of a year or more. Advertisements regularly include the *motto* "Your satisfaction is guaranteed." So if there is a problem with the product, customers can take it back. The customer service representative will often allow them to exchange the item or return it for a *full refund*. Here's a *trivia* question: Do you know what's the busiest time for most customer service representatives? The week after Christmas.

For many American customers, service is everything. If a person receives poor service from a store, he probably will avoid shopping

在美国，顾客服务在成交之后仍持续良久，很多货品都是保证可以退款的，像是车子、电脑或音响这类高价位的商品，通常会有保证期限，以保证1年或更久的时间内使用该产品没有任何问题。广告中通常会有"保证让你满意"的标语。所以产品若是有问题，顾客可以把它送回去，而客户服务人员通常会让他们换商品或是全额退钱。这里有一个小问题：你知道什么时候是大部分顾客服务人员最忙的时候吗？圣诞节过后的那个礼拜。

对许多美国的顾客而言，服务就是一切，如果有人在某一家店里受到很糟的服务，他以后可能就会尽量不再去那家店购物。另外一方面，一家店若提供上乘的服务，就算价钱高一点，顾客们通常会保持对该店的忠诚度。美式的顾客服务源于一个信念：顾客永远是对的。这不见得全对，但是，就像有人说过的，顾客就是顾客！

我要去美国当上帝

美国的服务顾客之道

Would you like to be a king or queen? To have people *waiting on* you *hand and foot*? Many Americans experience this royal treatment every day. How? By being customers. The American idea of customer service is to make each customer the center of attention. Need proof? Just listen to the *commercials*. Most of them sound like the McDonald's ad: "We do it all for you."

People going shopping in America can expect to be treated with respect from the very beginning. Most places don't have a "furniture street" or a "computer road" which allow you to compare prices easily. Instead, people often use the telephone and "let their fingers do the walking" through the Yellow Pages. From the first "hello," customers receive a *courteous* response to their questions. This initial contact can help them decide where to shop.

When customers get to the store, they are treated as honored guests. Customers don't usually find store clerks sitting around watching TV or playing cards. Instead, the clerks greet them warmly and offer

你想当国王或皇后吗？想让人对你进行无微不至的服侍吗？然而美国人却每天都享受着皇室般的待遇。他们是如何办到的呢？当顾客就可以了。美式的顾客服务就是使每一个顾客成为关注的焦点。需要任何证据吗？听听广告就知道了。大部分广告就像麦当劳的广告一样：我们全心全意为您服务。

在美国逛街，顾客们可以从一开始就享受到被尊重的感觉。大部分的城市不会有"家具街"或是"计算机路"让你可以轻松地比价一番；取而代之的是人们会用电话，让手指头在黄页上"比价"。从第一声"你好"开始，顾客们的疑问都收到礼貌的回答。这个初步的接触，可以帮助他们决定去哪里采买。

当顾客们来到店里的时候，他们会受到贵宾般的款待。他们通常不会看到店员坐在那儿看电视或是玩扑克牌。相反的，店员会亲切地打招呼，

情侣的节日——情人节

情人节为何要送玫瑰花

Most of the items linked to Valentine's Day came from *old-fashioned* customs that used lace handkerchiefs and *floral bouquets* to pass on *non-verbal* messages.

When the custom went out of style for everyday use, the *original* meaning was lost and eventually they became part of the Valentine's Day tradition.

Giving flowers dates back to the 1700s when Charles II of Sweden introduced the Persian custom of "the language of flowers" to Europe. Books about the meanings of particular flowers were published, and entire conversations could be carried out using only a bouquet of flowers.

The rose has become the traditional Valentine's Day flower. As it has always been a popular flower, the meaning of the red rose is still well known as the flower of passion and love. The red rose is also the favorite flower of Venus, the goddess of love, which helped give the rose its symbolic meaning.

与情人节相关的大部分物品都来源于旧日习俗，在这些习俗中，多用蕾丝手绢和鲜花花束来传达无声的信息。

当这一习俗与日常生活脱节，不再流行的时候，其最初的意义也就流失了，最终也只是成为了情人节的一部分传统。

送花要追溯到18世纪初期，那时瑞典的查理斯二世将波斯"花语"的习俗引入欧洲。于是有关于特定花朵的含义图书出版，这样所有的交谈仅用一束花就能进行。

玫瑰花是传统的情人节花朵。由于红玫瑰一直非常流行，它作为热情和爱情之花的含义至今广为人知。红玫瑰也是爱神维纳斯最爱的花，这也给予了玫瑰象征性的意义。

单词释义

old-fashioned 老式的	floral 花的	bouquet 花束
non-verbal 非语言的	original 原始的	

情人节元素有哪些

Lace

Centuries ago, a woman would drop her handkerchief in front of the man she liked. This was a form of encouragement to him, and if he picked it up for her an introduction could be made. Lace has always been part of women's handkerchiefs, and it has since been *linked* to romance.

Cupid

He is the *winged* child whose *arrows* are shot into the hearts of potential lovers. His victims are supposed to fall deeply in love with someone. In both Greek and Roman mythology Cupid is the son of the goddess of love and Cupid has always played a role in the celebrations of love and lovers.

Why does an X mean a kiss?

In the Middle Ages, a lot of people couldn't read or write. When they had to *sign a document*, they would make an X in place of their name. In front of witnesses the signer would kiss the X to show themselves *trustworthy*. The kiss has since come to be represented by an X.

Love knots

A love *knot* is a symbol of *everlasting* love, because its *winding loops* have no beginnings or ends. In times past, they were made of ribbon or drawn on paper to prove one's *undying* love.

蕾丝

几个世纪以前，一个女人在她心仪的男性面前会丢下手绢。这是一种鼓励，如果他为女子捡起手绢，那么初次相识也就达成了。自从把蕾丝与浪漫联系在一起之后，女性的手绢上就都有蕾丝了。

丘比特

他是一个有翅膀的孩子，经常会向互有爱意的人们射出丘比特之箭。被他射中的人都会坠入爱河。在希腊和罗马神话中，丘比特是爱神的儿子，一直扮演着庆祝爱情与爱人的角色。

为什么X代表着一个吻

在中世纪，很多人都不识字，也不会写字。当他们需要签署文件的时候，他们会在他们的姓名处写个X。在目击者面前，签字的人会亲吻这个X来表示他们是值得信赖的。从此吻就由X来表示了。

爱情同心结

爱情同心结象征持久的爱情，因为缠绕的圆圈既没有开始也没有终点。在古代，同心结可以用丝带制作，也可以在纸上绘出以证明某人永恒的爱。

link 连接

sign a document 签合同

everlasting 永恒的

undying 不朽的

winged 有翅膀的

trustworthy 可靠的

winding 卷绕的

arrow 箭

knot 结

loop 环

美国特色文化

特色表达One

常言道，"有情人终成眷属。"这句话用英语说即是：All shall be well, Jack shall have Jill. 这里的Jack和Jill是欧洲的童话形象，象征金童玉女。有时候，如果有男生对女生说这句话，则暗含男生有意中人了，想要拒绝表白的女生。

☆ 实景链接

A：You are exactly my type. I think I have a crush on you. 你就是我喜欢的类型。我觉得我迷恋上你了。

B：**All shall be well, Jack shall have Jill.** 我已经心有所属了。

A：Who is she? Is she your girlfriend now? 她是谁？她现在是你女朋友了吗？

B：Not yet. But we are not the right fit. 还没有。但咱俩不合适。

特色表达Two

要在情人节约会的朋友可得注意了，一定要给对方留下好印象。而不是 leave a bad taste in one's mouth。可别把这个俚语理解成"在别人嘴巴里留下不好的味道"，它的真实意思是"给人留下不好的印象"。

☆ 实景链接

A：Maria means the world to me. I miss her from the moment I wake up. 玛利亚是我的一切，我从早上睁开眼就开始想她。

B：Are you an item now? 你们现在是一对了吗？

A：No. but I am gonna ask her on a date on Valentine's Day. 没呢，但我想在情人节那天约她出去。

B：Good luck. By the way, you'ood luck. By the way, yo **leave a bad**

taste in her mouth. 祝你好运。顺便说一句，你可得聪明着点。别给她留下不好的印象。

拓展特色句

1. I will declare my love for her on Valentine's Day. 我打算在情人节那天向她告白。

2. Did you get a lot of chocolates on Valentine's Day? 你在情人节有收到很多巧克力吗？

3. My husband sent me a bouquet for Valentine's Day. 我老公情人节送我一束花。

"聊" 美国特色文化

A: What gift will you give to your girlfriend for the Valentine's Day?

B: I will give her a gift card of her favorite brand.

A: That's great. I want to give her something I made. Do you think it is a good idea?

B: What is it?

A: It's a model plane, which can be put on the desk.

B: Well, does she like planes?

A: I'm not sure. But it is good-looking.

B: I'm afraid most girls are hard to be attracted by model planes. What girls love are things with lace, roses and chocolates.

A: 情人节你会给女朋友送什么礼物？

B: 我给她送一张她最喜欢的牌子的礼品卡。

A: 这个主意不错。我想送她亲手做的礼物。你觉得这个想法怎么样？

B: 你做的是什么？

A: 是一架模型飞机，可以放在书桌上。

B: 呃，她喜欢飞机？

A: 我也不确定。但它看起来不错。

B: 恐怕大多数女孩很难被模型飞机吸引。女孩喜欢的是有蕾丝的东西、玫瑰花和巧克力。

"问" 美国特色文化

情人节只能是情人专享吗?

以前,2月14日原本是女孩对男孩倾诉情意的日子,女孩可以送情人节巧克力、手工曲奇给男孩。但是发展到最后,情人节由谁主动送礼已经不重要了。因为情人节这天送出的不仅是情人之间的爱情期盼与甜蜜,也有朋友间的祝福与美好愿望,更有家人间的欢乐聚会,这一天,传达的是各种满满的爱。

阅读笔记

欢庆美国独立日

独立日有哪些庆典活动

Independence Day is the national day of the United States.

Similar to other summer-themed events, Independence Day celebrations often take place outdoors. Independence Day is a federal holiday, so all non-essential federal *institutions* (like the postal service and federal courts) are closed on that day. Many politicians *make it a point* on this day to appear at a public event to praise the nation's *heritage*, laws, history, society, and people.

Families often celebrate Independence Day by hosting or attending a picnic or barbecue and take advantage of the day off and, in some years, long weekend to gather with relatives. Decorations (e.g., streamers, balloons, and clothing) are generally colored red, white, and blue, the colors of the American flag. Parades are often in the morning, while *fireworks* displays occur in the evening at such places as parks, *fairgrounds*, or town squares.

美国独立日的庆典方式和其他夏日主题的活动别无二致,大多数也是户外活动。独立日属于联邦节日,所以不太重要的联邦机构(比如邮电服务和联邦法院等)在那天都不营业。很多政客都很在意这一天,他们会在公开场合露面,歌颂祖国的文化传统、法律、历史、社会及其人民。

一般家庭会举行野炊或者烧烤活动来庆祝独立日,充分利用这一天假期,而在有些年,这一天的假期会和周末连成小长假,可以去和亲人团聚。人们通常会给装饰品（比如横幅、气球和服装上）涂上美国国旗的红、白、蓝三色。游行一般在上午举行,晚上则会在公园、游乐场或者广场等地放烟花。

单词释义

institution 机构　　　　make it a point 对……特别注意　heritage 传统
firework 烟火　　　　　fairground 露天市场

"独立日"碎碎谈

In 1775, people in New England began fighting the British for their independence. On July 2, 1776, the Congress secretly voted for independence from Great Britain. The *Declaration of Independence* was first published two days later on July 4, 1776. The first public reading of the Declaration of Independence was on July 8, 1776. Delegates began to sign the *Declaration of Independence* on August 2, 1776. In 1870, Independence Day was made an unpaid holiday for federal employees. In 1941, it became a paid holiday for them.

The first *description* of how Independence Day would be celebrated was in a letter from John Adams to his wife Abigail on July 3, 1776. He described "*pomp* and parade, with shows, games, sports, *guns*, bells, *bonfires*, and *illuminations*" throughout the United States. However, the term "Independence Day" was not used until 1791.

Interestingly, Thomas Jefferson and John Adams, both signers of the *Declaration of Independence* and presidents of the United States, died on July 4, 1826—exactly 50 years after the *adoption* of the declaration.

1775年，新英格兰人为了自由，开始与英国对抗。1776年7月2日，国会秘密投票从大不列颠独立出来。两天之后，也就是1776年7月4日，《独立宣言》问世。1776年7月8日，《独立宣言》第一次面向公共宣读。1776年8月2日，代表们开始签署独立宣言。1870年，联邦雇员在独立日那天可以享受无薪假期。而从1941年之后，那天变成了带薪假期。

约翰·亚当斯于1776年7月3日写给他妻子阿比盖尔的一封信中头一次描述了如何庆祝独立日。根据他的描述，美国在那天会有"游行盛况、表演、游戏、运动、礼炮、铃铛、篝火和灯饰"。然而，直到1791年，大家才开始使用"独立日"这个名词。

托马斯·杰弗逊和约翰·亚当斯都是《独立宣言》的签署者，同时也是美国总统。有意思的是他们都于1826年7月4日逝世——正好是这份宣言正式通过后的50年。

单词释义

description 描述   pomp 盛况   gun 礼炮

bonfire 篝火   illumination 灯饰   adoption 正式通过

"品" 美国特色文化

特色表达One

美国人喜欢在独立日欢庆，但欢乐要有分寸，better safe than sorry，不要犯二high过头。better safe than sorry的字面意思是"安全总比遗憾好"，在俚语中指"最好不要冒险"，在劝说朋友时常用这句话。

☆ 实景链接

A: How would you celebrate the Independence Day? 你打算怎么庆祝独立日？

B: How about setting off fire-crackers? 放爆竹怎么样？

A: It would be dangerous. It's **better safe than sorry**. 这可能很危险。最好不要冒险。

B: You said it. There would be many other wonderful events. 你说得对。一定还会有其他精彩的活动。

特色表达Two

每年的7月4日是美国独立日，在这个举全美之力欢庆的日子里，美国人常常心怀感恩地祝贺生日快乐。但是美国人在给祖国欢庆生日的时候，经常会说Happy Birthday, Uncle Sam!（山姆大叔，生日快乐！）在这里，Uncle Sam（山姆大叔）常被用来代指"美国"或"美国政府"。

☆ 实景链接

A: I really like vacations. I feel so good. 真喜欢放假啊。我感觉真好。

B: I propose to make a toast on the Independence Day. 我提议为独立日干一杯。

A: I agree. Here, happy Birthday to **Uncle Sam**! 我同意，来，祝山姆大叔生日快乐！

B: Happy Birthday to Uncle Sam! 祝山姆大叔生日快乐！

拓展特色句

1. I say we have some wine to celebrate the Independence Day. 我建议我们喝点红酒来庆祝独立日。

2. Happy Independence Day! Use it well. 美国独立日快乐啊！好好过假期哦。

3. Independence Day is a paid holiday. 独立日是有薪假期。

"耶" 美国特色文化

A: Which day is the National Day of America?

B: It is July 4th, which is known as the Independence Day.

A: Will you hold celebrating events?

B: Of course. We often have a picnic or barbecue on that day.

A: It sounds interesting. Are there any other events?

B: If it is on Friday, we spend the day off and the following weekend as a long weekend.

A: How would you spend the long weekend?

B: We will gather with relatives.

A: 美国的国庆节是哪一天？

B: 7月4日，这一天被称作独立日。

A: 你们会举办庆祝活动吗？

B: 当然。我们在那一天会去野炊或者烧烤。

A: 听起来很有意思。还有其他的活动吗？

B: 如果那天是星期五，我们就会把这一天和随后的周末当作小长假。

A: 你们怎么度过这个小长假呢？

B: 我们会和亲人相聚。

"问" 美国特色文化

《独立宣言》是如何产生的?

　　1776年7月4日是美国独立日，在这一天，大陆会议在费城正式通过《独立宣言》。这份宣言由托马斯·杰弗逊起草，经大陆会议专门委员会修改后通过，并由大陆会议主席约翰·汉考克签字生效。《独立宣言》是具有世界历史意义的伟大文献，它开宗明义地阐明所有人生而平等，具有追求幸福与自由的天赋，受到美国人民的极力追捧，这份宣言也对法国大革命及法国的《人权宣言》产生了深远的影响。

西方鬼节——万圣节

万圣节怎么过

Halloween is a holiday celebrated on the night of October 31. The word Halloween is a *shortening* of All Hallows' Evening also known as Hallowe'en or All Hallows' Eve. Traditional activities include trick-or-treating, bonfires, *costume* parties, visiting "*haunted* houses" and *carving* jack-o-lanterns.

Some families carve lanterns with "*scary*" faces out of pumpkins or other vegetables or decorate their homes and gardens in Halloween style. These were traditionally intended to ward off *evil spirits*. If you are at home on Halloween, it is a good idea to have a *bowl* of small presents or sweets to offer to anyone who knocks on your door. This will help you to please the little spirits in your neighborhood!

The *commercialization* of Halloween started in the 1900s, when postcards and *die-cut* paper decorations were produced. Halloween costumes started to appear in stores in the 1930s and the custom of "trick-or-treat" appeared in the 1950s. The types of products available in Halloween style increased with time. Now Halloween

万圣节是在10月31日晚上庆祝的节日。Halloween这个单词是All Hallows' Evening的简写，有时候也可以称作Hallowe'en或者All Hallows' Eve。传统活动包括"不给糖就捣乱"、烟花、化装舞会、夜访"鬼屋"或者雕刻南瓜灯。

有些家庭会把南瓜或者其他蔬菜挖空，在上面雕刻"鬼脸"，有的也会把自己的屋子和花园装扮成万圣节风情。这样做是为了抵御恶魔。如果万圣节那天你在家，在碗里装些小礼物或者糖果来打发那些敲门的人是一个不错的建议。这能让附近的小精灵们高兴！

在20世纪初期，万圣节开始变得商业化，明信片和打孔纸装饰品开始投入生产。20世纪30年代，万圣节服饰开始在各大商店出现，"不给糖就捣蛋"的风俗出现于20世纪50年代。万圣节风情的产品也越来越多。现

is a very profitable holiday for the **manufacturers** of costumes, yard decorations and candy.

在，对于那些服装、院落装饰品和糖果商来说，万圣节是一个非常有利可图的节日。

不给糖就捣蛋

Trick-or-treating or "*Guising*" is a customary practice for children on Halloween. Children in costumes travel from house to house in order to ask for treats such as candy with the question "Trick or treat?" The "trick" is a (usually *idle*) threat to perform *mischief* on the homeowners or their property if no treat is given. In North America, trick or treat has been a customary Halloween tradition since at least the late 1950s. Homeowners wishing to participate in it usually decorate their private entrance with plastic spider webs, paper *skeletons* and Jack-O-Lanterns.

Some rather *reluctant* homeowners would simply leave the candy in pots on the porch. In the more recent years, however, the practice has spread to almost any house within a neighborhood being visited by children.

不给糖就捣蛋或者乔装打扮是孩子们的万圣节习俗。乔装打扮的孩子们挨家挨户询问"是给糖，还是要捣蛋？"以获得糖果之类的款待。而"捣蛋"威胁如果得不到糖果，就要对屋主或他的财产进行破坏(通常只是说说)。在北美，"不给糖就捣蛋"至少从20世纪50年代末期开始就已经是万圣节习俗。通常想要参加这个活动的屋主会在万圣节那天用塑料蜘蛛网、纸骷髅和南瓜灯来装饰房子的门口。

一些不愿参加活动的屋主会把糖放在门廊的罐子里。但是近年来，该活动广泛流传，几乎临近的每户人家都会被孩子们光顾。

单词释义

guise 伪装　　　　　idle 使空闲　　　　　mischief 恶作剧

skeleton 骨架　　　　reluctant 不情愿的

 美国特色文化

 **特色表达One**

　　万圣节是开展恶作剧的好日子，但不是每个人都喜欢被恶搞，尤其是被捉弄的人。他们会说It is totally for the birds! 别以为这句话的意思是恶作剧都是为小鸟们准备的，在俚语里，这句话的常用意思是"这真的很无聊"。

⭐ **实景链接**

A：Are you scared by that? 你没被那个吓到吗？

B：Not at all. **It is totally for the birds!** 一点都没有。这真的很无聊！

A：Most of the tricks shock the hell out of me. 很多恶作剧都能吓到我。

B：Why are you so chicken? 你怎么就那么胆小呢？

 **特色表达Two**

　　万圣节这一天，最令人期待的要数化装舞会了吧，舞会上"鬼怪横行"，经常会听到有人说"吓死我了""你吓坏我了""天啊，太恐怖了"等等。这些话用英文怎么说呢？比如你在惊魂不定时可以来一句You scared me!或者是I am freaked out! 意思是"你吓死我了！"若要表示被吓得够呛，久久不能回神，可以说I am frightened out of my wits!（我的魂都被吓飞了！）

⭐ **实景链接**

A：Happy Halloween's Day! 万圣节快乐啊！

B：Sweet Jesus. Mother of God! You scared me! Where did you get this costume? 我的天哪，你吓我够呛！你从哪里搞到这么一身衣服？

A：It looks great, isn't it? 看起来很棒，不是吗？

B：**I am frightened out of my wits.** 我的魂儿都被它吓跑了。

拓展特色句

1. Let's have pumpkin pie. 我们吃南瓜派吧。
2. Are you going trick-or-treating? 你要去"不给糖就捣蛋"吗？
3. Our school holds a masquerade party every Halloween. 我们学校每年万圣节都会举行化装舞会。

美国特色文化

A：How will you dress up for the Halloween party?

B：I'd like to wear the costume of zombie.

A：That's so cool.

B：What about you?

A：I'll go as a vampire. Vampires are very popular recently.

B：Yeah. I love watching the TV drama **The Vampire Diaries** and I like the heroine.

A：I need to do the dressup now. See you later.

B：See you.

A：你万圣节聚会上怎么打扮？

B：打扮成僵尸。

A：这真是太酷了。

B：你打扮成谁呢？

A：我要打扮成吸血鬼。吸血鬼现在挺流行的。

B：是啊。我喜欢看《吸血鬼日记》的电视剧，而且我喜欢女主角。

A：我现在要去打扮了。我要走了。一会儿见。

B：一会儿见。

"问" 美国特色文化

万圣节为什么要化装游行？

万圣节的晚上，你会看到一群奇妙的生物悠闲地游走在大街上，比如喷满番茄汁的吸血鬼、带着尖尖帽子的巫婆、穿着白大褂的幽灵、蹦跳着行走的僵尸、搞怪的独眼海盗、打扮新潮的外星人等，不要以为你穿越了，这只是万圣节的传统嘉年华。据说在中世纪，人们穿上动物造型的服饰、戴上可怕的面具是为了在万圣节前夜驱赶黑夜中的鬼怪。如今人们盛装cosplay，举行精彩的游行只是为了庆祝节日的到来。

一年中最重要的节日——圣诞节

庆祝耶稣诞生

Many people in the United States celebrate Christmas Day on December 25. The day celebrates Jesus Christ's birth. It is often combined with customs from pre-Christian winter celebrations. Christmas is both a *sacred* religious holiday. For two *millennia*, people around the world have been observing it with traditions and practices that are both religious and *secular* in nature. Christians celebrate Christmas Day as the *anniversary* of the birth of Jesus of Nazareth, a *spiritual leader* whose teachings form the basis of their religion. Popular customs include exchanging gifts, decorating Christmas trees, attending church, sharing meals with family and friends and, of course, waiting for Santa Claus to arrive. December 25—Christmas Day—has been a federal holiday in the United States since 1870.

很多美国人都会在12月25号庆祝圣诞节，这一天是为了庆祝基督诞生，这一天的活动还包括基督诞生之前的冬日庆典习俗。圣诞节也是一个充满神圣色彩的宗教节日。2000年来，全世界的人都以神圣而不朽的传统习俗来庆祝这个节日。基督徒将圣诞节作为拿撒勒的耶稣的生日来庆祝，他是一位精神领袖，他的教义形成了基督教的基石。流行的习俗包括互换礼物、装饰圣诞树、去教堂做礼拜、与家人和朋友一起吃饭，当然还有等待圣诞老人到来。自1870年起，12月25日的圣诞节成为了美国的联邦假期。

单词释义

sacred 神圣的	millennia 一千年（复数） secular 世俗的
anniversary 周年纪念	spiritual leader 精神领袖

圣诞节庆祝活动

Many Sunday schools, churches and communities organize special events. These can include decorating the neighborhood or a shopping mall, putting up a Christmas tree and planning a Nativity display, concert or performance. A lot of plays and songs have an aspect of Christmas as a theme. Some groups arrange meals, *shelter* or *charitable* projects for people without a home or with very little money.

Government offices, organizations, businesses and schools are closed, almost without exception. Many people visit relatives or friends and are out of town. This may cause *congestion* on highways and at airports. Public transit systems do not run on their regular schedules. In general, public life closes down completely.

A wide range of people and objects represent Christmas. These include baby Jesus, the Nativity and the Three Kings, but also Santa Claus, reindeer and elves. Common objects at this time of year are pine trees, holly, decorations, fairy lights, candles and presents. Christmas Day is now truly a mix of religious celebration and commercial interests.

许多主日学校、教堂和社团都会组织特别活动，包括装扮街区或购物广场、搭造圣诞树或筹备"耶稣诞生"展览、演唱会或表演等。许多游戏和歌曲都与圣诞节主题相关。有的组织会为那些无家可归或者身无分文的人们发放食物、安排住宿或者给予其他的慈善。

政府机关、组织、商户以及学校几乎都无一例外不营业。很多人都会出城拜访亲戚朋友。这会引发高速公路或者机场的拥堵。公共交通系统无法在那天按照正常的时刻表运营。总之，那天的公共生活几乎是完全停止的。

有很多人和物品都象征着圣诞节。包括婴儿耶稣、耶稣诞生雕像、三圣，当然还有圣诞老人、驯鹿和小精灵。在一年中的这个时候，随处可见松树、冬青树、装饰品、圣诞树小彩灯、蜡烛和礼物。现在，圣诞节这一天几乎已经演变成宗教庆典和商业利益的结合。

单词释义

shelter 避难所　　　　charitable 慈善事业的　　　　congestion 拥堵

 美国特色文化

特色表达One

有些工作狂即使到了圣诞节也要埋头苦干，好不容易吃顿午餐，他居然说Let's do lunch together. 这句话的本意是"咱们一起去吃饭吧"，不要理解为一起去做饭。然而do lunch并不是单纯的吃饭，通常指"一边吃饭一边谈公事"。

☆ 实景链接

A：Do you have arrangement during the lunch break? 你午休的时候有什么安排吗？

B：Just come to the point. What do you want to do? 你直说吧。你想干什么？

A：If you have no plan, let's **do lunch** together. 如果你没什么计划，咱们一块吃饭吧。

B：Forget it! Don't you know it is time for a rest? 没门儿。你不知道该休息了吗？

特色表达Two

圣诞节一到，香港、伦敦等地的商铺在圣诞节期间会挂起Xmas这样的招牌，而不是Christmas，这是怎么回事呢？因Christ一词的希腊文 Χριστος的第一个字母的大写写法很像英文的X，初期的基督徒因为使用希腊文，确实常常以X作为基督的缩写，语言发展成英语系后，有人索性将Christmas写成Xmas。因此，Xmas是希腊文和英文的混合体，并不是有人为了避免圣诞节的宗教元素而故意要用X代替Christ。

☆ 实景链接

A：I can't wait to open my present. That's so nice of you to give me this. 我等不及要拆我的礼物了，你真好，还送我礼物。

B：I hope you have the best Christmas ever. 我希望你有个最棒的圣诞节。

B：Oh, thank you and the same to you. And please don't forget to tell Jane **Merry X'mas** for me. 谢谢，你也是。还有，别忘了代我向简说声圣诞快乐啊。

A：Sure, I will. 好的，我会的。

拓展特色句

1. We decorated the house for Christmas. 我们为过圣诞节把房子装饰了一番。

2. What do you want for Christmas this year? 今年圣诞节你想要什么礼物？

3. Let's sing some Christmas Carols. 我们来唱圣诞赞歌吧。

"聊" 美国特色文化

A：Have you got any ideas what you're getting for your husband as Christmas gift?

B：What did you get?

A：I just bought a shirt of his favorite brand.

B：How much is that?

A：200 dollars.

B：The price is a bit expensive. I'd better wait for the holiday sales.

A：You'd better not to wait. The fancy items are sold out quickly in this season.

B：Well, I'll go to choose a gift for him.

A：你想好给你老公买什么圣诞节礼物了吗？

B：你买什么了？

A：我买了他最喜欢的牌子的衬衫。

B：多少钱？

A：200美元。

B：价钱有点贵。我还是等着节日促销吧。

A：你最好不要等。在这个时期，好东西卖完得很快。

B：嗯，那我去给他挑礼物吧。

"问" 美国特色文化

圣诞老人到底是何方神圣？

　　每逢圣诞节，圣诞老人会骑着驯鹿，圣童手持圣诞树降临人间。但是圣诞老人又是何方神圣呢？圣诞老人原名叫作圣·尼古拉(Saint Nicholas)，4世纪的时候，出生于小亚细亚巴大拉城，家庭富有，父母亲是非常热心的天主教友，不幸他的父母早逝。尼古拉长大以后，便把丰富的财产，全部捐送给贫苦可怜的人，自己则出家修道，献身教会，终生为社会服务。在他一生当中，他暗暗帮助了很多困难的贫民。在北美洲，荷兰和英国殖民者把圣尼古拉送给人们礼物的传统融入圣诞节日的庆祝里，荷兰语圣尼古拉(Sinterklaa)传入英语，就成了我们熟悉的Santa Claus。

Part 6

那些年我们追过的影视作品

《绝望主妇》

《绝望主妇》演绎别样主妇

Since the first *episode* was aired in 2004 the American TV series *Desperate Housewives* has *triumphed* in over 150 countries. The leading idea, invented by producer Marc Cherry, *initially* was that modern-day women face surprising difficulties. Those hardships can be *depicted* cleverly by using drama, comedy, *satire* and even crime. Linguistically the series operates on many levels, from higher to lower register, using vocabulary and speech as a *stylistic device*.

There is a certain *pattern* in which all of the seasons of *Desperate Housewives* thus far have worked. In each seasons first episode a new neighbor moves on to the mentioned street. With their moving *van* they always bring a secret that is kept from the viewers until the season *finale*. The newcomers are depicted in a *sinister* way to *evoke* the viewers imagination. It is the carrying idea of the show that the women with their families are often superficially blissfully happy, but have awful and embarrassing secrets behind the fade. Each of the housewives has her own way of keeping the secrets.

美国电视剧《绝望主妇》自2004年播出第一集后，已在150多个国家取得了巨大的成功。制片人马克·切利最初的指导思想是表现现代女性面临的意想不到的困难。这些困难可以通过戏剧、喜剧、讽刺剧甚至犯罪剧勾勒出来。在语言上，该剧横跨多个层次，从上层社会到下层社会都有涉及，将词汇和语言作为修辞手法来使用。

迄今为止，每一季的《绝望主妇》都遵循一个特定的模式。在每一季的第一集总有一个新邻居搬到剧中提到的街道。和他们搬家的货车一起来的，总会有一个不为观众所知的秘密，直到所在的一季完结才会揭晓。剧中总是用邪恶的手法描述新来者，以充分激发观众的想象。该剧表达的观念是已成家的女人通常只是表面上看起来幸福快乐，在日渐衰老的背后却有着令人害怕和尴尬的秘密。每个家庭主妇都有自己保密的方式。

单词释义

episode 一集   triumph 成功   initially 最初

depict 描述   satire 讽刺   stylistic device 修辞手法

pattern 模式   van 面包车   finale 结局

sinister 阴险的   evoke 引发

《绝望主妇》中的美国味道

The series also utilizes cultural references and language that has its roots in American culture, history, brand names and popular culture. These references may be difficult to recognize without the cultural *insight*, for example Beantown, the nickname for Boston, *apparently derived from* the local tradition of eating beans.

The language used in the series is *vivid* and *variable*. Every character has a unique way of speaking; the use of language is clearly designed to characterize the person in question. Of the four main characters three are Caucasian white females who use generic American English. One character has Latin-American roots, but uses very few Spanish words. Vernacular language is seldom spoken by any of main characters. However, the nationality of *Desperate Housewives* can be noticed through language attached to American culture and comparisons with Standard British English.

该剧集还利用了扎根于美国文化、历史、品牌和流行文化的背景和语言。在缺少文化认知的情况下很难看懂这些背景，例如波士顿的昵称豆城显然是源于当地吃豆子的传统。

剧中使用的语言生动而多变。每个角色都有独特的说话方式，语言的使用完全是为了体现所讨论的角色的个性。四个主妇中有三个都是说通用美式英语的高加索白人女性。另一个主妇带有拉丁美洲人血统，但只说极少的西班牙单词。主要角色很少说方言，但通过对比依附在美国文化的语言与标准的英式英语，就可以看出绝望主妇的国籍。

单词释义

insight 洞察力　　　　apparently 显然地　　　derive from 源自

vivid 生动的　　　　　variable 多变的

 美国特色文化

特色表达One

常看《绝望主妇》的朋友一定耳熟能详一个词语就是bad egg，这是"坏的鸡蛋"的意思吗？首先，在中国，常用"坏蛋"指坏人或小偷，如今也常用在亲密的朋友之间，或情侣间打情骂俏。在美国也有类似说法，bad egg就是"坏蛋"的意思。

☆ 实景链接

A：Why does Lily break up with Tom? 莉莉为什么和山姆分手？

B：Tom is a **bad egg** who can't be trust. 汤姆是个不可信的坏蛋。

A：Poor Lily. She must be very sad. 可怜的莉莉。她一定很伤心。

B：But it's good for her to leave him early. 不过她能及早离开他也是好事。

特色表达Two

《绝望主妇》里几位女主们常说That face rings a bell, where have I seen him before? 尤其是遇见帅气的绅士时，这句话出镜率要不要太高。为什么face能响铃了？这里可不是响铃的意思，ring a bell在这里指的是"让人记起或想起什么东西，但又不确定"。

☆ 实景链接

A：Your face **rings a bell**. Have we seen each other before? 我看你眼熟。我们之前见过吗？

B：I'm afraid no. 恐怕没有。

A：Well, I want to make a friend with you. Can you give me your phone number? 嗯，我想和你做个朋友。你能给我你的电话吗？

B：Sorry, I'm waiting for my boyfriend and he is coming. 抱歉，我在等我男朋友，他就要来了。

拓展特色句

1. Desperate Housewives is produced by ABC Studios. 《绝望主妇》是由美国广播公司制作播出的。

2. I like the character Gaby Solis in Desperate Housewives which was played by Eva Longoria. 我喜欢《绝望主妇》中伊娃·朗格利亚扮演的角色加比·索利斯。

3. The sentence is from Desperate Housewives. 那句话是《绝望主妇》里的台词。

 "聊" 美国特色文化

A: How do you view the TV play **Desperate Wives**?

B: I'd say the characters in this play are well depicted.

A: I agree with you. The stories of the housewives make me think about my own experiences.

B: Yeah. As women, we all feel confused and desperate sometimes.

A: Thus we will resonate with the characters.

B: Who is the favorite character of yours?

A: Lynette. I admire able women like her.

B: But she failed to balance her work and life.

A: 你如何看待《绝望主妇》这部电视剧?

B: 我要说这部剧中的角色都被刻画得很出色。

A: 我同意。这些主妇的故事让我想起我自己的经历。

B: 是啊。作为女人,我们在有些时候都会觉得困惑和绝望。

A: 这样我们就会与角色产生共鸣。

B: 你最喜欢的角色是哪个?

A: 利奈特。我很佩服她这样的女强人。

B: 但她没能平衡好工作和生活。

 美国特色文化

《绝望主妇》讲的是什么故事呢?

《绝望主妇》主要讲述四个家庭主妇的生活与工作中的故事。剧中,每一季都有一个令人心痒痒的悬疑,叫人想继续追剧,并对此爱不释手。这部美剧感情丰富,剧情展开方式轻松愉快,很容易让人联想到生活中的点滴。虽然人物刻画或许不够完美,但每个角色都那么生动活泼,会让你觉得,原来她们的生活也是这样,原来我也遇见过这样的事情,总之很能引人共鸣。

阅读笔记

《老友记》——美国人生活的"写真"

讲述年轻人自己的生活

The *sitcom Friends*, which has ended its 10-year run on TV will be remembered as one of those rare shows that marked a change in American culture.

Friends stands out as a sign that we are now living in a culture where youth *rules*, where the image of youth has become the *dominant* image of our culture. *Friends* will be remembered as the show that made America aware that being in your 20s is really being in the *prime* of life.

Friends was among the first shows to depict young people who were very much on their own, without significant parental interaction. Prior sitcoms were almost always centered on the lives of *nuclear families*, where father and mother knew best.

The characters in *Friends* pretty much were running their own lives and looked to each other for *moral guidance*.

情景喜剧《老友记》已经结束了在电视上为期10年的播出，作为为数不多的标志着美国文化变迁的电视剧之一，必将为人们所铭记。

《老友记》是一个明确的符号，即我们生活在一个年轻人统治的文化中，年轻人的形象已经成为我们文化的主导。《老友记》让美国人认识到二十多岁的年纪正是生命的黄金期，由于这一点，这部剧将为人们铭记。

《老友记》是最早体现年轻人的我行我素，以及与父母之间缺乏明显交流的电视剧之一，以前的情景喜剧几乎全都着眼于小家庭的生活，而这种生活正是父母们最了解的。

《老友记》中的人物几乎都过着他们自己的生活，并以道德准则互相依靠。

单词释义

sitcom 情景喜剧	rule 统治	dominant 占优势的
prime 全盛时期	nuclear family 小家庭	moral guidance 道德准则

公寓生活莫严肃

The characters in *Friends* lived in apartments, not in houses, where the characters were not *upwardly mobile*, and where they had the same friends forever and never grew up.

The *premise* of this show often centered on *trivial* matters in the characters' lives—sending the message that it's okay to not be serious about anything because nothing really bad is likely to happen in a young person's life.

Since 9/11—and with the country's current economic problems—that attitude has changed, which may be one reason why sitcoms like *Friends* are not in style anymore and are in decline as a major ratings draw.

"What we are seeing now instead is the *immense* popularity of TV reality shows, with their depictions of *corporate*, *cut-throat* values, whose characters are concerned solely with competing and getting ahead of other people."

《老友记》中的人物住在公寓里，而不是家里，他们的地位没有上升的趋势，因而可以永葆友谊，永葆年轻。

该剧的前提往往关注主角生活中的琐事——传达的信息是年轻人的生活不太可能发生真正糟糕的事，因此没有必要太过严肃。

自从"9·11"事件以后，美国的经济发展面临诸多问题的观念已经改变，这也是像《老友记》这样的情景喜剧不再流行，收视率下跌，且与主流电视剧相比优势不再的原因之一。

"我们现在爱看广受欢迎的电视真人秀节目，它们关注的是企业和残酷拼杀的价值观，节目中的角色只关心竞争和超过别人。"

单词释义

upwardly 向上地	mobile 移动	premise 前提
trivial 琐碎的	immense 巨大的	corporate 企业的
cut-throat 残酷的		

 **美国特色文化**

特色表达One

《老友记》里有一集是莫妮卡对瑞秋有怨言，因为瑞秋steal her thunder。为什么瑞秋要偷莫妮卡的雷呢？其实是说莫妮卡觉得瑞秋抢了她要结婚的风头，很不高兴，所以steal one's thunder在俚语里是说"抢了某人的风头"。

☆ 实景链接

A：How was the party? Did you enjoy yourself? 聚会怎么样？你玩得高兴吗？

B：Lily **stole my thunder**, and I don't want to see her anymore. 莉莉抢了我的风头，我不想再看见她了。

A：What happened? 怎么了？

B：She wore a same dress with me. 她穿了和我一样的裙子。

特色表达Two

记得有一集里罗斯气冲冲地找瑞秋理论，很生气地说着I have a bone to pick with you. 难道是说罗斯要找瑞秋一起去找骨头吗？这句话在俚语里是指"某人有话与某人说"，一般暗指说话人的情绪非常愤怒，口气也不好，有烦人的事情必须马上解决。

☆ 实景链接

A：**I have a bone to pick with you.** Do you have a minute? 我有话要跟你说。你有时间吗？

B：Yes. What's the problem? 有。出什么事了？

A：There are many mistakes in your report. It is awful. How did you do it? 你的报告里有很多错误。糟透了。你怎么做的？

B：How do you define "awful"? I will check it myself. 你如何定义"糟透了"？我得自己看看。

拓展特色句

1. I love Friends. The writers are brilliant. 我非常喜欢看《老友记》，编剧实在太有才华了。

2. Friends is the highest-rated sitcom on television at that time. 《老友记》在那个时候是超高收视率的情景喜剧。

3. What attracted me most about Friends was the friendship between the roommates. 《老友记》最吸引我的地方是室友间的友情。

"聊" 美国特色文化

A: In my opinion, **Friends** is the most classical sitcom which is both funny and profound.

B: I have the same view with you.

A: I love it for it reflected the life of the young people.

B: Yes. It is exactly the life of yours and mine.

A: I was deeply moved by the story of the main characters.

B: I also learned a lot from them.

A: In a word, it conveys positive thinking.

B: I can't agree more with you.

A: 在我看来，《老友记》是最经典的情景喜剧，既有趣又深刻。

B: 我和你的观点相同。

A: 我喜欢这部情景喜剧，是因为它反映了年轻人的生活。

B: 是啊。这就是你我的生活。

A: 我被几位主角的故事深深地打动了。

B: 我也在他们身上学到了很多。

A: 总之，它传达着积极的思想。

B: 我完全同意。

"问" 美国特色文化

《老友记》让人感动吗?

曾经《老友记》中的那批演员红遍了全球，也收获了各自的幸福，但在剧迷眼里，瑞秋永远是那个大大咧咧的大小姐；莫尼卡还是一如既往地强硬到底，争强好胜；菲比一贯反应迟钝；乔伊还是花花公子；钱德勒就像降温空调，每天冷笑话不断；而罗斯则一直是瑞秋的那个人。能在电视上与这样一批人认识，体会他们生活中的酸甜苦辣，可谓是《老友记》给人的无尽感动，很多粉丝都会永远记得他们，那些欢声笑语总能令人会心一笑。

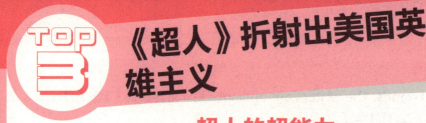

《超人》折射出美国英雄主义

超人的超能力

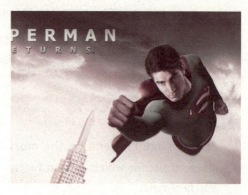

Superman is a perfect example of a contemporary *mythical* hero. No other character better *exemplifies* myth as *paradigm*: a mythical model that *embodies* the cultural reality of an era.

Like every mythical hero Superman has a super-natural *origin*. The story is that of an alien baby placed by his parents on a small rocket and shipped across millions of light-years to earth as the only survivor of a "wonderful race" on the eve the planet Krypton's *destruction*. The baby finally *lands* in a Midwestern corn field. He is found by Jonathan and Martha Kent who raise the child like their own son. They soon find out that Clark is no ordinary being.

In the early issues of *Superman* the hero was seen *leaping* tall buildings. A few years later he began to fly. As cars and airplanes became popular means of *transportation* it increased the *overall* mobility of the American people. As American's mobility increased so did Superman's. Through the years his powers increased until Superman became a godlike figure which also matched

超人是当代神话英雄的完美典范。没有其他角色能比超人更能证明神话的范例：反映一个时代的文化现实的虚构典范。

超人和所有其他的神话英雄一样，都有着超自然的出身。超人是一个外星婴儿，被他的父母放在小火箭里，穿越数百万光年的距离到达地球，在氪星球的毁灭前夕，成为经历了"惊险时速"的唯一幸存者。这个婴儿最后降落在中西部的玉米田里，被乔纳森和玛莎·肯特夫妇发现，他们像对待自己的亲生儿子一样将他抚养成人。但很快他们就发现，克拉克并不是凡人。

在早期的《超人》剧集中，主人公可以在高楼间跳跃。几年后，他开始飞翔。随着汽车和飞机日渐成为流行的交通工具，美国人民的整体流动性都有所增加；随着美国人民整体流动性的增加，超人的流动性也开始增

the US' status as the world's military super-power.

Accordingly, Superman's most *singular trait* is that of his split personality. One part relates to his super-natural powers and the other to the profane reality of the everyday world; a yin and yang so to speak. The first symbolizes the ideals of individual freedom and power.

加。他的超能力在几年内迅速变强，直至后来成为神一般的人物，与作为世界军事大国美国的地位相匹配。

因此，超人最奇异的特质在于他分裂的人格。其中一部分与他超自然的力量相关，另一部分则与世俗的现实世界有关；或者也可以说成是"阴阳"。是第一个将个人自由与超能力的理念结合起来的形象。

mythical 神话的	exemplify 例证	paradigm 范例
embody 体现	origin 出身	destruction 破坏
land 降落	leap 跳跃	transportation 运输
overall 全体的	singular 单一的	trait 特性

超人——一个神话典范

As we have seen, Superman is more than just a *vigilante* taking upon himself to rid Metropolis of its criminals. As the prefix "super" in his name *implies* he is "above" the ordinary "man": a *sacred* and *inaccessible* being that *roams* the heavens. These godlike qualities represent the super-natural origin that is typical of all mythical heroes. Myth therefore plays a major role in the *edification* of a cultural model that *transcends* all cultural and ethnical diversities. As such, the hero fosters an ideal to which all can identify; in this case an American

正如我们所看到的那样，超人不仅仅是个依靠自己消除都市犯罪的义务警员。超人这个名字的前缀"超"意味着他"超越"了普通"凡人"：是一个在天堂徘徊的神圣且难以接近的存在。其神一般的品质代表了所有超自然神话英雄的出身。因此神话在超越所有文化和种族多样性的文化模

ideal. As a result Superman embodies a civil religion that transcends all other religions. A civil religion that is concerned with the cultural *identity* and *integrity* of America.

Therefore, Superman was a mythical paradigm of an era. A model that promoted the cultural reality of a ruling group during post World War II.

式的启迪方面起到了重要的作用。正是如此，神话人物塑造了所有人都能认识到的理想；在《超人》中，这就是美国的理想。所以，超人体现着超越所有其他宗教的公民信仰，这种信仰关注美国的文化一致性和完整性。

因此，超人是一个时代的神话典范，一个第二次世界大战后促进统治集团的文化现实的典型。

单词释义

vigilante 义务警员	imply 暗示	sacred 神圣的
inaccessible 难接近的	roam 流浪	edification 启迪
transcend 超越	identity 一致	integrity 完整

美国特色文化

特色表达One

要是有可能，很多人都会期待能像超人一样厉害，可以拯救地球吧？可若是没有那份超能力，就不要招惹是非了，否则就有the devil to pay等着你。这个短语的字面意思是"魔鬼付账"。在美国俚语里的意思是"很大的麻烦"，或是"自讨苦吃"。

⭐ 实景链接

A： Are you taking a day off? I didn't find you in the office. 你今天请假了？我在办公室里没找到你。

B： I skip off work today. 我今天逃班了。

A： You mean, you didn't ask your manger before? 你是说，你之前没有跟经理请求过？

B： Yes. I just don't want to be there although it will be **the devil to pay**. 是。虽然我知道我会有麻烦，但我就是不想去。

🗨 特色表达Two

即使是拥有超能力，能够一飞冲天的超人可能也会犯糊涂，搞出误会。所以，超人其实也是普通人，他也需要一个机会去clear the air。可不要以为超人打完坏人又去清理空气了，clear the air在俚语里是"消除误会"的意思。

☆ 实景链接

A：Have Lucy forgiven you? 露西原谅你了吗？

B：Not yet. She refused to give me a chance to **clear the air**. 没有。她不给我消除误会的机会。

A：You should only apologize to her. 你应该跟她道歉。

B：I apologized many times. And I will try another time. 我道歉了许多次。不过我要再试一次。

拓展特色句

1. The leading actor in *Superman* is very attractive and handsome. 《超人》里的男主角非常吸引人也很帅气。

2. How many versions does *Superman* have? 《超人》这部电影有几个版本？

3. Producers invest a lot on *Superman*, but as a result the box office is very high. 投资商在《超人》上投资了很多，但是同时它的票房也很高。

🗨 "聊" 美国特色文化

A：Among the movie characters in, who is the real hero in your mind?

B：I think the Superman is the real hero.

A：I appreciate the Superman most too because he is the embodiment of justice.

B：The Superman is brave so I admire him very much.

A：在所有的电影形象中，谁是你心目中真正的英雄？

B：我认为超人是真正的英雄。

A：我最欣赏的也是超人，因为他是正义的化身。

B：超人很勇敢，因此我很佩服他。

A：而且他可以跳得很高，还能飞，这是我也希望拥有的能力。

A: And he can jump high and fly, which are abilities that I also want to have.

B: Why do you want to have such abilities?

A: It would be cool if you can save the world with these abilities.

B: Yeah. It's good to obtain freedom and power.

B: 你为什么想要这样的能力？

A: 如果你能凭借这些能力拯救世界会很酷。

B: 是啊。能获得自由和力量就太好了。

 美国特色文化

超人拍摄过程相当艰辛?

《超人》这部影片的拍摄可谓历经千辛万苦。首先，本片的选角过程一波三折：达斯汀·霍夫曼拒绝扮演鲁瑟；罗伯特·雷德福因名气过旺而不适合扮演超人；伯特·雷诺兹和西尔维斯特·史泰龙也相继回绝；最终，马龙·白兰度以370万片酬签约出演乔·艾尔。另外，《超人》的剧本相当恢宏，于是制片方又重新修改剧本，后来预定的导演档期不够，制片方只好又找来莱斯利·纽曼为片中的部分人物重写对白，而为了效果，在拍摄场景上更是下了很大的力气。

阅读笔记

《阿甘正传》中流露的美国信仰

努力就能获得成功

Forrest Gump contains *recurring* representations of American ideals that *manifest* national culture. The use of common *archetypal* characters in the film represents norms emphasized by Hollywood and *embedded* into the national *narrative*. The title character Forrest Gump is the classic *underdog*, or the archetype of the unlikely yet lovable hero who overcomes the *odds* and succeeds eventually. Despite his low IQ, physical disability, and modest background, Forrest works hard and *thrives*, becoming successful in *battle*, at ping-pong, at running, and eventually in business with his shrimp company. Jenny, his childhood sweetheart, fits into the damsel in *distress* archetype, since Forrest must continually save her from risky situations *stemming from* her *misguided* relationships with men.

Recurrent themes in *Forrest Gump* depicts the dominant national culture. The film emphasizes the theme of determination—the concept that hard work will lead to success. Determination has long been a value depicted in American society, due to the necessity of this value to flourish in a free market, capitalist economy.

《阿甘正传》反复提到了代表美国理想的民族文化。电影中利用普通的原型人物，这一点符合好莱坞的标准，也深深地融入到故事的叙述当中。主人公阿甘是典型的弱势者，或者说这个形象虽然毫无希望，但却是可爱的，是一个克服了各种的不平等，并最终获得成功的英雄人物。尽管阿甘智商低、身体残疾，背景朴实无华，但他通过努力日益成长，在乒乓球、跑步以及后来的捕虾公司中都获得了成功，在战斗中取得了胜利。他的青梅竹马珍妮则是个不幸的少女形象，她与男人的不当关系使阿甘必须不断帮助她脱离险境。

《阿甘正传》中反复出现的主题描绘了主导的民族文化。这部电影强调了决心这一主题——努力就能成功。决心是美国社会强调的价值，因为资本主义经济自由市场需要这种价值，才能蓬勃发展。

单词释义

recur 重现　　　　　　manifest 显示　　　　　　archetypal 原型的

embed 使嵌入　　　　　narrative 叙述　　　　　　underdog 不被看好的人

odds 不平等　　　　　　thrive 繁荣　　　　　　　battle 战役

distress 不幸　　　　　stem from 源自　　　　　misguided 被误导的

阿甘的乐观与希望

The theme of determination *illustrated* in *Forrest Gump* has even become a cultural *artifact* itself, with the phrase "Run, Forrest, run!" signifying determination against the odds (in this case, the bullies chasing Forrest). The theme of optimism and hope is displayed by Forrest, who never loses hope in his *quest* for Jenny's love nor in his expectation of the goodness in others. Optimism is another distinctly American value, often represented when describing the idealized "American dream" or the vision of America as a *refuge* for those seeking freedom and opportunity. The film also has a strong *undercurrent* of *patriotism*, a prominent factor shaping the national culture. Forrest fights for his country and sees his best friend die for his country. The willingness to die for your country displays a level of nationalism. Now film serves as a *platform* for visually representing these patriotic values.

Through the use of archetypes,

而《阿甘正传》中阐释的决心这一主题本身也成了一个文化产物，"跑，阿甘，快跑！"的话语标志着克服苦难的决心(片中是恶霸追着阿甘跑)。阿甘演绎着乐观和希望的主题，无论是追求珍妮的爱，还是对他人的善良抱有期望，他都没有丧失过希望。乐观是另一个特色鲜明的美国价值观，通常在描述理想化的"美国梦"，或者美国被视为追求自由和机遇者的庇护所的形象时，这种价值就会体现出来。《阿甘正传》也隐隐地表达着强烈的爱国主义，这个塑造了民族文化的重要因素。阿甘为他的国家而战，并眼睁睁地看着他最好的朋友为国家牺牲。愿意为国家牺牲在某种程度上体现着民族主义。现在，电影提供了一种从视觉上体现这些爱国

nationalistic themes, and historical references, Forrest Gump reinforces and *perpetuates* a dominant American culture. The film also becomes part of that American culture, serving as an artifact and reference itself.

主义价值观的平台。

通过利用原型、民族主义主题和历史背景，《阿甘正传》加强并发扬了美国主流文化，作为美国文化的产物和参考，这部影片本身也是美国文化的一部分。

单词释义

illustrate 阐明
refuge 庇护所
platform 平台

artifact 人工制品
undercurrent 暗流
perpetuate 使不朽

quest 追求
patriotism 爱国主义

  **美国特色文化**

特色表达One

《阿甘正传》中有一句这样的台词"Jenny and I was like peas and carrots." 为什么阿甘要将他与珍妮比作豌豆与胡萝卜呢？因为美国人烹饪的时候，习惯用豌豆与胡萝卜来装饰主菜，所以这两种蔬菜是同时出现的，在俚语里引申为"形影不离"。

☆ 实景链接

A： Who is your best friend in this place? 你在这里最好的朋友是谁？

B： Agnes. We are **like peas and carrots**. 艾格尼丝。我们形影不离。

A： Why do you love her best? 你为什么最喜欢她？

B： We can cooperate well with each other. 因为我们能很好地互相合作。

特色表达Two

朋友们，可还记得剧中猫王与阿甘母亲的对话吗？当时，阿甘跳了一支可笑的舞，于是猫王说：Let me show you a thing or two on the guitar here. 显而易见，这里的a thing or two不是一件事或两件事，而是指"露一手"。

⭐ **实景链接**

A：Are you good at cooking? 你擅长做饭吗？

B：Of course. I will show you a **thing or two** this afternoon. 当然。我今天中午就给你露一手。

A：I'm afraid that you would light up the kitchen. 我怕你把厨房点着了。

B：It's impossible. 那不可能。

拓展特色句

1. The film Forrest Gump won Hanks his second Best Actor Oscar. 电影《阿甘正传》为汤姆·汉克斯赢得了第二个奥斯卡最佳演员奖。

2. If I love a film very much I will watch it again and again, like Forrest Gump. 如果我非常喜欢一部电影，我会反复地看，比如《阿甘正传》。

3. Forrest Gump was an inspiring piece of cinema. 《阿甘正传》是一部励志影片。

💬 **"聊"美国特色文化**

A：I watched **Forrest Gump** and I was encouraged by the main character.

B：I love this movie for it revealed the importance of perseverance.

A：When I meet difficulties, I will remember "Run, Forrest, run!"

B：And then we can take actions to pull through.

A：Forrest Gump's story lets me know that if you work hard, you will succeed.

B：So it is important to be determined.

A：And even if we fail, we shouldn't lose heart.

B：Yes. We should be optimistic under any circumstances.

A：我看了《阿甘正传》，受到了主角的鼓舞。

B：我喜欢这部电影，因为它揭示了坚持的重要性。

A：当我遇到困难时，我会想到那句"跑，阿甘，快跑！"

B：然后我们就会采取行动，渡过难关。

A：阿甘的故事让我知道，只要你努力就能成功。

B：所以坚持很重要。

A：而且就算我们失败了，也不能灰心。

B：是的。在任何情况下都要保持乐观。

"问" 美国特色文化

《阿甘正传》中的阿甘与珍妮象征着什么?

在《阿甘正传》中,阿甘是一个操着美国南方口音且有智障的青年,他时常深情地凝视着他的女神珍妮,给人感觉他仿佛是《喧哗与骚动》中的傻子班吉穿越而来。可是他们两者毕竟是不同的,班吉是个真正的傻子,而阿甘的傻却体现在很多人所不屑的"诚信""勇敢""义气"等方面,简直是对当今社会的莫大讽刺。他的女神珍妮则象征着堕落,她吸毒、放纵,甚至因某种病毒而死亡,或许这里影射的是艾滋病毒。而阿甘却始终爱着她,而这更体现了他的纯真和善良。

阅读笔记

《欲望都市》演绎"阴盛阳衰"

当女性像男性一样

"Women have the right to behave every bit as badly as men" is not a claim made by the big-screen version of the television hit *Sex and the City*—it is the film's *presupposition*. In the world of Carrie, Miranda, Samantha, and Charlotte, women are every bit as *callous*, *petty*, unforgiving, and sexually promiscuous as any man. It's not an *aberration*, the film reveals, it's just the way things are.

Tension was bound to increase. If women were the new guardians of *virtue*, then a moral man, a *tamed* man, must, in some ways, be an *emasculated* man. Men resisted. The moral divide deepened, and an economic divide widened. Eventually it boiled over. Modern feminism devalued home life, and encouraged women to abandon the home in favor of careers. In a short time, many of the morals that western culture *took for granted* were *imperiled*. Women would be like men: ambitious, lacking *self-restraint*, sexually *promiscuous*—remarkably like the women in the film. Carrie, Miranda, Samantha and Charlotte have all arrived just in time to apply an *upscale* sense of style to a city in ruins.

"女人有权完全和男人一样行为不端"并不是热播电视剧《欲望都市》的电影版所要表达的东西，这只是该电影给人的错觉。在凯莉、米兰达、萨曼莎和夏洛特的世界里，女人和男人一样冷酷无情、小气、不宽恕别人以及乱搞男女关系。电影告诉我们，这不是失常，情况本来就是这样的。

不安感必然会增加。如果女人是美德的卫道士，那么有道德的男人和顺从的男人，必定在某种程度上是个柔弱的人。男人抵触这一点。道德的分化越加深，经济的分化就越大。最终这一切都失控了。现代女权主义轻视家庭生活，鼓励女人为追求事业而放弃家庭。很快，许多西方文化认为理所当然的道德都受到了威胁。女人也会和男人一样：雄心勃勃、缺乏自制、乱搞男女关系——就像电影中的女人一样。凯莉、米兰达、萨曼莎和夏洛特及时出现，给这个废墟般的城市带来一种高消费的风格。

单词释义

presupposition 假定	callous 无情的	petty 琐碎的
aberration 失常	virtue 美德	tamed 驯服的
emasculated 柔弱的	take for granted 认为理所当然	imperil 危及
self-restraint 自制	promiscuous 混杂的	upscale 高消费阶层的

《欲望都市》充斥着物质主义

In a *materialist* culture, marriage cannot be sacred, because nothing is. Marriage, despite being the focus of the *endgame* in this movie, is more often the object of *scorn*. Miranda tells Big that "marriage ruins everything." For her, marriage is discussed more as a legal protection against *untimely* house hunting than a lifelong spiritual *commitment* to the well-being and happiness of a spouse.

The goal of the women in *Sex and the City* is to live in a place that will make your girlfriends *jealous*, to view and purchase high-fashion clothing with designer price tags that would *bankrupt* most viewers, to reject anything other than the life of a sexual Olympian, and to pay attention to the circumstances of life while ignoring issues of character.

In a world *devoid* of spiritual *connotations*, adultery become "indiscretions," serial relationship failure magically is argued to be a herald of marital success; after all, as

在物质主义的文化里，婚姻并不神圣，因为没有什么是神圣的。尽管婚姻在电影《欲望都市》的尾声部分成为重点，但往往会被蔑视。米兰达告诉比格，"婚姻毁掉了一切。"对她来说，婚姻被讨论更多的是一种法律保护，能保证自己不会提前被赶出去找房子，而不是对配偶的终身健康和幸福的精神承诺。

在《欲望都市》中，女人的目标是生活在一个让女性朋友嫉妒的地方，浏览并购买那些标价高昂、足以让大多数人望而却步的高端时尚服饰，排斥除了性爱生活之外的其他东西，以及仅关注生活的环境，而不在意个性的问题。

在精神内涵匮乏的世界里，外遇就变成了一种"轻率之举"，几段爱情

Carrie tells Big, "We've already done everything we can to *screw it up*." But G.K. Chesterton would disagree, "It is always simple to fall; there is an infinity of angles at which one falls, only one at which one stands." The tough part of life, that this film wants to ignore, is the difficult task of determining how to stand.

连续受挫，却被神奇地看作婚姻成功的前奏；毕竟，正如凯莉告诉比格的那样，"我们已经做尽了能把它搞砸的事情。"但G·K·切斯特顿却不同意，"跌倒是很容易的；跌倒的角度有无限多个，但是站立的角度却只有一个。"而这部电影力图忽略的正是生活中最艰难的部分，即决定如何站立。

单词释义

materialist 物质主义者	endgame 尾声	scorn 蔑视
untimely 不合时宜的	commitment 承诺	jealous 嫉妒的
bankrupt 破产	devoid 缺乏	connotation 内涵
screw sth. up 把……搞砸		

美国特色文化

特色表达One

《欲望都市》里有一集凯莉问那些面试者是不是喝醉了，其中一个说：Never made it to bed last night. 从字面意思可知，这句话大概是说某人昨晚没去床上，其实引申意义就是"一晚没睡觉"。而make it在口语里指"成功达成目标"的意思。

☆ 实景链接

A：You look pale. Are you OK? 你看起来脸色苍白。你还好吗？

B：I think so. I **never made it to bed last night**. 我觉得还好。我昨天一宿没睡。

A：Oh, no. It's harmful to your health. 哦，不。这样对你的健康有害。

B：But I have to finish my work before the deadline. 但是我必须在截止日期之前完成工作。

特色表达Two

《欲望都市》里那帮女人既活泼狡猾又感性。在一集的剧情里，米兰达见到许久没联系的前男友忍不住哭了起来，忏悔当年的所作所为，突然男方说：You got a bat in the cave. 难道哪个洞里来蝙蝠了吗？其实他说的是米兰达"边哭边流鼻涕"。

☆ 实景链接

A：**You got a bat in the cave.** What makes you so upset? 你怎么哭得直流鼻涕？什么事让你这么烦恼？

B：I failed the exam. 我考试挂了。

A：Don't cry over split milk. I didn't pass it, either. We can prepare for the make-up exam. 别为打翻的牛奶哭泣。我也挂了。咱们可以准备补考。

B：OK. We must work hard and pass the make-up exam. 好的。我们必须努力通过补考。

拓展特色句

1. I was in high school when Sex and the City premiered on HBO. 《欲望都市》在美国家庭影院首播时我在读高中。

2. I am the one of the followers of US TV series Sex and the City. 我是美剧《欲望都市》的粉丝。

3. Have you watched all six seasons of Sex and the City? 六季《欲望都市》你都看了吗？

"聊" 美国特色文化

A：Do you agree with the view that women have the right to behave as badly as men in **Sex and City**?

B：No. I don't think anyone have the right to do so.

A：But there are many people act like this.

B：It doesn't mean that they are right.

A：你同意《欲望都市》里，女人可以和男人一样行为不端的观点吗？

B：不。我认为任何人都没有权利这样做。

A：可是很多人就是这样的。

B：这不能说明他们就是对的。

A：有时候我也想和剧中人物一样，过着奢侈的生活。

A: Sometimes I want to lead a luxurious life as the characters in the play.

B: Come on. You know it is impractical.

A: I just have such an illusion.

B: You should face the reality.

B: 拜托。你知道这是不切实际的。

A: 我只是有这样的幻想。

B: 你应该面对现实。

 美国特色文化

《欲望都市》曾掀起纸杯蛋糕风暴？

据说，《欲望都市》曾是全美人民最喜爱的电视剧，有一集女主角凯莉·布拉德肖在纽约布利克大街的马格诺利亚面包店外品尝纸杯蛋糕的形象深深吸引了观众的目光，于是纸杯蛋糕开始在纽约流行起来。至今，仍有众多人士慕名来到马格诺利亚面包店，品尝纸杯蛋

糕。很多游客说："我喜欢《欲望都市》，所以我想尝尝纸杯蛋糕。"另外，纸杯蛋糕本身小巧美丽，尤其吸引女顾客。

阅读笔记

《美国丽人》
让观众反思美国文化

《美国丽人》追求美式幸福

Happiness exists in *American Beauty* as a myth, as a goal, and as a *disguise*. All of the characters are engaged in the pursuit of happiness, although they have very different ideas about what happiness is and how to find it. This is one of the qualities that truly make American Beauty a film about the modern American experience: if being American means having the *intrinsic* right to the pursuit of happiness, why is the "typical" American so deeply unhappy?

Ultimately, *American Beauty* endorses the pursuit of happiness as the only thing worth living for. At the end of the film, Lester's murder seems almost *inconsequential*; how can Lester's end be viewed as a tragedy when he was lucky enough to know true happiness in the months before he died, and when so many others never know it at all?

《美国丽人》中的幸福是神话、目标，也是一种掩饰。电影里的所有角色都在追求幸福，尽管他们对何为幸福以及如何找到幸福有着完全不同的见解。这是《美国丽人》探讨的现代美国历史的特点之一：如果作为美国人就意味着拥有追求幸福的固有权利，那"典型的"美国人为什么极端地不开心？

最重要地是，《美国丽人》将追求幸福作为生活的唯一值得的理由。在影片的结尾，莱斯特被谋杀似乎无关紧要；可是莱斯特在死前的几个月里幸运地知道了幸福的真谛，而其他人却根本不了解，那他的死又怎么能被视为悲剧呢？

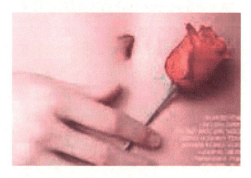

单词释义

disguise 掩饰 　　intrinsic 本质的 　　inconsequential 不重要的

《美国丽人》反映出的美国文化

From its title to its allusions to several *iconic* American texts, *American Beauty* explores different aspects of American culture and American identity. The title refers to three different symbols of American culture: American Beauty roses (a popular variety), Angela as a representative of youthful, innocent, "American" loveliness, and the American *aesthetic* of beauty, as represented by Ricky's films. Lester Burnham has distinct similarities to Willy Loman, the everyman *protagonist* of Arthur Miller's *Death of a Salesman*. Lester, *cognizant* of his situation, *reinvents* his life in order to save himself from a similar end. Carolyn Burnham represents American consumerism and the unfortunate belief that things can replace relationships. Lester's job at a fast-food restaurant and Jane's participation on the cheerleading team (both "typical" American roles) inject a humorous note into Mendes' discussion of American culture. All the same, *American Beauty* forces the viewer to consider whether there is anything worth saving at the root of this culture. When *American Beauty* was released abroad, many critics were surprised that Americans

从标题，到其暗含意义，再到标志性的美国主题，《美国丽人》探究了美国文化与特性的不同方面。电影的标题引用了三个不同的美国文化符号：美国美人玫瑰(一个流行品种)，代表年轻、无邪和美国式魅力的安琪拉，以及瑞奇电影所代表的美国美学。莱斯特·伯恩汉姆与阿瑟·米勒的电影《推销员之死》中平凡的主角威利·罗曼有明显的相似性。莱斯特知道自己的处境，就改造自己的生活以自我解救，避免类似的结局。卡洛琳·伯恩汉姆代表美国的消费主义，以及事物可以替代人际关系这一令人遗憾的观念。莱斯特在快餐店工作，简加入了拉拉队(两者都是"典型"的美国元素)，为门德斯关于美国文化的讨论加入了幽默的成分。尽管如此，《美国丽人》仍然迫使观众去思考美国文化中是否真有值得拯救的东西。当《美

responded so positively to a film that seemed so critical of traditional American values. Americans, it seems, were ready to question these values much as Lester does in the film, and move towards a more satisfying, emotionally fulfilling existence.

国丽人》在国外上映时，令许多评论家感到奇怪的是美国人竟然对这部看似批评美国传统价值观的电影给予了如此积极的评价。也许美国人和影片中的莱斯特一样希望去怀疑这些价值观，并向着更满足、情感更充实的方向前进。

单词释义

iconic 标志性的
cognizant 已认知的

aesthetic 审美的
reinvent 彻底改造

protagonist 主角

 美国特色文化

 ### 特色表达One

在中国，我们常称呼朋友的女朋友为"他的另一半"，那美国人会如何说呢？在《美国丽人》中有一句话：Everyone here is with their spouse or significant other. 意思是"这里每个人都带了他们的另一半。"所以，在美国俚语里，significant other就是"另一半"的意思。

☆ 实景链接

A：Do you bring your **significant other** with you? 你带你的另一半来了吗？

B：Yes. Look at there, she is dancing. 是的。看那边，她在跳舞。

A：Wow, she looks pretty with great figure. 喔，她看起来很美，身材很好。

B：Yeah. I'm mad about her. 是啊。我为她疯狂。

特色表达Two

平日里我们常用no double来表达"毋庸置疑"，那美国俚语里是怎么说的呢？在《美国丽人》里用到了hands down这个词组，如剧中的台词I mean, your firm is hands down the Rolls Royce of local real estate firms.（你的公司毋庸置疑是房地产界的劳斯莱斯。）此外，这个短语还有"容易地，唾手可得地"的意思。

☆ 实景链接

A: Do you have any problem when doing the job? 你做这项工作有什么问题吗？

B: Yes. I have no idea about how to start it. 是的。我没有头绪，不知道该如何开展工作。

A: I know it is **hands-down** a difficult job. If you have any question, you can turn to me. 我知道这确实是很难做的工作。如果你有问题，你可以来找我。

B: OK. Thanks a lot. 好的。太感谢了。

拓展特色句

1. American Beauty is an Oscar Award winner. 《美国丽人》是一部奥斯卡获奖影片。

2. Whose part do you think was best played? 你认为哪个角色演得最好？

3. How did the American Beauty finally come out? 《美国丽人》最后的结局如何？

"聊" 美国特色文化

A: What do you think about the movie **American Beauty**?

B: It is a blow and a shout to the middle class American.

A: I can understand the situation and the feeling of emptiness.

B: Especially when we see the main characters are facing various problems.

A: Do you feel depressed when watching it?

B: A little bit, it makes people feel hopeless.

A: We should reinvent when we are not satisfied with ourselves.

B: Yeah, just like Lester did in the movie.

A: 你如何看待《美国丽人》这部电影？

B: 这对美国中产阶级是当头棒喝。

A: 我能想象那种处境，以及那种空虚的感觉。

B: 尤其是当我们看到主角面临各种问题的时候。

A: 你在看这部电影时会觉得压抑吗？

B: 有一点，这部电影让人感到绝望。

A: 当我们对自己不满的时候，应该想办法改变自己的处境。

B: 是的，就像电影中莱斯特那样。

"问" 美国特色文化

《美国丽人》是部怎样的影片？

《美国丽人》这部影片重点强调的不是道德问题，而是讨论人生哲学，在一定程度上讽刺了世界的荒诞性。比如说，影片中莱斯特虽然在无意中发觉了比尔的心疾，却没放在心上，可最后却被疑心的比尔枪杀了。影片揭示某种荒诞，却没有谴责这种荒诞，反而告诉人们这是每个人都无法控制的冲动，这也是一种美。于是整部影片弥漫着一股浓烈的存在主义的意味。

阅读笔记

"艾滋"话题破冰者《费城故事》

冒险尝试"艾滋"话题

More than a decade after AIDS was first identified as a disease, *Philadelphia* marks the first time Hollywood has risked a big-budget film on the subject.

Philadelphia is quite a good film, on its own terms. And for *moviegoers* with an *antipathy* to AIDS but an enthusiasm for stars like Tom Hanks and Denzel Washington, it may help to *broaden* understanding of the disease. It's a ground-breaker like *Guess Who's Coming to Dinner* (1967), the first major film about an *interracial* romance; it uses the chemistry of popular stars in a reliable *genre* to *sidestep* what looks like *controversy*.

The story involves Hanks as Andrew Beckett, a skillful lawyer in a big, old-line Philadelphia law firm. We know, although at first the law firm doesn't, that Beckett has AIDS. Visits to the clinic are part of his routine. Charles Wheeler, the senior partner (Jason Robards) hands Beckett a case involving the firm's most important client, and then, a few days later, another lawyer notices on Beckett's forehead the *telltale* lesions of the skin cancer associated with AIDS.

在艾滋病首次被确定为疾病的十多年后,《费城故事》是好莱坞第一次冒险尝试以艾滋病为主题的大制作电影。

从内容来看,《费城故事》是部好电影。对于反感艾滋病,却热捧汤姆·汉克斯和丹泽尔·华盛顿这样的明星的观众,本片有助于人们进一步认识艾滋病。这是一部旷世之作,就像第一次探讨跨种族爱情的《猜猜谁来吃晚餐》(1967年);它借用了明星的影响力,以一种可靠的方式回避了可能的争议。

汤姆·汉克斯在本片中饰演安德鲁·贝克特,费城一家历史悠久的大律师事务所的律师。起初,这家律师事务所并不知道贝克特染上了艾滋病,而去诊所看病变成了他日常生活的一部分。贝克特的上司查尔斯·惠勒交给了他一个涉及事务所最重要客户的案件,而在几天后,另一位律师注意到贝克特前额的皮肤癌病变与艾滋病有关。

故事情节让观众感同身受

The film was directed by Jonathan Demme, who with Nyswaner finds original ways to deal with some of the *inevitable* developments of their story. For example, it's obvious that at some point the scales will fall from the eyes of the Washington character, and he'll realize that his *prejudices* against homosexuals are wrong; he'll be able to see the Hanks character as a fellow human worthy of affection and respect. Such changes of heart are *obligatory* (see, for example, Spencer Tracy's acceptance of Sidney Poitier in "Guess Who's Coming to Dinner").

But *Philadelphia* doesn't handle that *transitional* scene with *lame* dialogue or *soppy extrusions* of *sincerity*. Instead, in a brilliant and original scene, Hanks plays an aria from his favorite opera, one he identifies with in his dying state. Washington isn't an opera fan, but as the music plays and Hanks talks over it, passionately explaining it, Washington undergoes a conversion of the soul. What he sees, finally, is a man who loves life and does not

《费城故事》由乔纳森·戴米指导，他和编剧内斯万尼尔共同处理了本片情节发展中不可避免的问题。例如，很明显，在某种程度上，在华盛顿饰演的角色将会改变看法，他将意识到对同性恋者的偏见是错误的，并将汉克斯饰演的角色当成值得爱与尊重的普通人来看待。这样的转变是义不容辞的(比如《猜猜谁来吃晚餐》中斯潘塞·特雷西接纳了西德尼·波蒂埃)。

但《费城故事》并没有用无力的对话或勉强装出的真挚来设置过渡场景。相反，就是在原先华丽的场景中，汉克斯演奏了他最爱的歌剧中的一首咏叹，将自己将死的状态也融入到演奏中。华盛顿不是歌剧迷，但随着音乐响起，汉克斯慢慢的演绎和用热情的阐释，华盛顿的灵魂也随之升华了。他最终看到的是一个热爱生命

want to leave it. And then the action cuts to Washington's home, late at night, as he stares sleeplessly into the darkness, and we understand what he is feeling.

而不愿放弃的人。然后镜头切换到了华盛顿的家中，在深夜里，他凝视着黑夜难以入眠，这样观众就能体会到他此刻的感受。

单词释义

inevitable 不可避免的
transitional 过渡的
extrusion 挤出

prejudice 偏见
lame 差劲的
sincerity 诚挚

obligatory 义不容辞的
soppy 多愁善感的

美国特色文化

特色表达One

《费城故事》涉及了很多有关法律、人权、同性恋、艾滋病等敏感话题。电影里的人常说No sweat, buddy. 这句话直译就是"别出汗，伙计"，而一般让人出汗的事大多很麻烦，且令人担忧。所以这句话可以引申为"别担心，伙计"的意思。

☆ 实景链接

A：I can't find my passport. 我找不到护照了。

B：**No sweat, buddy.** Have you checked the little bag? 别担心，伙计。你检查小包了吗？

A：Let me see... Oh, it's here. 我看看……哦，在这儿呢。

B：When you can't find something, you need to calm down first. 如果你找不到东西了，首先要冷静。

特色表达Two

在《费城故事》中，法官会对情绪失控的人们说：Let's not go off the deep end. 这句话是什么意思呢？deep end是"深渊，困境"的意思，而go off the deep end就有"走入深渊，走入困境"的意思，引申为"走极端"的意思。

☆ 实景链接

A：I will give up. There is no chance to do it well. 我放弃了。我没可能做好了。

B：**Let's not go off the deep end.** 不要走极端。

A：But it is beyond my ability. 但这超出了我的能力范围。

B：You can ask others for help. 你可以向其他人求助。

拓展特色句

1. What's the film Philadelphia about? 《费城故事》这部电影讲的是什么?

2. It was a real tear-jerker. 这真是个赚人眼泪的情节。

3. This film is well worth seeing. 这部电影很值得一看。

"聊" 美国特色文化

A：Have you seen the movie **Philadelphia**?

你看过《费城故事》这部电影吗?

B：Yes. I think AIDS as the theme is worthy of attention.

看过。我认为艾滋病这个题材值得关注。

A：You can say that again. The movie is enlightening indeed.

你说得没错。这部电影能给人很大的启发。

B：Can you explain more specifically?

你能详细解释一下吗?

A：Some people think this disease disgusts, but after seeing the movie, I realize that we shouldn't discriminate the patients.

一些人认为这种病是令人厌恶的,可是看完这部电影后,我认识到我们不应该歧视这些病人。

B：Yes. The movie taught us that we should respect everybody.

是的。这部电影教导我们要尊重每一个人。

A：And we shouldn't discriminate others who are different with us.

我们也不应该歧视与我们不同的人。

B：That's true.

确实如此。

"问" 美国特色文化

《费城故事》反映了美国司法现状吗?

影片很好地反映了美国的司法现状,从其中的各种细节,都可以强烈地感受到美国司法制度的严谨。首先,在电梯门关上的时候,可以看到电梯门上写的几个粉笔字:NO JUSTICE, NO PEACE. 这似乎在告诉人们,在美国当时的司法制度下,只要正义没有得到伸张,诉讼就会永不停息地进行下去,无论是种族歧视,还是对同性恋抑或是艾滋病的歧视。这也为之后的剧情展开埋下了一个伏笔。

阅读笔记

Part 7

为何美国没有"北漂"现象

旧金山，昔日淘金者的天堂

旧金山何以形成

Perched *atop* hills and filled-in *marshland* at the entrance to one of the Pacific's largest natural harbors, San Francisco has had an *outsize* influence on the history of California and the United States. Originally a Spanish (later Mexican) mission and *pueblo*, it was conquered by the United States in 1846 and by an invading army of prospectors following the 1848 discovery of gold in its hinterland. The Gold Rush made San Francisco a *cosmopolitan* metropolis with a frontier edge. The great 1906 earthquake and fire destroyed much of the city but barely slowed its *momentum*; San Francisco barreled through the 20th century as a center of wealth, military power, progressive culture and high technology.

San Francisco is one of those cities that need no introduction; like Hollywood and New York, this city already enjoys international renown for everything from sightseeing to shopping to entertainment.

Construction of the Central Pacific Railroad—funded by the "Big Four" businessmen Charles Crocker, Mark Hopkins, Collis P. Huntington and Leland Stanford—drew

旧金山所在的位置是太平洋最大的自然海湾入口之一，城市坐落在沼泽遍布的山顶上。旧金山给加利福尼亚乃至美国的历史造成了巨大的影响。最初这个地方只是西班牙人(后来是墨西哥人)使团和村落所在的地方，1846年，这里被美国征服，在随后的1848年，一个地质勘探队伍在旧金山腹地发现了金子。然后，淘金热让旧金山成为了极富优势的世界性大都市。1906年的地震和大火摧毁了这座城市大部分的地区，但这不能阻挡其发展势头；20世纪，作为财富、军事力量、进步文化和高科技中心，旧金山的发展十分迅速。

旧金山是一座无需介绍的城市；和好莱坞、纽约一样，无论是观光、购物还是娱乐，这座城市的一切在国际上都声名显赫。

查尔斯·克罗克、马克·霍普金斯、

thousands of laborers from China. Although many were later forced to leave by **exclusionary** U.S. policies, San Francisco's thriving Chinatown quickly became the largest Chinese settlement outside of Asia.

科里斯·P·亨廷顿以及利兰·斯坦福这四位商界"巨头"出资修建中央太平洋铁路，吸引了上千名中国劳工。尽管由于美国随后的排他政策，许多人被迫离开，但旧金山繁荣的中国城也迅速变成了亚洲之外最大的中国人定居地。

单词释义

atop 在……顶上
pueblo 村落
exclusionary 排除在外的

marshland 沼泽
cosmopolitan 世界性的

outsize 特大的
momentum 势头

有名的淘金热

In January of 1848, James Marshall had a work crew **camped** on the American River at Coloma near Sacramento. The crew was building a saw mill for John Sutter. On the cold, clear morning of January 24, Marshall found a few tiny gold **nuggets**.

Within months, San Francisco became the central port and **depot** of the frenzied Gold Rush.

Thus began one of the largest human migrations in history as a half-million people from around the world **descended upon** California in search of instant wealth.

The first printed notice of the discovery was in the March 15 issue of "The Californian" in San Francisco. Shortly after Marshall's discovery, General John Bidwell discovered

1848年1月，詹姆斯·马歇尔及一群工人在萨克拉门托附近的克罗马的美洲河上安营扎寨。这些工人在为约翰·萨特修建木材厂。在1月24日那个寒冷而晴朗的清晨，马歇尔发现了一些小金块。

在几个月之内，旧金山变成了疯狂的淘金者们的中心港口和仓库。

于是，这导致了人类历史上最大规模的移民，有50万人从世界各地蜂拥而至，来到加利福尼亚州，希望能够一夜暴富。

第一则公布找到了金子的新闻报道刊登在3月15日在旧金山发行的《加利福

gold in the Feather River and Major Pearson B. Reading found gold in the Trinity River. The Gold Rush was soon in full sway.

尼亚人》报上。在马歇尔发现金矿之后不久，约翰·彼得威上将和皮尔森·B·雷丁少校也分别在羽毛河和特里尼蒂河发现金矿。淘金热就此迅速全面展开。

单词释义

camp 露营　　　　　　　nugget 矿块　　　　　　　depot 仓库

descend upon 突然到达　　exclusionary 排他的

 ## "品"美国特色文化

特色表达One

淘金者在淘金时，会先用盆从河流中淘水，然后把水慢慢倒出去，如果运气不错，就会看到好结果，也就是pan out well。后来淘金热逐渐消退，可是pan out这个用法却流传了下来，比喻"成功，奏效"。

☆ 实景链接

A：His plans never **pan out**. 他的计划从来没有成功过。

B：He is always out of luck. 他的运气总是不好。

A：But I never see him taking any action. 但我从来没见他采取过任何行动。

B：Maybe you are right. He doesn't work hard enough. 或许你说得对。他不够努力。

特色表达Two

和当初的淘金者一样，每个人都希望能做出一番事业，因此我们一定要有一个切实的计划，不能have our head in the clouds。美国人用这个俚语表示"满脑子幻想，不切实际"。此外，in the clouds在口语里可以表示"心不在焉"。

☆ 实景链接

A：Have you heard his business plan? 你听说他的创业计划了吗？

B：Yes. What do you think about it? 听说了。你觉得怎么样？

A：He'll never be able to run the business because he is always **had**

his head in the clouds. 他根本就做不了生意，他只会做白日梦。

B：I agree with you at there. 在这件事上我和你的看法一样。

拓展特色句

1. There is a large population in San Francisco. 旧金山人口众多。

2. San Francisco has a gay night life. 旧金山的夜生活很热闹。

3. San Francisco has many appealing attractions, including the Golden Gate Bridge, Fisherman's Wharf, and the Exploratorium museum. 旧金山有很多吸引人的景点，包括金门大桥、渔人码头，还有探索博物馆。

"聊" 美国特色文化

A：What is the symbol of San Francisco?

B：Of course the Golden Gate Bridge which looks magnificent.

A：Yes. The design of its structure is excellent.

B：And its color makes it can be seen clearly in the fog.

A：Are there any other fascinating places in San Francisco?

B：Maybe you'd love to go to the Fisherman's Wharf.

A：I've been told that it is a wonderful place.

B：If you were there, you must try the Boudin Sourdough Bakery's sourdough.

A：旧金山的象征是什么？

B：当然是金门大桥，它看起来很宏伟。

A：是啊，它的结构设计非常出色。

B：而且它的颜色让它在雾中也清晰可见。

A：旧金山还有其他吸引人的地方吗？

B：也许你会喜欢渔人码头。

A：我听说那是一个很棒的地方。

B：如果你到那里去，一定要尝尝波丁酸面包工厂的酸面包。

美国特色文化

去渔人码头干什么？看渔人网鱼吗？

"渔人码头(Fisherman's Wharf)"是旧金山的著名景点，它的标志是画有大螃蟹的圆形广告牌。这里原是渔民出海捕鱼的港口，当这里不再作为码头使用之后，经过商业包装，形成了独具特色的休闲、文化景点。来到渔人码头，一定要体验39号码头旁边的"海底世界"。在这里，你可以一边吃着波丁酸面包工厂生产的酵母面包，一边站在缓缓前移的走道上，抬头仰望豹纹鲨潇洒地游弋、各色小鱼活泼地嬉戏，可谓妙趣横生。

阅读笔记

拉斯维加斯，玩客的天堂

拉斯维加斯：从沙漠演变成"天堂"

Shimmering from the desert *haze* of Nevada like a latter-day El Dorado, Las Vegas is the most dynamic, *spectacular* city on earth. At the start of the twentieth century, it didn't even exist; now it's home to two million people, and *boasts* nineteen of the world's twenty-five largest hotels, whose *flamboyant*, no-expense-spared casinos lure in thirty-seven million tourists each year.

Las Vegas has been *stockpiling superlatives* since the 1950s, but never rests on its *laurels* for a moment. Many first-time visitors expect the city to be kitsch, but the casino owners are far too *canny* to be *sentimental*. The current trend is for *high-end* properties that attempt to *straddle* the line between screaming ostentation and "elegant" sophistication.

Although Las Vegas is an unmissable destination, it's one that palls for most visitors after a couple of (hectic) days. If you've come solely to gamble, there's not much to say beyond the fact that all the casinos are free, and open 24 hours per day.

拉斯维加斯是地球上最动感、最壮观的城市，它像一座现代的宝山一样闪耀在内华达荒漠的薄雾中。20世纪初期还没有这座城市；而现在它是200万人的家，世界上最大的25家酒店中有19家都在这里，这些酒店的赌场有着炫耀和一掷千金的风气，每年会引诱3700万游客前往。

自20世纪50年代起，高手们就云集在拉斯维加斯，但是他们不会因为荣誉而松懈片刻。许多第一次前来的游客都以为这座城市会很媚俗，但赌场的拥有者们却十分谨慎，不会感情用事。目前的趋势是使用高端道具试图跨越引人发笑的卖弄和"优雅"的老练间的界限。

尽管拉斯维加斯是一个不可错过的目的地，但对于那些在此（兴奋地）度过几日的游客来说，它令人厌烦。如果你来这里只是为了赌博，那么只有一句话要说：所有的赌场都是免费入场的，而且24小时全天开放。

单词释义

- shimmer 闪烁
- boast 以有……为豪
- superlative 最佳者
- sentimental 感情用事的
- haze 薄雾
- flamboyant 炫耀的
- laurel 荣誉
- high-end 高端的
- spectacular 惊人的
- stockpile 贮存
- canny 狡猾的
- straddle 跨过

赌城花样多

There are many rules for common Las Vegas table games, it took a while to get the *gist* of gaming in this town, but with this guide to Table Game Rules you'll have a *jump start* that lots people never did.

Arguably the most popular table game in Las Vegas, and my personal favorite, blackjack is a *relatively* simple game to understand with many *subtleties* to truly master. Nothing can make or break a table more than the people you're gambling with.

With the explosion of poker *tournaments* across the country it is of little surprise that casinos across Las Vegas have invested millions into their poker rooms. Poker is a true mental sport, where a player's skill and ability to bluff trump the cards in their hands.

Roulette is the game that most *newbies* play first. It is *deceptively* simple and my guess is that the spinning ball's hypnotic power helps soothe the nerves of the newbie

拉斯维加斯常见的桌游有很多规则，了解在这个小镇赌博的要点，你需要花点时间。但看完这个指南，你就占据了领先地位，这是许多人从来没有过的体验。

可以证明，21点是拉斯维加斯最受欢迎的桌游，是我个人最喜欢的。对于真正的高手来说，21点相对较简单，有容易掌握的技巧。赌博的对手非常重要，他们有可能成就你的一盘赌局，也可能会毁掉它。

由于扑克比赛在全国范围内爆炸般地举办，因此拉斯维加斯的赌场投资上千万来打造扑克室也就不足为奇。扑克是一项纯脑力运动，玩家们需要凭借自己的技巧和实力，虚张声势地打出手中的牌。

轮盘赌局是多数新手感觉上手最快的游戏。它本身有种魔力，让人能够一学就会。我认为旋转球具有的催眠的功

gambler. While not possessed of the best odds out of the various Las Vegas casino games, roulette remains popular for its easy play and low stress *approach*.

能，有助于新手放松紧绷的神经。尽管在数目繁多的拉斯维加斯赌场游戏中，轮盘赌局不是最容易赢钱的游戏，但由于容易上手，且给人的压力不大，它仍然是颇受欢迎的桌游。

单词释义

gist 要点
subtlety 微妙
deceptively 欺骗地

jump start 抢跑
tournament 比赛
approach 方法

relatively 相对地
newbie 新手

 美国特色文化

特色表达One

我们都知道，赌博有风险，下手需谨慎。然而赌徒却好像并不以为然，他们都习惯了stick their neck out。从字面意思来看，这个俚语的意思是"伸出头"，汉语里常说"枪打出头鸟"，把头伸出来可是很危险的，因此这个俚语就是"冒风险"的意思。

☆ 实景链接

A：I bet you will regret about buying the virtual currency. 我敢打赌你会后悔买这种虚拟货币。

B：But its revenue is quite high. 但它的收益真的很高。

A：Why do you always **stick your neck out**? 你怎么总是爱冒风险呢？

B：I'm eager to get rich. 我十分渴望变富。

特色表达Two

stake有"赌注"的意思，如果一样东西at stake，说明它可能随时会被输掉，所以这个短语可以引申为"处于危险中，利害攸关"的意思，也可以指事物"得失难料"。

★ **实景链接**

A: The game is so exciting. 比赛太让人激动了。

B: Yeah, I was almost trembling when the player scored a goal. 是啊，当运动员进球的时候我激动得都要发抖了。

A: I feel nervous too while watching. 我在看的时候也感觉很紧张。

B: The tension was naturally high because the game is **at stake**. 这场比赛成败难料，所以自然紧张度很高。

拓展特色句

1. Las Vegas is the city which swings all year. 拉斯维加斯是那种一年到头都很热闹的城市。

2. You can find many kinds of adult entertainment in Las Vegas. 在拉斯维加斯你能发现各种成人娱乐消遣。

3. People nickname Las Vegas as Sin City. 人们给拉斯维加斯起绰号为"罪恶之城"。

"聊" 美国特色文化

A: Do you like Las Vegas table games?

B: No. I don't like games that involve mental sport.

A: You can start with the easy ones. For example blackjack.

B: It's still difficult for me.

A: How about Roulette? It is relaxing.

B: Actually, I have no interest in gambling. And I'm afraid I may lose control.

A: You won't. It's just a game.

B: I'd better not to try.

A: 你喜欢拉斯维加斯的桌游吗？

B: 不喜欢。我不喜欢那些涉及脑力活动的游戏。

A: 你可以从简单的玩起。比如21点。

B: 这对我来说还是太难了。

A: 那轮盘赌局呢？这个很能让人放松。

B: 其实，我对赌博没兴趣。而且我怕我会失去控制。

A: 不会的。这只是游戏。

B: 我最好还是别试了。

"问" 美国特色文化

拉斯维加斯缘何得名"Las Vegas"？

Las Vegas来自西班牙语，意思为"肥沃的青草地"。过去这里曾是荒凉的石漠与戈壁地带，只有拉斯维加斯是一片有泉水的绿洲。由于有泉水，以及美国大兴铁路，这里逐渐成为了周边公路的驿站和铁路中转站，各地的淘金客都期待来这里醉生梦死，于是这样一个如海市蜃楼般的不夜城在沙漠之中崛地而起，尽显极致奢华。

阅读笔记

纽约城的千姿百态

小谈纽约

New York City is the most *beguiling* place there is. You may not think so at first—for the city is admittedly mad, the *epitome* in many ways of all that is wrong in modern America. But spend even a week here and it happens—the pace, the adrenaline take hold, and the shock *gives way to* myth. Walking through the city streets is an experience, the buildings like icons to the modern age, and above all to the power of money. Despite all the *hype*, the movie-image sentimentalism, Manhattan—the central island and the city's real *core*—has *massive* romance: whether it's the *flickering* lights of the *midtown* skyscrapers as you speed across the Queensboro bridge, the 4am half-life in Greenwich Village, or just wasting the morning on the Staten Island ferry, you really would have to be made of stone not to be moved by it all.

纽约城是最迷人的地方。一开始你可能并不会这样认为，不可否认，这座城市有疯狂的特质，而且在现代美国，它在许多方面都是错误的典型。但只要在这里待一个礼拜，你就会感受到它的迷人之处——城市的节奏，肾上腺素不断上升，你为此震惊，并被这神话般的城市折服。走在这座城市的街道上是一种体验，这里的建筑是当今时代的象征，也是金钱的力量的象征。尽管有那些浮夸的宣传，有电影形象的感伤主义，但曼哈顿作为纽约的中心地带，以及这座城市真正的核心，这里仍然是一个非常浪漫的地方：无论是匆匆走过皇后区大桥，望见商业区的摩天大厦闪烁着光芒，还是格林威治村初见晨光的凌晨4点，或者只是在史丹顿岛的轮渡上度过的一个早晨，除非你是铁石心肠，否则怎么可能不为这些所动。

单词释义

beguiling 令人陶醉的　　epitome 象征　　give way to 为……让步
hype 大肆宣传　　　　core 核心　　　　massive 巨大的
flickering 闪烁的　　　midtown 市中心区

不可错过的4个纽约印象

Located on one of the world's largest natural harbors, New York City consists of five **boroughs** which were consolidated in 1898: The Bronx, Brooklyn, Manhattan, Queens, and Staten Island.

Manhattan is the most **densely** populated borough and is home to Central Park and most of the city's skyscrapers. The borough is the financial center of the city and contains the **headquarters** of many major corporations, the UN, a number of important universities, and many cultural attractions.

Brooklyn, on the western tip of Long Island, is the city's most populous borough and was an independent city until 1898. Brooklyn is known for its cultural, social and **ethnic** diversity, an independent art scene, distinct neighborhoods and a distinctive architectural **heritage**.

Queens is geographically the largest borough and the most ethnically diverse county in the United States, and may **overtake** Brooklyn as the city's most populous borough due to its growth.

The Bronx is New York City's northernmost borough, the location of Yankee Stadium, home of the New York Yankees, and home to the

纽约城位于世界最大的自然港湾，由布朗克斯、布鲁克林、曼哈顿、皇后和史丹顿岛五个区组成，并于1898年统一。

曼哈顿是人口密度最大的区，这里有中央公园，这座城市大部分的摩天大楼都在这里。该区还是这座城市的金融中心，许多大型企业的总部、联合国、众多高校，以及许多文化景观都在这里。

布鲁克林位于长岛最西边，是这座城市人口最多的区，这里在1898年之前曾经是一个独立的城市。布鲁克林因其文化、社会和种族多样性，独立艺术现场、独特的社区和与众不同的建筑遗产而闻名。

皇后区是占地面积最大的区，也是美国种族最多样的一个县，而且由于人口数量上升，它可能超越布鲁克林，成为人口最多的一个区。

布朗克斯是纽约城最北部的区，

largest cooperatively owned housing complex in the United States, Co-op City. Except for a small section of Manhattan known as Marble Hill, the Bronx is the only section of the city that is part of the United States mainland.

这里是纽约扬基人的家乡，扬基体育馆就在这里。这里还有美国最大的合作公寓地区、合作公寓城。除了曼哈顿的马布尔希尔这一小部分地区以外，布朗克斯是这座城市唯一在美洲大陆的部分。

单词释义

borough 区　　　　densely 稠密地　　　　headquarters 总部
ethnic 种族的　　　heritage 遗产　　　　overtake 超过

美国特色文化

特色表达One

　　行走在纽约街头，面对这个庞大的国际化都市，常常会有恍若隔世的感觉，感到一切都美好极了。而out of the world就可以形容这种美好的感觉，它的字面意思是"世界之外"，引申为"极其精彩，极好的"等含义，多用来形容电影、美食、音乐等让人感觉很精彩。

☆实景链接

A：What do you think about the artsy concentrations in New York? 你觉得纽约的艺术聚集地怎么样？

B：These places are **out of the world**. 这些地方真是棒极了。

A：I have strong interest in arts. Maybe I should pay a visit. 我对艺术有着浓厚的兴趣，或许我应该去看一看。

B：Believe me. They are worth visiting. 相信我。那些地方值得一看。

特色表达Two

　　纽约是一个节奏很快的城市，这里的人们行色匆匆，甚至不愿意停下来。然而在过去，人们一般骑马外出，如果马走得时间太长，马蹄就会发热，骑马人必须停下来让马休息，等到马蹄凉了再走。人也是一样，走得时间长了脚后跟

(heels)也会发热，需要cool one's heels，停下来休息片刻。后来，这个俚语被引申为"苦等，久候"的意思。

☆ 实景链接

A：Why are you standing outside the boss's office? 你为什么一直站在老板的办公室外？

B：I have to **cool my heels** until he comes back. 在他回来之前，我只能等着。

A：You can make a time with him next time, thus you don't need to be waiting. 你下次可以和他约个时间，那样就不用等了。

B：Yes. You are right. 是啊，你说得对。

拓展特色句

1. I dream that I can live in New York. 我梦想自己能在纽约生活。

2. New York is just dazzling! 纽约真是繁华耀眼啊！

3. Welcome to New York in the beautiful autumn. 欢迎各位在这美丽的秋季来到纽约。

"聊" 美国特色文化

A：What is your impression of the New York City?

B：New York is a charming city. Everybody would be fascinated by it.

A：Is the pace of life fast here?

B：Yes. People on the streets seem to be busy.

A：Well, I can't imagine life like this. I want to have more leisure time.

B：If you could roam around the New York City, you can also enjoy the beautiful scenery there.

A：你对纽约城的印象是什么？

B：纽约是一个很有魅力的城市。每个人都会被它吸引。

A：这里的生活节奏快吗？

B：是的。街上的人看起来都很忙碌。

A：呃，我很难想象这样的生活。我希望有更多的休闲时间。

B：如果你能在纽约城闲逛，你也会欣赏到这里美丽的风景。

A：除了摩天大楼以外，这座城市有美丽的自然景观吗？

B：当然。你可以去曼哈顿的中央公园。

A: Except for the skyscrapers, does this city have wonderful natural scenery?

B: Of course. You can go to the Central Park in Manhattan.

 美国特色文化

为何称纽约为Big Apple?

为什么纽约会被称作Big Apple（大苹果）呢？根据历史记载，这个称谓最早在爱德华·马天尼于1909年写的《旅人在纽约》中出现。作者在书中用树来比喻国家经济，由于纽约"吸取了国家经济的大部分汁液"，所以它就是树上的一个"大苹果"。这个名称是指责纽约每年得到的国家财政数额都过大，但纽约市民却认为，生活在纽约就意味着享受繁荣经济带来的好处。而1971年的一次宣传活动将"大苹果"的称号广泛推广，希望人们对纽约有一个更正面的认识，就此，"大苹果"的名称才得到了官方承认。

阅读笔记

政治中心华盛顿

集政治和生活于一身的华盛顿

Washington, DC is not only the home to the *federal* government, but is also a *vibrant* city where people live, work and play. The city is known for its *monuments* and museums, national landmarks, cultural events, musical and theatrical entertainment and sporting events. The District of Columbia has a population of about 599,000 however, with the surrounding *suburbs* the metropolitan area has a population of more than 5.3 million making it the ninth-largest metropolitan area in the country.

Like any city, DC has its problems. There is still violence in its streets. There is still a *gigantic* wealth gap: within the same 61.4 square miles, Washington is home to both *affluent* Georgetown and poverty-stricken Anacostia, and it's surrounded by very prosperous areas in Virginia and Maryland. There is also a gigantic perception gap in that Washington is seen as a merciless overseer, not unlike the Capitol in The Hunger Games, living off the effort of the rest of the country while *oppressing* it into *submission*.

华盛顿特区不仅是联邦政府所在地，同时也是一个活跃的城市，人们在这里生活、工作、娱乐。这里的各种古迹、博物馆、国家地标性建筑、文化活动、音乐和戏剧活动、体育赛事都十分有名。哥伦比亚特区的人口超过599000人，再加上四周的郊区，该城市范围内的人口就能超过530万人，这样，华盛顿特区便成为了美国第九大城市。

和任何一座城市一样，华盛顿特区也有自己的问题。在这里仍然可见街头暴力。贫富差距依然巨大：无论是生活在乔治城的富人和生活在安那卡斯提亚的穷人都以这61.4平方英里的华盛顿为家，且周围还有弗吉尼亚州和马里兰州这样的繁华地区。在这里还存在着认知差异，华盛顿就像《饥饿游戏》中的国会大厦，它被认为是一个无情的监督者，汲取着其他国家努力换来的成果，并迫使它们屈服。

单词释义

federal 联邦的   vibrant 充满生气的   monument 遗迹

suburb 郊区   gigantic 巨大的   affluent 丰富的

oppress 压迫   submission 屈服

华盛顿必游景点

The neighborhood surrounding the U.S. Capitol Building is the largest residential historic district in Washington, DC with many 19th and 20th century *row* houses that are listed on the National Register of Historic Places. Capitol Hill is the most *prestigious* address in Washington, DC and the political center of the nation's capitol.

Georgetown served as a major port and commercial center during colonial times because of its *prime* location on the Potomac River. The neighborhood of *restored* row houses is a popular tourist destination because of its *upscale* shops, bars and restaurants. Georgetown University is located on the western edge of the neighborhood. The Chesapeake and Ohio Canal begins in Georgetown and runs 184 miles to Cumberland, Maryland.

Adams Morgan is the center of Washington DC's liveliest nightlife and is popular with young professionals. The neighborhood has a wide variety of restaurants, nightclubs, coffee houses, bars, bookstores, art galleries

美国国会大厦周围邻近地区是华盛顿特区最大的历史住宅区，这里的19世纪和20世纪的排屋已经登上国家历史名胜名录。国会山则是华盛顿特区最富名望的地方，也是美国国会的政治中心。

在殖民时代，乔治城是主要港口和商业中心，因为这是波托马克河上最好的位置。修复后的排屋附近也是很受欢迎的旅游景点，因为这里有高档的商店、酒吧和餐厅。乔治城大学位于城市西部。切萨皮克-俄亥俄运河也发源于乔治城，并延伸到184英里外的马里兰坎伯兰。

亚当斯摩根是华盛顿特区最具活力的夜生活中心，在年轻的职业人士间很受欢迎。附近还有各种各样的餐

and unique *specialty* shops. The nearby U Street Corridor is home to some of the city's best nightclubs and theaters and is rapidly changing into an arts and entertainment district.

厅、夜店、咖啡店、酒吧、书店、美术馆和独特的专卖店。附近的U街走廊上有一些这个城市最好的夜店和剧院，而这里也正在迅速变成艺术和娱乐区域。

单词释义

row 排	prestigious 有名望的	prime 最好的
restored 修复的	upscale 高档的	specialty 专业，专长

 美国特色文化

特色表达One

在美国付款时，你可以使用dead president，这里不是"死去的总统"的意思，dead president在美国俗语中指的就是"美钞"。在美国，一美元的纸钞与一美分硬币上都印有开国元勋华盛顿总统的头像，因为他们认为小面值的货币流通性最大，这样才能彰显总统的影响力。

☆ 实景链接

A: I have spent all the **dead presidents**. I have gone broke. 我的钱都花完了。我身无分文了。

B: What? You just got paid last week, right? 什么？你上周刚发的工资，对吧？

A: Yes, but I bought a new game console. 是，但我买了一台新游戏机。

B: So you deserve it. Don't expect that I would lend you money. 那你就是活该。别指望我会借你钱。

特色表达Two

华盛顿特区作为首都，是美国的政治中心。政界人士具备出色的把控事物走向的能力，让所有的事情都under the thumb，才能天下太平。俚语under the thumb就是"受控制"的意思，其字面意思是"在大拇指下"，比喻将事物牢牢地控制在手中的状态。

☆ 实景链接

A：Why don't we call Tom out? We can go to a pub, drink and dance. 咱们把汤姆叫出来吧。我们去酒吧喝酒跳舞。

B：Forget it. He cannot go out recently. 别想了。他最近出不来。

A：What happened? 发生什么了？

B：He won't be able to go to pub without his wife's permission. He's **under the thumb**. 没有他老婆允许他不能去酒吧。他被控制着呢。

拓展特色句

1. This is my first visit to Washington, DC. 这是我第一次到华盛顿特区旅游。

2. The capital city of the United States, Washington, DC, is named for the first U.S. president. 美国首都华盛顿特区是以美国第一任总统的名字命名的。

3. I would like to go to the National Museum of Natural History. 我想去国家自然历史博物馆看看。

"聊" 美国特色文化

A：What are the must-see attractions in Washington, DC?

B：I think it should be the Capitol Hill.

A：I know Washington, DC is the political center of the United States, but I'm not interested in politics.

B：If you want something historic, you can visit the row houses.

A：Wow? Can you say more about the row houses?

B：They are listed on the National Register of Historic Places, which are worth seeing.

A：It seems that Washington, DC is also

A：华盛顿特区必看的景点有哪些？

B：我认为应该是国会山。

A：我知道华盛顿特区是美国的政治中心，但我对政治不感兴趣。

B：如果你想看一些有历史意义的景点，可以去看看排屋。

A：喔？你能再说说关于排屋的事情吗？

B：它们已经登上了国家历史名胜名录，值得一看。

A：看来华盛顿特区也是一个有活力的城市。

B：是的。这座城市也有浓厚的文化气息。

a dynamic city.

B：Yes. The city also has a strong cultural
atmosphere.

 **美国特色文化**

华盛顿纪念碑有何代表意义?

无论从任何方向进入华盛顿，首先
映入眼帘的都是这座高耸入云的方尖碑。
这就是著名的华盛顿纪念碑(Washington
Monument)，它的作用是纪念乔治·华盛顿的
功绩。这座方尖碑是华盛顿的地标性建筑，
整体为石质，碑柱为正方体，顶端则是四面

三角形的尖顶，看起来锐气逼人。在纪念碑顶层，通过8个观览窗口可以一览华
盛顿的美景。整个碑身上没有一个字母，仿佛在告诉人们，华盛顿一生的卓越成
就是难以用文字来表达的。

阅读笔记

享受听觉盛宴，去纳什维尔

音乐之城纳什维尔

Nashville is located in the north-central part of Tennessee along the Cumberland River. Aside from being the capital of the state of Tennessee, Nashville is also known as "Music City." Nashville earned its *reputation* as "music city" due to being a focal point for the music industry. Nashville's musical reputation started back in the 1920s with the radio broadcast of what would eventually become the *Grand Ole Opry* and continues today to be a hub for all types of music from country to rock to gospel.

Nashville began to earn a reputation as a center for music publishing as early as the turn of the 20th century. In 1925, however, the future "Music City" truly started to unfold when WSM radio station started broadcasting. Among the first programs sent over the *airwaves* on radio WSM were broadcasts of the *Grand Ole Opry*. The nickname "Music City" was born during the 1920s and 1930s and has been *associated* with Nashville ever since. The *Grand Ole Opry* has also continued to be broadcast live from Nashville every week since its first broadcast.

纳什维尔位于田纳西州北部中心地区，沿着坎伯兰河延伸。纳什维尔除了是田纳西州首府以外，"音乐之城"的名字也为人熟知。由于这里是音乐产业的焦点，纳什维尔赢得"音乐之城"的美誉。纳什维尔在音乐方面的声誉始于20世纪20年代，当时收音机里广播着如今的"奥普里大剧院"节目，这档节目如今仍然是从乡村乐到摇滚乐，再到福音音乐等各种音乐类型的集合。

纳什维尔赢得音乐出版中心的美誉是从20世纪初开始的。然而在1925年，当WSM广播开始播音的时候，未来的"音乐之城"确实就已开始呈现。WSM广播通过电波播放的第一批节目就有"奥普里大剧院"。而"音乐之城"的昵称也是在20世纪二三十年代出现的，并从此与纳什维尔密切关联。自首次播出以后，"奥普里大剧院"在纳什维尔至今每周仍有直播。

单词释义

reputation 名誉   airwave 电波   associate 联系

纳什维尔衍生副产业

Of all of the products *manufactured* in the city, music is what makes Nashville most famous. The local *recording* industry and its offshoots have not only brought worldwide *recognition* to what was once a sedate southern city, but they have also *pumped* billions of dollars into the local economy, created a *thriving* entertainment business scene *ranked* behind only New York and Los Angeles, and given the city a distinctly *cosmopolitan* flavor. Nashville music—country, pop, gospel, and rock—generates well over a billion dollars in record sales each year.

As a result, spin-off industries have flourished: booking agencies, music publishing companies, promotional firms, recording studios, trade publications, and performance rights associations such as BMI, the Broadcast Music Inc. As Nashville remains a center for the music industry, it continues to draw support businesses and industry to the area. Local music-related advertising firms bring in vast *revenues*, music video production in the city is at an all-time high, while a burgeoning radio,

在纳什维尔生产的所有产品中，音乐最能使其扬名天下。当地的唱片业及周边衍生行业不仅让这个曾经的安静南方小城变成世界闻名的城市，还为当地带来了数十亿美元的经济收入，创造的繁荣的娱乐商业景象仅仅排在纽约和洛杉矶之后，并为这座城市带来了鲜明的世界风情。纳什维尔制作的音乐形式包括乡村音乐、流行音乐、福音音乐和摇滚乐，这些每年可以带来超过10亿美元的唱片销量。

因此周边衍生行业也开始繁荣：包括预订机构、音乐出版公司、宣传公司、音乐工作室、商业出版物和BMI，即广播音乐公司这样的演出版权协会。纳什维尔是音乐产业的核心，因此仍能吸引到商业和工业支持。音乐广告片在这里可以带来很大的收

television, and film industry has *enticed* some of the country's top producers, directors, and production houses to set up shop in Nashville. The music industry in Nashville is responsible for a good chunk of the city's tourism activity.

益，时时刻刻都在制作大量音乐录影带。迅速增长的广播、电视和电影业也引诱着美国顶级的制作人、导演和制作公司前来纳什维尔展开业务。此外，纳什维尔的旅游活动也有很大一部分与音乐产业有着密切的关系。

单词释义

manufacture 制造	recording 唱片	recognition 认识
pump 汲取	thriving 繁荣的	rank 排名
cosmopolitan 世界性的	revenue 国家的收入	entice 诱使

  美国特色文化

特色表达One

　　如果你厌倦了现在的生活，可以换个环境，换个生活方式。但是，你不能bury your head in the sand。把头埋在沙子里是鸵鸟经常干的事儿，遇到危险时，它们就会这样做，以为自己看不见敌人，敌人也就看不见它了。这是典型的自欺欺人，而这种不愿正视现实的做法，在英语里就叫bury one's head in the sand。

☆ 实景链接

A : Will you go to work tomorrow? 你明天会去上班吗？

B : No. I don't want to face the pile of work. 不去。我不想看见那一堆的工作。

A : You can't **bury your head in the sand**. You must learn to face it. 你不能逃避现实。你必须学会面对现实。

B : You'd better leave me alone. 你最好让我一个人待着。

特色表达Two

　　在去看演出或音乐会时，观众往往会用鼓掌的方式来对表演表示欣赏。但如果演出水平太低，观众就会sit on their hands，也就是"不鼓掌"的意思。现在，sit on one's hands已经不局限于文艺界，引申为"按兵不动，不作为"的意思。

⭐ **实景链接**

A: Do you know why she **sits on her hands**? 你知道她为什么不采取行动吗？

B: Maybe she doesn't like the plan? 也许她不喜欢这个计划？

A: No. Actually she thought that she should be the person in charge. 不是。其实她觉得自己才应该是负责人。

B: Come on. There is a slim chance. 拜托。那机会很渺茫啊。

拓展特色句

1. She's set to perform in Nashville. 她计划会在纳什维尔市登台演出。

2. The singer will be in Nashville on Saturday for the Academy of Country Music awards. 周六该歌手会在纳什维尔市出席乡村音乐颁奖典礼。

3. The home of American country music was Nashville, Tennessee. 美国乡村音乐的故乡就是田纳西州的纳什维尔。

"聊" 美国特色文化

A: Why Nashville is called "Music City?"

B: Because it is famous for its music industry.

A: Are there many celebrities of the music industry in Nashville?

B: Yes. The city attracts many music producers and to set up studios here.

A: What kinds of music are produced in this city?

B: The genres involve country, pop, gospel, and rock music.

A: So we'd say that music is the core industry of this city.

B: You are right. It contributes a lot to its thriving economy.

A: 为什么纳什维尔被称作"音乐之城"？

B: 因为这里是以音乐产业而闻名。

A: 在纳什维尔有很多音乐界的名人吗？

B: 是的。这座城市吸引了许多音乐制作人来开设工作室。

A: 这座城市制作哪种类型的音乐？

B: 包括乡村乐、流行乐、福音音乐和摇滚乐这几种类型。

A: 所以，可以说音乐是这座城市的核心产业。

B: 你说得对。这为该城市繁荣的经济做出了很大的贡献。

 **美国特色文化**

乡村音乐名人堂是个怎样的地方？

乡村音乐名人堂(Country Music Hall of Fame and Museum)是纳什维尔最主要的景点之一，成立于1961年，作为历史博物馆和国际艺术组织，这里的藏品包括数以万计的唱片、电影带、电视录像、书籍、杂志、期刊和歌本。参观者可以观看电影，在电脑上进行互动操作，欣赏乐器、服装和明星们的私人物品。另外，这里还不时推出现场表演，让游客可以游走在乡村音乐的过去和现实之间。

阅读笔记

在洛杉矶邂逅文艺

走进洛杉矶

On the second Thursday of every month, something strange happens in Downtown LA. It starts in the morning, when owners of LA art galleries begin to *hustle* around making last-minute preparations—adjusting lighting, getting a *lineup* of drinks ready, choosing music. Come *nightfall*, the historic core of Downtown LA comes alive with *remarkable* energy.

For visitors who want a *taste* of where the locals go, the Downtown Art Walk, which takes place every second Thursday, usually from noon-10 pm, is a perfect example of Los Angeles at its best. The *sheer* electricity of the scene *explodes* from bass-pumping galleries, the eclectic crowd and the music groups that set up outside various galleries in Downtown LA. One thing is for certain: art lovers think it's one of the best shows in town.

在每月的第二个星期四的晚上，在洛杉矶市中心都会发生奇怪的事情。从早上开始，画廊的拥有者们便会匆忙奔走，做着最后的准备——调好灯光，备好酒水，以及选择音乐。当夜幕降临时，洛杉矶市区这一历史的核心就会带着巨大的能量活跃起来。

对于想要体验当地市区生活的游客们来说，洛杉矶的Art Walk活动是最好的范例。Art Walk活动于每月的第二个周四举行，通常从中午一直持续到晚上10点。一些画廊举办现场音乐演出，从中会爆发出电贝司纯粹的声音，折中主义的人们和音乐团体也会一起在洛杉矶市区开办各类户外画展。有一件事是肯定的：艺术爱好者们会认为这是这座城市最好的演出活动之一。

单词释义

hustle 匆忙，赶紧	lineup 一组	nightfall 黄昏
remarkable 非凡的	taste 体验	sheer 纯粹的
explode 爆发		

爱上文艺的她

For those seeking *masterpieces* of art, Los Angeles is a *must-see* destination filled with cultural treasures from around the world. Many of these *iconic* works are unexpectedly in Los Angeles, from Van Gogh's *Irises* and Diego Rivera's *Flower Day* to *The Thinker* and *The Blue Boy*.

Angelenos and visitors alike depend on LA's freeways to *navigate* the *sprawling* metropolis, and it's no surprise that they've provided inspiration to generations of authors. Joan Didion's 1970 novel *Play It as It Lays* centers on the fringes of Hollywood and in particular the *faded* actress Maria Wyeth, who tries to find *solace* by driving aimlessly on LA's freeways.

LA's freeways are often referred to as "*arteries*" and other organic terms. In his poem Night Song of the Los Angeles Basin, Pulitzer Prize-winning Beat poet Gary Snyder contrasts the "*calligraphy* of cars" with the sounds of nature. Snyder describes the LA basin and hills as "*Checkered* with street ways".

Like Los Angeles, the art represents a range of tastes, but much of it takes on the energy of the city and the emotions of life Downtown.

对那些希望寻找艺术杰作的人们来说,洛杉矶拥有来自世界各地的文化瑰宝,因此是必去的地方。让人意想不到的是,许多代表性作品都收藏在洛杉矶,比如梵高的《鸢尾花》,迭戈·里维拉的《花卉节》,以及《思考者》和《蓝衣少年》。

无论是洛杉矶人还是游客,人们都同样地依赖着这里四通八达的高速公路,它们为一代又一代的作家提供了灵感。比如琼·迪迪翁于20世纪70年代创作的小说《顺其自然》、这部小说讲述好莱坞边缘人物的生活,尤其是淡出人们视线的女演员玛利亚·怀斯的故事,她开着车子漫无目的地沿着洛杉矶的高速公路驶去,希望找到慰藉。

洛杉矶的高速公路常被认为是城市的"动脉"或其他器官。在普利策奖得主,诗人加里·斯奈德的诗歌《洛杉矶流域的夜曲》中,对比了"车灯画出的光线"和自然的声响。根据斯奈德的描述,洛杉矶的山河"与街道互相交错"。

和洛杉矶本身一样,这里的艺术也代表着一系列的品位,但大多数

Urban *counterculture* expresses itself through *graffiti* styles, while artists tap into emotions ranging from inspiring to sexual to playful.

都借助着城市的能量，以及市区生活的情感。墙上涂鸦风格的画作表达着反主流文化，而艺术家会挖掘各种情绪，从灵感，到性，再到玩乐。

单词释义

masterpiece 杰作　　　　must-see 必看的　　　　iconic 标志性的

navigate 驾驶　　　　　sprawling 不规则伸展的　　faded 淡出人们视线的

solace 慰藉　　　　　　artery 动脉　　　　　　calligraphy 笔迹

checker 画成棋盘型方格　counterculture 反主流文化　graffiti 涂鸦

美国特色文化

 特色表达One

　　洛杉矶的Art Walk如此精彩，一定不能错过，就算"赴汤蹈火也在所不惜"，美国俚语come hell or high water就可以表达类似的含义，这个俚语是"就算天崩地裂"的意思。如果你决心要办一件事，就可以这样说。不过这个俚语虽然主要表达克服困难的决心，但有时也有"无论如何"的意思。

☆ 实景链接

A： Will you be at the family reunion this year? 今年你会回去和家人团聚吗？

B： Yes. It's important for me to go back. 是啊。回去对我来说非常重要。

A： But the airline ticket is expensive during holidays. 但是节日期间机票很贵。

B： I'll be there, **come hell or high water**! 无论如何我也都回去！

特色表达Two

　　在洛杉矶这样的艺术之城，千万不能做一个老套的人哦，如果你总是in a rut，可能会让人感觉枯燥乏味。rut作名词是"车辙，槽，凹痕"，以及"常规，惯例"的意思。如果某物陷入了深深的车辙，那一定是寸步难行，无法进展，所以in a rut就是"千篇一律"的意思。

☆ 实景链接

A: Why did you quit your job? 你为什么辞职了？

B: My life was **in a rut** and I can't stand anymore. 我的生活千篇一律，我再也无法忍受了。

A: Oh, I really envy you. What is your next plan? 噢，我真羡慕你。你下一步的打算是什么？

B: I will travel to India. 我要去印度旅行。

拓展特色句

1. L.A. attracts millions of tourists a year. 洛杉矶每年能吸引上百万的游客。

2. We can have a motorcycle trip up the road linking Los Angeles and San Francisco. 我们可以在连接洛杉矶和旧金山的公路上骑车兜风。

3. Why don't we go to the L.A .Art Museum to improve our taste in art! 咱们去洛杉矶美术博物馆逛逛，提升一下自己的艺术修养吧！

"聊" 美国特色文化

A: Have you been to the Art Walk in Los Angeles?

B: Yeah. I was there last week. It was marvelous!

A: Can you say something about it in details?

B: There are many exhibitions hosted by the owners of the galleries. And we had the foods and drinks provided by them.

A: Sounds interesting. And are there any live show?

B: Yes. You can enjoy shows held in some galleries.

A: When will the next Art Walk start?

A: 你参加过洛杉矶的Art Walk活动吗？

B: 参加过。我上周还去了。那活动非常棒！

A: 你能详细地说说吗？

B: 画廊老板们会举办许多的展览。而且我们可以享用他们提供的食物和饮料。

A: 听起来很有趣。那有没有现场演出呢？

B: 有的。你可以在一些画廊里看到演出。

A: 下次的Art Walk什么时候举办？

B: 每月的第二个周四举办。你要等到下个月了。

B：It was held on the second Thursday of each month. You need to wait until next month.

 美国特色文化

洛杉矶的迪士尼乐园怎么样？

洛杉矶不仅是美国西海岸边的一座风景秀丽的海滨城市，更是一个老少皆宜的人间乐园。在这里，你可以参观世界上第一座迪士尼乐园，体验睡美人城堡的爱与梦幻，或者与蹦蹦跳跳的米老鼠、唐老鸭结伴而行，乘坐优雅的华丽马车，品尝古色古香的茶点小餐，畅游童话般的迪士尼世界。

阅读笔记

星巴克的故乡，文化之城西雅图

西雅图在哪里

Seattle lies on a narrow *strip* of land between the salt waters of Puget Sound and the fresh waters of Lake Washington. Beyond the waters lie two *rugged* mountain ranges, the Olympics to the west and the Cascades to the east. It is a city built on hills and around water, in a mild marine climate that encourages *prolific vegetation* and *abundant* natural resources.

White settlers came to the Seattle area in 1851, establishing a *town site* they first called New York, and then, adding a word from the Chinook *jargon* meaning "by-and-by," New York-Alki. They soon moved a short distance across Elliott Bay to what is now the historic Pioneer Square district, where a protected deep-water harbor was available. This village was soon named Seattle, honoring a Duwamish Indian leader named Sealth who had *befriended* the settlers.

西雅图位于普吉特海湾的咸水水域和华盛顿湖的淡水水域之间的狭长地带。水边是两座崎岖的山脉，西边是奥林匹克山脉，东边是卡斯卡德山脉。这是一座依山傍水的城市，有着温和的海洋性气候，适合植被的茂盛生长，并且有着丰富的自然资源。

白人们于1851年来到西雅图定居，建立了最初被他们称为纽约的城址，随后他们在这个名字中加上了表示"将来"的切努克人的行话Alki。他们很快就以很短的距离横渡了艾略特湾，来到了如今历史上著名的先锋广场，这里有一个保护良好的深水海湾。这个村子很快被命名为西雅图，这是为了纪念一位名为西尔斯的杜瓦米什印第安领袖，他曾经如同朋友一般帮助过这些定居者。

单词释义

strip 带，条状　　　　rugged 崎岖的　　　　prolific 多产的
vegetation 植被　　　　abundant 丰富的　　　　town site 城址
jargon 行话　　　　　　befriend 如朋友般对待

受教育程度最高的城市

Seattle is both the most highly educated and most *literate* city in the United States. Some might say that Seattle's dreary weather keeps everyone indoors, a condition *conducive* to intellectual *pursuits*! It may very well be the weather to blame for the *pervasive* passive-aggressiveness encountered among many who call Seattle home.

Seattle's population has expanded dramatically over the past few decades as job seekers in technology-based fields swarmed into Seattle to take jobs at Microsoft and other corporations.

Scientists also flock to Seattle to take advantage of its blooming biotech industry, *buoyed* by the University of Washington, several excellent hospitals, and the Fred Hutchinson Cancer Research Center.

While Seattle is well-known as the home of Starbucks, the streets of Seattle are *thick with* independent coffee shops, many of which roast their own coffee. Be on the lookout for Espresso Vivace, Hotwire, Uptown Espresso, Caffe Ladro, Diva Espresso, and many other only-in-Seattle beaneries.

几乎可以说西雅图是美国教育程度最高的城市，也是最有文化的城市。可能有人会说，这是由于西雅图阴沉的天气让人们只能待在室内，而这样的环境适合深造学业！可能确实是出于天气的问题，住在西雅图的人们都很不愿意积极进取。

在过去几十年，西雅图的人口迅速扩张，这是由于许多科技领域的求职者纷纷来到西雅图，以便到微软或其他企业工作。科学家们也聚集在西雅图，充分利用这里蓬勃发展的生物科技产业，华盛顿大学、一些顶尖医院及弗雷德·哈钦森癌症研究中心都在支持这里的科技产业。

众所周知，西雅图是星巴克的故乡，在西雅图的街道上，自营咖啡馆随处可见，且多数提供自己烘焙的咖啡。这里还可以看到Espresso Vivace, Hotwire, Uptown Espresso Caffe Ladro, Diva Espresso等咖啡店，以及其他一些只在西雅图有的经济小店。

单词释义

literate 受过教育的　　　conducive 有益的　　　pursuit 追求
pervasive 普遍的　　　　buoy 支撑　　　　　　thick with 满是……
beanery 经济小吃店

 美国特色文化

特色表达One

西雅图处处弥漫着小资情调，是pub crawl的必去之处。pub crawl或a gin crawl源自19世纪，可以指喜欢泡吧的人，或者是在酒吧间走来穿去的行为，甚至还能指代酒吧或咖啡馆。

☆ 实景链接

A： Do you have any plan for today after work? 你今天下班后有什么安排吗？

B： Nothing special. How about you? 没什么特别的。你呢？

A： Why don't you go to the bar and have a drink? 我们去酒吧喝一杯怎么样？

B： Actually you want to go on a **pub crawl**! I love the idea! 其实你想串着酒吧去喝吧。我喜欢这个主意！

特色表达Two

西雅图的天气总是阴沉多雨，如果雨下得很大，我们可以说rain cats and dogs。这个俚语是"下倾盆大雨"的意思，这个说法的来源是由于17世纪人们使用的地下排水系统非常简陋，导致排水能力极其有限。一旦下起暴雨，地下水沟里便会积满污水，随着雨越下越大，污水便会四处横流，随着污水流出的除了各种垃圾外，还有死猫死狗之类的小动物尸体。之后rain cats and dogs就表示下很大的雨。

☆ 实景链接

A： Will you go out? It's **raining cats and dogs**. 你要出门吗？外面下着倾盆大雨呢。

B： I have to buy some salt, or we can't cook meal. 我去买点盐，否则咱

们没法做饭。

A: Don't forget your umbrella. 别忘了带伞。

B: Thanks for reminding. But I don't think I would forget since it rains such heavily. 谢谢提醒。不过雨这么大，我觉得我是不会忘的。

拓展特色句

1. In 1971, the first Starbucks over the world was founded in Seattle. 1971年全球第一家星巴克在西雅图创办。

2. The software developer comes from a Seattle company of the same name. 该软件开发商来自于美国西雅图的一家公司。

3. Seattle Olympic Sculpture Park is a public art center in Seattle. 西雅图奥林匹克雕塑公园是西雅图的一个公共艺术中心。

"聊" 美国特色文化

A: Are citizens in Seattle the most highly educated ones in the country?

B: It was said to be like this.

A: Why most of the citizens are well-educated?

B: The city provides many job opportunities, which are attractive to the job seekers in the technology-based fields.

A: You said it. And he headquarters of Microsoft is here.

B: Maybe it is good for us to move to Seattle.

A: I agree with you. Another reason that I love Seattle is the numerous cafes.

B: Yeah. So it is not surprising that the city is the hometown of Starbucks.

A: 西雅图的市民是受教育程度最高的人群吗？

B: 人们是这样说的。

A: 为什么这里的市民大多数都接受过良好的教育？

B: 这座城市提供许多工作机会，而这对那些科技领域的求职者们来说很有吸引力。

A: 你说得对。而且微软的总部也在这里。

B: 也许搬到西雅图对我们来说很不错。

A: 我同意。还有一个我喜欢西雅图的理由是这里有数不清的咖啡店。

B: 是啊。所以这里是星巴克的故乡也不足为奇。

 美国特色文化

星巴克遇上西雅图?

在西雅图,有一个地方是世界各地的咖啡迷们"朝圣"的圣地,那就是咖啡连锁店星巴克(Starbucks)的总部。那是一座红砖砌成的九层老建筑,中央的钟楼上,四面各立着一面星巴克的标志——羞涩的美人鱼。星巴克诞生于美国西雅图,靠出售咖啡豆起家,在这个进口远东咖啡的港口城市创造了一个  风靡全球的咖啡王国,如同灰姑娘收获了幸福的魔法,实现了人生的华丽转身。

阅读笔记

Part 8

不可不看的美国特色地标

自由女神像

自由女神漂洋过海来到纽约

The Statue of Liberty National Monument officially celebrated her 100th birthday on October 28, 1986. The people of France gave the Statue to the people of the United States over one hundred years ago in *recognition* of the friendship established during the American Revolution. Over the years, the Statue of Liberty's *symbolism* has grown to include freedom and *democracy* as well as this international friendship.

Lady Liberty, representative of freedom to the world, shines bright in New York Harbor. Created by Frenchman Frederic Auguste Bartholdi, the Statue was a gift from France to the United States. Visitors can now view the inside of the statue through a glass *ceiling* and *capture* a better image of Lady Liberty through the *enhanced lighting* and video system surrounding the statue. Ferries *depart* from Battery Park. With a *torch* and a book in her hands, Lady Liberty has generously welcomed immigrants and visitors for over a century.

1986年10月28日，自由女神像国家纪念碑正式迎来了她的100岁生日。法国人民在100多年前将该雕像赠予美国人民，来认可两国在美国革命中建立起来的友谊。多年来，自由女神像的象征意义已经发展到不仅象征着这种国际友谊，还象征着自由和民主。

自由女神，代表通往世界的自由，在纽约港口闪闪发光。由法国人弗雷德里克·奥古斯特·巴特勒迪创作，这座雕像是法国赠予美国的礼物。游客现在可以通过玻璃天花板看到雕像的内部，并通过雕像周围的光影强化系统感受到更美的自由女神形象。自由女神手持火炬和一本书，慷慨地迎接移民和游客已超过了一个世纪。

单词释义

recognition 认可	symbolism 象征	democracy 民主
ceiling 天花板	capture 捕获	enhanced 加强的
lighting 闪电	depart 离开	torch 火炬

法国集资造"女神"

Sculptor Frederic Auguste Bartholdi was *commissioned* to design a *sculpture* with the year 1876 in mind for completion, to *commemorate* the *centennial* of the American Declaration of Independence. The Statue was a joint effort between America and France and it was agreed upon that the American people were to build the *pedestal*, and the French people were responsible for the Statue and its *assembly* here in the United States. However, lack of funds was a problem on both sides of the Atlantic Ocean. In France, public fees, various forms of entertainment, and a *lottery* were among the methods used to raise funds. In the United States, benefit *theatrical* events, art *exhibitions*, *auctions* and prize fights assisted in providing needed funds.

Financing for the pedestal was completed in August 1885, and pedestal construction was finished in April of 1886. The Statue was completed in France in July, 1884 and arrived in New York Harbor in June of 1885 on board the French frigate "Isere" which transported the Statue of Liberty from France to the United States. In transit, the Statue was reduced to 350 individual pieces and packed in 214 crates. The Statue was re-assembled on her new pedestal

雕塑家弗雷德里克·奥古斯特·巴特勒迪奉命设计并在1876年完成一座雕像，用以庆祝美国独立宣言颁布100周年。这座雕像是通过美国和法国共同的努力建成的，双方一致同意由美国人来建造底座，法国人负责设计雕像，最后安置在美国的纽约。然而，这两个大西洋两岸的国家都遇到了资金不足的问题。在法国，公共收费、各种名目的娱乐和彩票等形式都用来筹集资金。在美国，公益性的戏剧活动、艺术展、拍卖会和职业拳击赛帮忙筹集资金。

底座的资金募集于1885年8月完成，其建筑于1886年4月竣工。雕像于1884年7月在法国完工，并于1885年6月由法国护卫舰"伊泽尔"号运送抵达纽约港口。在运输途中，这尊雕像被拆成350块，装在214口箱子里。雕

in four months time. On October 28th 1886, the *dedication* of the Statue of Liberty took place in front of thousands of spectators. She was a centennial gift ten years late.

像重新安置在底座上花费了4个月的时间。1886年10月28日，自由女神像的落成典礼在成千上万的观众面前进行。作为百年纪念，她晚了10年。

单词释义

commission 委任　　　　sculpture 雕塑　　　　commemorate 纪念

centennial 百年纪念　　pedestal 底座　　　　assembly 集合

lottery 彩票　　　　　theatrical 戏剧性的　　exhibition 展示

auction 拍卖　　　　　dedication 奉献

  美国特色文化

特色表达One

对众多美国人来说，矗立在自由岛的自由女神像就是他们心中最美的女人，能够让他们发自内心地赞美She is a peach of a girl.（她是个迷人的女孩子。）这句话中的peach不是大家熟知的"桃子"，而是形容像桃子一样惹人喜爱的人。另外，美国人还习惯将"Gorgeous!"挂在嘴边，看到大美女时就会这样感叹一句。

☆ 实景链接

A：Wow, the Statue of Liberty. I finally got to meet you. 哇，自由女神，我终于见到你了。

B：**She is such a peach of a girl.** 她真是个迷人的女孩子。

A：Come on. Take a picture for us! 快点，给我们照张相！

B：OK, you go there...right, right. Stand right over there. 好，你去那边……对，对。就站在那儿。

特色表达Two

看到自由女神像不要过多询问它是由什么构成的，这些问题是the nuts and bolts。nuts是指"螺母，螺帽"，bolts是指"螺钉"，这两个搭档是常见的五金，因此nuts and bolts就用来指代"一些事情的具体细节或者是最基本的组成部分"。

☆ **实景链接**

A：I don't know how to know more about the company. 我不知道如何更加了解公司。

B：Then I advise you to learn **the nuts and bolts.** 那我建议你学习基本的具体工作。

A：What's the specific function of it? 它具体有什么作用呢？

B：It will make you know the business as a whole. 这会让你对整体的业务更加了解。

拓展特色句

1. The Statue of Liberty was a gift from the French. 自由女神像是法国人赠送给美国的礼物。

2. I can't believe that you in New York City and never been to the Statue of Liberty. 我真不敢相信你住在纽约却从来没看过自由女神像。

3. Lady Liberty reaches the height of 305 feet. 自由女神高达305英尺。

"聊" 美国特色文化

A：Can you tell me something about the Statue of Liberty?

B：It was presented by France to United States in 1886 to honor the friendship between these two nations. Nowadays we consider it to be a symbol of liberty throughout the world.

A：It is said that more than 5 million people visit the statue every year. It's a big number.

B：It's really popular among people around the world. It is a concept of personal freedom.

A：Can you tell me about its size? How

A：你能告诉我一些关于自由女神的信息吗？

B：它是1886年法国人民赠送给美国人民的礼物，目的是为了纪念两国之间的友谊。今天，我们把它看成是全世界自由的象征。

A：据说每年有500多万的游客来参观自由像。这是一个很大的数字。

B：它确实很受全世界人的欢迎，它传达的是个人自由的理念。

A：你能告诉我它的尺寸吗？它有多高？

B：自由女神高达305英尺。

A：真是高大啊。它是用什么做的？是由石头做的吗？

tall is it?

B：Lady Liberty reaches the height of 305 feet.

A：What a huge size. What is it made of? Is it made of stone?

B：Actually, it's made of steel coated with copper and the pedestal is made of granite.

B：事实上，它是由钢镀上铜做成的，底座是大理石。

 美国特色文化

到底哪里的女神才是"正宗"的？

自由女神像表达着美国人民争取民主、向往自由的崇高理想，是美国的象征，也受到世界各地人们的深切喜爱，至于这个喜爱有多深呢？数数就知道了，比如说拉斯维加斯的自由女神像、关岛的自由女神像、巴黎的自由女神像、阿尔萨斯的自由女神像、东京的自由女神像、广州的自由女神像……喂喂，你们够了！

阅读笔记

金门大桥

排入世界七大奇迹的金门大桥

Once called "the bridge that couldn't be built," today it is one the seven wonders of the modern world. This *magnificent span*, perhaps San Francisco's most famous *landmark*, opened in 1937 after a four-year struggle against *relentless* winds, fog, rock and *treacherous* tides. The Golden Gate Bridge has now long lost its record of the longest bridge, but it is still one of the world's most famous structures.

More than 10 years in planning due to *formidable opposition*, but only four years in actual construction, the Golden Gate Bridge brought the communities of San Francisco and Marin Country closer together.

International Orange was selected as the color of the bridge because it provided *visibility* in the fog for passing ships and also because it was a color that fit in naturally to the bridge's setting and the surrounding land area.

金门大桥曾被誉为"无法建造的桥"，今天，它是现代世界的七大奇迹之一。这座宏伟的桥梁也许是旧金山最著名的地标性建筑，它历时4年与风、雾、岩石和危险潮汐做出不懈的斗争后，于1937年开通了。今天金门大桥的最长纪录早已被打破，但它仍是世界上最著名的建筑之一。

由于遭到强烈的反对，金门大桥的计划被搁置10年之久，但实际建造只花费了4年时间。金门大桥将旧金山和马林县连接起来。

大桥的颜色选用国际标准橘色，因为它便于在雾中行驶的过往船只识别，同时它也与大桥的环境及周围的海域天然搭配，相得益彰。

单词释义

magnificent 壮丽的　　span 跨度　　landmark 地标
relentless 无情的　　treacherous 叛逆的　　formidable 强大的
opposition 反对　　visibility 可见度

261

最美金门

Construction of the Golden Gate Bridge started in 1933. The bridge, which was designed by engineer Joseph Strauss was built to connect San Francisco with Marin County across the 1600 meter wide *strait* known as the Golden Gate which links the San Francisco Bay with the Pacific Ocean.

Soon after its completion the Golden Gate Bridge already enjoyed worldwide *fame*, not only because the bridge was breaking records, but also *thanks to* the *elegant* Art Deco design of the two huge towers and the *magnificent* surroundings near the Pacific Ocean. The eye catching orange-red color of the bridge also helped its popularity. The color was suggested by engineer Irving Morrow, who thought the traditional gray color was too boring.

The Golden Gate is at its most *enchanting* in the morning when the bridge is often *shrouded* in *mist*. But the bridge is also *alluring* at night when the lighting makes it seem as if the *spires* of the towers *dissolve* in the darkness.

金门大桥于1933年开始建造，由工程师约瑟夫·施特劳斯设计，将旧金山和马林县连接起来，它穿越了1600米宽的海峡，从而通过金门海峡把旧金山湾和太平洋联系了起来。

金门大桥在建成后不久就享誉世界，不仅因为这座桥是打破了纪录，而且更是因为它那两个巨塔装饰的优雅设计，以及太平洋周围的景象非常壮观。吸引眼球的橙红色也使得金门大桥备受欢迎。大桥的颜色受工程师艾尔文·莫罗建议得来，他认为传统的灰色太过无聊。

清晨是金色大桥最有魅力的时刻，通常这个时候金门大桥都笼罩在薄雾中。但是夜幕中的大桥也非常具有诱惑力，尤其是在闪电的时候，桥拱突出的部分仿佛要融化在黑夜之中一般。

单词释义

strait 海峡	fame 民声	elegant 高雅的
magnificent 高尚的	enchanting 迷人的	shroud 覆盖
mist 薄雾	alluring 迷惑的	spire 尖顶
dissolve 融化	thanks to 多亏……	

美国特色文化

特色表达One

金门大桥一直被美国人视为自杀胜地，因此与这个桥相关的表达就有Dutch act，这个词并不是用来指代荷兰人的行为，Dutch act其实表示"自杀"，据说这个短语的来源是因为荷兰人遇事易怒、易走极端，习惯找上帝解决问题，因此用他们的举止引申为"自杀"。

☆ 实景链接

A：Do you know that Golden Gate Bridge is also known as "the bridge of death"? 你知道金门大桥还被称作"死亡之桥"吗？

B：No. Why? 不知道，为什么呢？

A：It is said that since the bridge was built 50 years ago, people who did the **Dutch act** on it were altogether over a thousand. 据说自从大桥建成以来的50多年来，从金门大桥上跳海自我了结者已超过1000人。

B：Oh, it is shocking. 啊，太令人惊讶了。

特色表达Two

有人看到金门大桥，喜欢take a wild guess这里有多少人跳下去了。wild是"宽广，无边无际"，所以wild guess就是"瞎猜"的意思。所以，take a wild guess这个短语的意思是"瞎猜一下"。

☆ 实景链接

A：I found you and Tom are very intimate. Are you in love recently? 我发现你最近和汤姆关系挺亲近的。你们最近是谈恋爱了吗？

B：Don't **take a wild guess**. We are just common friends. 不要瞎猜。我们只是普通朋友。

A：Really? But your relationship really becomes closer. 是吗？但是你们的关系真的亲近了。

B：That's because we are divided into a research group. 那是因为我们被分入了一个课题组。

拓展特色句

1. Jenny posted a photo of the Golden Gate Bridge on QQ zone. 詹妮在QQ空间上传了一张金门大桥的照片。

2. Muir Woods is just across the Golden Gate Bridge. 红木国家公园就在金门大桥的对面。

3. The Golden Gate Bridge is one of the most popular suicide spots. 金门大桥是最著名的自杀场地之一。

 美国特色文化

A: Have you joined in the golden gate bridge's 50th birthday?

B: I was really lucky to be part of the history of this bridge.

A: It's reported to be San Francisco's biggest event ever. As many as 800 thousand people crowded on this bridge.

B: That's true. The golden gate bridge was famous when it was built. Nowadays, it's a beautiful landmark of San Francisco.

A: Can you tell me something about its 50th birthday?

B: It began with walking through the bridge at sunrise.

A: Wow, it's meaningful. Do you have any other activities?

B: Then it came with a full day of games, concerts and a parade of cars.

A: 你参加了金门大桥50周年的庆典活动吗？

B: 我很荣幸自己能成为这所桥的一部分。

A: 据说这是旧金山规模最大的活动，有80万人聚集在这所大桥上。

B: 是这样的。金门大桥早在修建之初就声名远扬了。如今它更是旧金山美丽的标志。

A: 你能讲一下它50岁生日那天的事情吗？

B: 庆典的开始是在日出时穿越大桥。

A: 哇，真是太有意义了。还有其他的活动吗？

B: 紧接着是一天的游戏、音乐会和汽车游行。

 美国特色文化

金门大桥竟然是"自杀胜地"？

众所周知，金门大桥是世界上最著名的自杀场所之一。据说，在桥上，人们潜藏的自杀倾向可能会被唤醒。有人说，在金门大桥，你不需要思考，只需跳一下就可以见到上帝，跟他探讨一番当今世界的局势。

阅读笔记

华尔街

华尔街名景点

Wall Street is one of the world's most famous streets. *Historically* known as the center of New York's *financial* district, Wall Street is often associated with wealth and ambition in America.

By the late 19th and early 20th centuries, Wall Street was "the place" to be if you were a large financial *institution* or other big business. So many buildings *sprung up* on this tip of Manhattan that the Wall Street district began to *boast* its own distinct *skyline*, separate from the buildings in Midtown.

People like J.P Morgan built headquarters like the one at 23 Wall Street, which was—for decades—the most important financial institution in the country. (One can still see the *pockmarks* on the building, left there from an unsolved bombing that occurred in 1920.)

Other *notable* buildings include the *columned* Federal Hall, originally built to house City Hall and its offices. The New York Stock Exchange (NYSE) Building is also quite *grand*, built by George B. Post in a neoclassical style.

华尔街是世界上最著名的街道之一。历史上被称为纽约金融区的中心，华尔街在美国通常与财富和雄心联系起来。

在19世纪末和20世纪初，如果你就职于一个大的金融机构或其他大型企业，华尔街对你而言是非常值得一去的"地方"。曼哈顿顶部突然涌现大量的建筑，以至于华尔街区顶端都形成了自己独特的天际线，与市中心区分裂开来。

像J.P.摩根这样的公司会在华尔街23号这样的地方建立总部，几十年来，华尔街是美国最重要的金融机构。（人们可以在建筑上看到留下的"疮痍"，这是1920年的一场还没解决的轰炸引起的。）

其他著名的大楼还包括圆柱状的联邦大厅，最初是跟市政大厅及其办公间建在一起。纽约证券交易所(NYSE)是由乔治·B·波斯特设计的新古典风格，也非常雄伟壮丽。

单词释义

historically 从历史的角度   financial 金融的   institution 机构

boast 自吹自擂   skyline 地平线   pockmark 凹坑

notable 著名的   column 纵队   grand 宏伟的

spring up 涌现

游一游华尔街

On this unique walking tour of New York City, you will explore the world-famous financial district of Wall Street. Become *privy* to the secrets of the New York City financial *giants*. An *enthralling* and *intellectually* stimulating way to tour one of the world's most famous streets!

You will *meander* through the narrow, winding streets of Lower Manhattan led by Wall Street experts, who will tell you *exclusive* stories from inside the *trenches* that will inform and shock you! Learn how some traders made billion dollar profits while banks *collapsed*, and find out more about the *volatile* culture and lifestyle of the Wall Street Trader.

Explore the *fascinating,* historical district of Wall Street that it is a living, breathing body that still affects the world today. You will discover rich history and visit famous financial *landmarks*, such as the New York Stock Exchange, Federal Reserve,

纽约城的徒步旅行想必也是独特的，你可以探索世界级别的金融区域——华尔街。开始知悉纽约市金融巨头的秘密。以一种紧扣人心和启发心智的方式来浏览这个世界上最著名的街道之一。

你可以和华尔街的金融专家并肩漫步于曼哈顿下城蜿蜒狭窄的街道，他们会专门给你讲一些华尔街内部的故事，让你感到震惊。学习一些贸易者是如何在银行破产倒闭的时候仍能获利亿万，发掘更多有关华尔街交易者反复无常的文化和动荡的生活方式。

探索华尔街这个迷人的、历史性的街道，你会发现它是一个有着生命力、会呼吸的地方，并且至今仍然影响着整个世界。你可以发掘更多的历史并且探访其金融地标，比如：纽约证券交易所、（美国）联邦储备系统

and Charging Bull.

Even born and bred New Yorkers will gain valuable insight through storytelling and personal *interaction* with former Wall Street professionals.

以及华尔街铜牛。

甚至对于那些土生土长的纽约人而言，通过听以前的华尔街专业人士讲故事和私人交流，他们也会获得宝贵的洞察力。

单词释义

privy 私人的	giant 巨头	enthralling 迷人的
intellectually 理智上	meander 漫步	exclusive 独有的
trench 战壕	collapse 倒塌	volatile 不稳定的
fascinating 迷人的	landmark 地标	insight 洞察力

"品" 美国特色文化

特色表达One

华尔街有很多的big cheese。Cheese是"奶酪"的意思，常和big连用表示"一个重量级人物"。早在19世纪的西方，cheese表示"一流水平或极好的事物"。在如今的俚语里用cheese来比喻"重量级的事物或人物"。

☆ 实景链接

A：What's your dream? 你的梦想是什么？

B：I want to be **big cheese** in the Wall Street. 我想成为华尔街的大人物。

A：Can I understand it in the way you want to be a financier? 我能理解为你是想成为一名金融家吗？

B：A financier of riches and distinctions. 一名有财富和声望的金融家。

特色表达Two

熟悉股市的人，应该知道"牛市""熊市"，但是这两个词用英文如何表达呢？bear(熊)表示"抛售股票的卖空人"；而bull(牛)则指"哄抬价格的买进者"。因为bear更加冷静，比莽撞的bull善于思考。所以熊市是bear market(空头市场)，牛市为bull market(行情看涨的市场)。

☆ **实景链接**

A: Would you tell me something about stock? 能告诉我一些关于股票的信息吗？

B: Sure, what do you want me to start with? 没问题，你想让我从什么开始说起？

A: Uhh, you can start with the explanation of some terms like "a **bull market**" and "a **bear market**". 嗯，你可以从解释"牛市"和"熊市"这样的术语开始。

B: OK. A bull market is a situation in which share prices are rising while a bear market is a situation in which share prices keep falling. 好的。牛市就是股票价格一直上升，而熊市就是股价一直下降的情形。

拓展特色句

1. He is a fat cat from the Wall Street. 他来自华尔街，是个有钱有势的人。

2. This is one of the consequences of the Wall Street crisis. 这是华尔街危机造成的后果之一。

3. My uncle worked on Wall Street during the Crash of 1987. 1987年的经济危机期间，我叔叔就在华尔街工作。

"聊" 美国特色文化

A: I really want to visit Wall Street. Can you take me there?

B: What are you heading there for?

A: I want to experience the financial atmosphere. Maybe I can get some first-hand information.

B: Is that all? I had thought you wanted to touch the Wall Street Bull.

A: It would be part on my itinerary. But I really can't figure out why it is so

A: 我真想去华尔街。你能带我去吗？

B: 你为什么想去那里呢？

A: 我想去感受一下金融氛围。也许我还能获得一些最新的信息呢。

B: 就这吗？我还以为你想摸华尔街铜牛呢？

A: 这也是我的行程之一。但是我真的不知道为什么它那么受游客的欢迎。

B: 这只是迷信。据说如果摸铜牛可以给你带来好运。

popular to visitors.

B: It's just superstition. It is said it can bring you good luck if you touch the bull.

A: Then I have to go there because of this reason.

B: Alas, I will take you there tomorrow morning.

A: 那因为这个原因我也得去。

B: 哎，我明天上午带你去。

 **美国特色文化**

华尔街铜牛为什么这么受欢迎?

在华尔街，有一座铜牛雕像是外来游客必须观赏的景点之一。时常可以看到无数的观光客满怀期待地触摸铜牛的牛角，因为他们认为这样可以祈求好运。那这座铜牛又是从何而来呢? 以前有个叫狄摩迪卡的家伙炒股失利后没有自暴自弃，而是振作起来关心全美年轻人，于是捣鼓了一件自称为艺术品的铜牛雕像，宣传着这头牛是"美国人力量与勇气"的象征。当时，他将铜牛竖立在纽约证券交易所外，后因不被允许而移到几条街之外的鲍林格林公园现址。

阅读笔记

帝国大厦

纽约景标——帝国大厦

The Empire State Building is one of the most *iconic* landmarks in a city full of them. The tallest building in New York City has appeared in over 90 movies, and is the *key* piece of the NYC Skyline. The Empire State Building is also the key piece of any New York City vacation, so visitors should look to book a hotel nearby.

Its name is *derived from* the *nickname* for New York, the Empire State. The Empire State Building is generally thought of as an American cultural icon. It is designed in the *distinctive* Art Deco style and has been named as one of the Seven Wonders of the Modern World by the American Society of Civil Engineers.

帝国大厦是一个充满摩天大楼的城市里最具标志性的建筑之一。这座最高的大厦在90多部电影中出现过。它是纽约天际线中重要的部分。在所有纽约度假胜地中，帝国大厦是非常重要的环节，游客会考虑就近预订酒店。

帝国大厦的名字是由纽约的别称——帝国而来。通常大家会把帝国大厦当作是美国的文化图标。它是以独特的艺术装饰风格设计而成的，曾被美国土木工程师协会誉为世界现代七大奇迹之一。

单词释义

iconic 图标的　　　　　　key 关键的　　　　　　　derive from 源自
nickname 别称　　　　　distinctive 有特色的

帝国大厦有多高

A *feat* of true American *accomplishment*, the Empire State Building in New York City stands 1454 feet tall and is currently the 9th

纽约帝国大厦是真正的美国壮举，它有1454英尺高，是目前世界上第九高的建筑，美洲第四高的自立式结构建筑。这一纽约地标有102层，是

tallest building in the world and the 4th tallest *freestanding* structure in the Americas. This NY monument has 102 stories, and was the first building to have more than 100 stories.

The Empire State Building construction was completed in 1931, in the middle of the Great Depression in New York City. At the time, the Empire State Building held the *mantle* as the tallest building in the world, beating out the other *skyscraper* being built at the same time in New York City: the Chrysler Building. The project involved 3,400 workers, made up of mostly European immigrants, and hundreds of Mohawk iron workers. The first use of the lights at the top of the Empire State Building was to *signal* to New Yorkers that President Franklin Roosevelt had won the 1932 Presidential election.

第一个超过100层的建筑。

帝国大厦于1931年竣工，卷入了纽约经济大萧条。当时，帝国大厦享有世界上最高建筑的美名，超过纽约同时期建造的另一座摩天大楼：克莱斯勒大厦。该项目动用了3400名工人，主要是欧洲移民，也有上千的莫霍克钢铁工人。纽约帝国大厦的顶灯第一次点亮，是向纽约人通报消息，美国总统富兰克林·罗斯福赢得了1932年总统大选。

单词释义

feat 壮举	accomplishment 成就	freestanding 独立式的
mantle 地幔	skyscraper 摩天楼	signal 发出信号

 美国特色文化

特色表达One

帝国大厦是美国的摩天大楼，可不是科幻中的龙潭虎穴，需要你jump out of the frying pan into the fire。这个短语的字面意思是"跳出了平底锅，又掉进了火坑"，最早出现在16世纪一名英国作家的作品，他写是放在平底锅用油煎的鱼跳出了煎锅却又掉进了炉火中，难逃厄运，引申为"才脱龙潭又入虎穴"。

☆ 实景链接

A: Congratulations. I heard the customers are satisfied with your idea. 祝贺你！我听说顾客非常满意你的方案。

B: Don't say it too early. This idea is very hard to realize. 别言之过早，这个方案非常难以实现。

A: Then you can be said to **jump out of the frying pan into the fire**. 那你就是才脱龙潭又入虎穴啊。

B: You are too right. I had spent so much time on the idea. 太对了，我已经在这个方案上花了好长的时间了。

💬 特色表达Two

每年都有好多对情侣在"世界之顶"的帝国大厦举行婚礼，这里可谓是美国人爱情的见证地。在婚礼上，美国人常会祝贺新人Finally, you're getting hitched. 可别理解为你终于被勾住了(hitched)，其实这句话说的是你终于结婚了，通常是熟人之间使用，能让双方感到温馨与祝福。

☆ 实景链接

A: Hey, Jenny, I am getting married. 嘿，詹妮，我要结婚了。

B: **Finally, you're getting hitched.** When and where will the ceremony be? 你终于要结婚了。婚礼什么时候，在哪儿举行啊？

A: It will be hold in the Empire State Building on 24 September. Be sure to come please. 定在9月24号，在帝国大厦举行。你一定要来啊。

B: Of course I'll be there. 我当然会去了。

拓展特色句

1. Don't drop a penny off the top of Empire State Building. Even a penny can kill a person from here. 不要从帝国大厦的顶层扔硬币。即便是一分钱也有可能砸死人。

2. The Empire State Building is really an architectural icon. 帝国大厦真是一个建筑设计杰作。

3. It ranks within the top 10 in the world for building height. 它是全球十大最高建筑之一。

美国特色文化

A: This is the famous Empire State Building.

B: It's so tall and huge.

A: Dare you go to the top?

B: Of course. It's said many films have got scenes from there.

A: The Empire State Building has been in more than 90 films, including North by Northwest, Annie Hall, and of course, King Kong.

B: What's the height of it?

A: It stands 1454 feet tall. This NY monument has 102 stories, and was the first building to have more than 100 stories.

B: That's marvelous.

A: 这就是著名的帝国大厦。

B: 它真是又高又大啊。

A: 你敢去顶楼吗？

B: 当然，据说很多电影都在那里取过景。

A: 帝国大厦这一文化地标和纽约地标性建筑已经在90多部影片中出现，包括《西北偏北》《安妮·霍尔》，当然还有《金刚》。

B: 它有多高？

A: 它有1454英尺高。这一纽约地标有102层，是第一个超过100层的建筑。

B: 太了不起了。

美国特色文化

帝国大厦也是当红"影帝"一枚?

与其称帝国大厦为"影帝"，还不如称其为"影地"，顾名思义，就是拍电影的取景地。帝国大厦参与的大制作数不胜数，比如《北京遇上西雅图》，电影里男主角弗兰克与女主角文佳佳离别相会的地方就在这里。而10年前的大热片《西雅图夜未眠》，男女主角在片末也是在帝国大厦楼顶相见的。更别提美国风靡偶像剧《绯闻女孩》中的男主角恰克，在戏中扮演帝国大厦继承者。

时代广场

纽约之心

Times Square is a major *commercial intersection* and a neighborhood in Midtown Manhattan, New York City, at the *junction* of Broadway (now converted into a *pedestrian* plaza) and Seventh Avenue and stretching from West 42nd to West 47th Streets. Times Square — iconified as "The Crossroads of the World", "The Center of the Universe", and the "The Great White Way" –- is the brightly *illuminated hub* of the Broadway Theater District, one of the world's busiest pedestrian intersections, and a major center of the world's entertainment industry. According to Travel Leisure magazine's October 2011 survey, Times Square is the world's most visited tourist attraction, hosting over 39 million visitors annually. Approximately a third of a million people pass through Times Square daily, many of whom are either tourists or people working in the area.

At the end of the 19th century, New York City had expanded up to 42nd street and the area was becoming the center of the city's social scene. In 1904, the New York Times built the Times Tower on 43rd street just off Broadway to replace its downtown *premises*. The square in front of the

时代广场是个大型商业交叉点，位于纽约曼哈顿中城附近，在百老汇（现在是步行广场）和第七大道交会处，从西42大街延伸至西47大街。时代广场——缩小化的"世界的十字路口""宇宙中心"和"不夜城"——是百老汇剧院区的闪亮中心和全球娱乐产业的主要中心。《旅游与休闲》杂志2011年10月的调查显示，时代广场是世界上最热门的旅游景点，每年接待超过3900万游客。大约超过30万人每天经过时代广场，这些人当中的许多不是游客就是在那儿工作的人。

到19世纪末，纽约市已经扩大到第42街，时代广场所在的地区已成为城市的社交场所。1904年，《纽约时报》在离百老汇不远的第43大街修建了时代大厦，后者于是变成了市中心的标志性建筑。时代大厦前的广场叫

building was called Long *acre* square, but was soon renamed Times Square. The name is now used for the area between 40th and 53rd street and 6th and 9th avenue.

Today Times Square is a constantly *buzzing* tourist *magnet*; the square is even one of the most visited places in the world.

做长亩广场，但是后来被重新命名为时代广场。时代广场现在指第40大街到第53大街和第6大街到第9大街之间的区域。

今天的时代广场一直是一个繁忙的和吸引游客的旅游胜地，是世界上旅游量最大的地方之一。

单词释义

commercial 商业的	intersection 交叉	junction 连接
pedestrian 行人	illuminated 被照明的	hub 中心
premises 经营场址	acre 地产	buzzing 嗡嗡声
magnet 磁铁		

玩在世界中心

The most famous building at the square is *undoubtedly* the iconic Paramount Building. The building was home to the Paramount theater where stars such as Fred Astaire, Bing Crosby and Frank Sinatra performed in their *heyday*. Unfortunately the theater was *demolished* and the Paramount building is now merely an office tower.

Another former theater, the Embassy Theater, is now the home of Times Square's own visitor's center. Here you can get information about events and Broadway shows. There's also a small museum that tells the history of Times Square.

时代广场上最著名的建筑非派拉蒙大厦莫属。派拉蒙大厦是派拉蒙剧院的所在地，弗雷德·阿斯泰尔、平·克劳斯贝和弗兰克·辛纳屈巅峰时期表演的地方。不幸的是，派拉蒙剧院后来被毁，派拉蒙大厦现在只是一座办公大楼。

另一个以前的大使剧院现在就是时代广场的游客中心。这里可以获取到活动及百老汇演出的信息。还有一个小型博物馆介绍纽约时代广场的历史。

许多人来到时代广场只为感受这种氛围和目睹广告牌的景象，但这里也有许多餐馆和商店——超过100家——包括吸引游客的迪士尼商店和大型玩具反斗城。但时代广场最出名

Many people come to Times Square for the *ambiance* and the *billboards spectacle*, but there are also many restaurants and shops—well over 100 - in the area including some crowd-pullers such as the Disney Store and a large Toys"R"Us. But Times Square is best known for its entertainment, and plenty of visitors come here to attend a Broadway show. Times Square is also home to MTV's headquarters and ABC's Good Morning America' is broadcast in front of a *live* audience from its office at 44th and Broadway.

的还是它的娱乐，大量的游客来到这里观看百老汇演出。时代广场也是MTV总部的所在地，ABC的"早安美国"就在第44大街及百老汇的办公室里现场播出。

单词释义

undoubtedly 毋庸置疑地　　heyday 全盛期　　demolish 拆除

ambiance 气氛　　billboard 广告牌　　spectacle 景象

live 现场的

 美国特色文化

 特色表达One

时代广场寸土寸金，即使如此，很多商家也宁愿在这里租一些elbow room的地方。最早源自一句话"Please give me some elbow room." 意思就是希望对方能让出一旦空间，让他的胳膊活动活动。所以后来引申为用elbow room来表示"更大的空间"。

⭐ **实景链接**

A：Have you decided to order yet? 你决定是否下订单了吗？

B：The price you offer is too high. **Please give me some elbow room.** 你们提供的价格太高了，希望你们能再给点空间。

A： Sorry, it's the best we can do. 对不起，这已经是我们的最低价了。

B： Then I am afraid we can't accept the price. 那我担心我无法接受你的价格了。

💬 特色表达Two

时代广场汇聚世界名牌，这里出售的商品也是昂贵奢华，你可能时不时听着有人嘀咕This dress costs me an arm and a leg. 这里的cost me an arm and a leg强调的是商品价格贵得惊人，得花大笔钱才能拿下，比普通的expensive更生动。当然，你可以用This bag was dirt cheap. 说明某件商品太便宜了。

☆实景链接

A： Jesus, you look like a million dollars in this dress. Where did you grab that? 天哪，你穿这件裙子实在太美了，你从哪里得来的?

B： I bought it from Times Square last week. And **it cost me an arm and a leg**. 我上周在时代广场买的，花了我好大一笔钱呢。

A： But it worth it, isn't it? You really look great in it. 但是值了，不是吗? 你穿着很漂亮。

B： Thanks. 谢谢夸奖。

拓展特色句

1. I have never been to New York and don't know what Times Square looks like. 我从来没有去过纽约，不知道时代广场是什么模样。

2. It is a block from here to the heart of Times Square. 这里距时代广场中心还有一个街区。

3. Times Square is in Midtown Manhattan. 时代广场在曼哈顿市中城。

💬 "聊"美国特色文化

A： Do you have any place in your mind?

B： Times Square. Can you tell me something about Times Square?

A： It's the very center of Manhattan Island. Times Square is often referred

A： 你想去哪里?

B： 时代广场。你能告诉我关于时代广场的事情吗?

A： 它是曼哈顿岛的中心。时代广场通常被称为娱乐区的中心。

to as the heart of the entertainment area.

B: What does it have?

A: In that area you will find hotels, clubs, over a thousand restaurants and at least a hundred and fifty theaters.

B: Does the big New Year's Eve celebration take place there?

A: Believe it or not, five hundred thousand people from all over the world will come there to celebrate the New Year's Day.

B: I go there to watch the New Year's Eve carnivals.

B: 那里有什么?

A: 在那儿你可以看到旅馆、俱乐部、数以千计的饭店和至少150座剧院。

B: 纽约大型的新年庆祝会是不是就在那儿举行?

A: 也许你不知道,有50万来自世界各地的人们聚集到这里来庆祝新年。

B: 我去那里也是去看新年嘉年华的。

 美国特色文化

这里为什么被称作世界的十字路口?

时代广场是美国纽约市曼哈顿的一块街区。在这里,你会发现来自世界各地的熙熙攘攘的游客,大家摩肩接踵在这小小的十字路口,而四周是缤纷炫目的大屏广告牌,变换的创意广告。周围店铺林立,流光溢彩,叫人眼花缭乱,又让人感叹世界的变幻莫测。来到这里,人们会禁不住来一句,"这就是纽约啊,真是世界的十字路口啊。"

阅读笔记

五角大楼

名为五角大楼

The Pentagon is the headquarters of the United States Department of Defense. It houses more than 23,000 employees, both military and civilian.

The design was straightforward but very efficient: a 5 acre (2ha) central courtyard is surrounded by five pentagonal rings. The five different wedges forming the pentagonal shape were created one by one and as soon as a wedge was finished, it would be occupied. The first occupants moved in the Pentagon in April 1942 and the building was completed in January 1943.

In a span of just 16 months, an immense building with a floor size of 6.6 million sq.ft. or 600,000 sqm was created. It was almost twice the size of the largest office building at the time, the Merchandise Mart in Chicago and has three times the office space of the Empire State Building in New York, then the tallest building in the world. The Pentagon has 17.5 miles / 28 km of corridors spread over 5 floors. Due to its efficient structure, it takes never more than 7 minutes to walk from one point to another in the building.

五角大楼是美国国防部总部，大楼里有23000多名文职和武职人员。

设计简单却非常有效：5英亩(2公顷)中央庭院的四周是五个五边形的圆环。五个不同的楔形个个相连构成了五角形状，楔形一旦安装完毕，则互相相连。1942年4月，第一批入住者搬入五角大楼，1943年1月五角大楼竣工。

前后历时16个月，一幢占地面积为660万平方英尺，即60万平方米的巨大建筑拔地而起。它几乎是此前芝加哥最大办公大楼"商品市场"的两倍大，其办公空间是当时世界上最高建筑物纽约帝国大厦的3倍。五角大楼的五层走廊面积加起来有17.5英里（28千米）长，但是由于其结构高效，你从这栋大楼的任意一个地方到另一个地方都不会超过7分钟。

单词释义

house 给……房子住　　civilian 平民　　　　　straightforward 直白的
efficient 高效的　　　courtyard 庭院　　　　pentagonal 五角形的
wedge 楔形物　　　　occupant 居住者　　　　corridor 走廊

惊梦9·11

By September 11, 2001, the *renovations* were in their final stages. That day, American Airlines Flight 77 crashed into the Pentagon's first floor west wall at 9:37 a.m. Traveling 529 miles per hour at the time of the *impact*, the *hijacked* Boeing 757 made a *gash* 30 yards wide and 10 yards deep, *puncturing* the three outer rings of the building. The resulting fire *raged* for 36 hours, and by the time it was *extinguished*, 189 people were dead.

A $501 million repair and renovation *initiative*, dubbed the Phoenix Project, began in early October 2001. Its leader, declared on October 5 that the goal was to have repairs completed by September 11, 2002. His team's *considerable* efforts were largely successful.

The Phoenix Project was officially completed in February 2003 at a total cost of some $5 billion. The renovations included sweeping security *upgrades*, including a move of the Defense Department's command centers to the basement. In March 2003, designs were revealed

2001年9月11日，翻新已到了最后阶段。当天上午9:37，美国航空公司第77航班撞向五角大楼第一层的西墙。在时速529英里的巨大冲击下，这驾被劫持的波音757将大楼撞出了30码宽、10码深的大裂缝，击穿了建筑的三个外环。之后的大火持续了36个小时，等到大火熄灭后，有189人丧生（包括5名恐怖分子）。

价值5.01亿美元的修复和改造项目，被称为"凤凰项目"，在2001年10月开始了。项目负责人在10月5日宣布，目标是2002年9月11日前完成修复工作。他的团队付出的巨大努力取得了极大的成功。

"凤凰项目"于2003年2月正式完工，其总成本约为50亿美元。翻新包括全面的安全升级，例如将国防部的

for a September 11 *memorial*, including 184 *illuminated* benches, one for each victim, set above a series of illuminated pools. Ground for the memorial project was broken in June 2006, and it was opened to the public on September 11, 2008.

指挥中心转移到地下室。2003年3月，9·11纪念馆的设计曝光，包括184个照亮的长椅，每位受害者一个，放置在连续的照明池上面。2006年7月，纪念馆的地下部分遭到了破坏，2008年9月11日再次向公众开放。

单词释义

renovation 革新	impact 影响	hijack 劫持
gash 划入	puncture 刺穿	rage 愤怒
extinguish 熄灭	initiative 主动	considerable 重要的
upgrade 升级	memorial 纪念碑	illuminate 说明

美国特色文化

特色表达One

五角大楼事件后，很多人都疑神疑鬼，是不是觉得to have a feeling in one's bones。千万不要以为to have a feeling in one's bones是"骨头酸痛"，其实这个短语的意思是"感觉要发生什么事情，但又难以解释"。

☆ 实景链接

A：Are you ok? You face turns pale. 你还好吗？你的脸都变白了？

B：**I have a feeling in my bone.** 我感觉有些事情要发生，但是又难以解释。

A：It must be your psychological effect. Don't think too much. 一定是心理作用。别想太多了。

B：But my instinct is pretty precise sometimes. 但是我的直觉有时候还挺灵的。

特色表达Two

当年美国人听闻五角大楼的惨案时，每个人都被shaken up。这里的shaken up不是指某人摇来移去，而是指某人在听到惊人的新闻或从未经历的事情时的震撼状态。如：She was completely shaken up.（她完全被震撼到了。）

☆ 实景链接

A: How did you feel when you hear that the pentagon was attacked? 你听说五角大楼被袭击的感受是什么？

B: **I was completely shaken up**. 我完全被震撼到了。

A: I felt the same with you. 我跟你感受一样。

B: That was just unbelievable. It is the headquarters of the United States Department of Defense. How come?! 太不可思议了。那可是美国的国防总部啊。怎么可能呢？！

拓展特色句

1. The Pentagon is one of the largest office buildings in the world. 五角大楼是世界上最大的办公建筑之一。

2. It's quite a scene of horror. 那真是恐怖的景象。

3. The final death toll is much higher than it was first reported. 最终死亡人数比之前报道的要多。

"聊" 美国特色文化

A: What's that Pentagon building?

B: Don't you know that? It's the famous The Pentagon.

A: What? Is that the building was attacked on September 11, 2001.

B: Actually it is.

A: Then what is it for?

B: It is the headquarters of the United States Department of Defense. It houses more than 23,000 employees, both military and civilian.

A: Can you show me around there?

B: Since the attacks on September 11, 2001 the tours have been restricted to US Residents.

A: What a pity!

A: 那个五角高楼是什么？

B: 你不知道吗？那就是有名的五角大楼。

A: 什么？它就是在"9·11"事件中被袭击的大楼吗？

B: 就是它了。

A: 它现在是做什么的？

B: 五角大楼是美国国防部总部，大楼里有23000多名文职和武职人员。

A: 你能带我参观一下那里吗？

B: 自从2001年"9·11"事件袭击后参观只限于美国公民。

A: 真是遗憾啊！

 美国特色文化

"9·11"事件恐怖到了何种地步？

　　"9·11"事件是美国最严重的恐怖袭击事件之一。美国东部时间2001年9月11日早晨8时40分，四架美国国内航班几乎被同时劫持，袭击了纽约曼哈顿的摩天大楼世界贸易中心和首都华盛顿五角大楼——美国国防部所在地。世贸大厦的两幢110层大楼在遭到攻击后相继倒塌，附近多座建筑也受震而坍塌，而五角大楼的部分结构被大火吞噬。很多人在这次事件中丧失了亲朋好友，可以说，它是美国人心中永远的伤痛。

阅读笔记

城市绿肺——中央花园

中央花园如何而来

When the *terrain* for Central Park was bought by the City of New York in 1853, it was *faraway* from *civilization*, somewhere between the City of New York and the village Harlem. The area contained *sheds* from *colonists*, quarries, pig farms and *swamps*.

In 1857, the city of New York organized a *competition* for the design of this new park, which had to *rival* with the great parks in London and Paris. A design by Frederic Law Olmsted and Calvert Vaux, named "the Greensward Plan" was chosen.

This plan featured an English style *landscape* with large meadows, several lakes and hills. Winding pedestrian roads were separated from main roads and the huge number of trees ensured the city's buildings were not visible from within the park.

纽约市在1853年买下了中央公园所在的区域，位置在纽约市和哈莱姆村之间，当时那里看不到任何现代文明的迹象。只有殖民者的棚屋、采石场、养猪场和沼泽。

1857年，纽约市组织了一场新公园设计大赛，目标是超过伦敦和巴黎的大型公园。弗雷德里克·劳·奥姆斯特德和卡尔弗特·沃克斯的"绿草坪"设计最终脱颖而出。

该设计以英式景观为特色，其中包括大草地、几处湖泊和山。蜿蜒的人行道从主干道分开，大量的树木遮挡了视线，使得在公园内看不清城市的建筑。

单词释义

terrain 地势　　　　faraway 遥远的　　　civilization 文明
shed 小屋　　　　　colonist 殖民者　　　swamp 沼泽
competition 竞争　　rival 对手　　　　　landscape 风景

聚景游园

There's plenty to see and do in Central Park. Sports facilities can be found all over the park but most of the interesting sights are found in the lower half of Central Park. You'll *come across* historical buildings, statues, *monuments*, beautiful bridges, and of course plenty of nature. Some of it is quite *rugged* like the forest-like Ramble while other parts of the park are more *manicured* and feature beautiful flowers and *shrubs*.

Many people enter the via the Scholars' Gate at Grand Army Plaza, near Fifth Avenue, which leads to a nice pond with a beautiful stone bridge. More to the north is one of the park's most popular attractions: Central Park Zoo. The zoo has *exhibits* divided into several regions such as a tropic zone and polar circle. Some of its popular residents include polar bears, snow *leopards*, red pandas and penguins. Just north of the Central Park Zoo is the Tisch Children's Zoo, where small children can see and touch domestic animals.

West of the Central Park Zoo is the Dairy, a Victorian style cottage created in 1870. The *picturesque* building houses a Visitor Center where you can get maps, guides, gifts, and information on events that

在中央公园可看和可做的事情很多。公园里随处可见体育设施，但大多数有趣的景点都位于中央公园的下半区。你可以看到历史性建筑、雕像、纪念碑、漂亮的大桥，当然还有大量的自然景观。其中有些崎岖不平，就像在森林漫步，而公园的其他地方则修剪整齐，有许多美丽的花朵和灌木。

许多人通过第五大道附近的大军广场的学者门进入中央公园，到达一个带有漂亮石桥的池塘。再向北是公园最受欢迎的景点之一：中央公园动物园。动物园划分成几个展区，例如热带区和极地圈。一些极受欢迎的动物包括北极熊、雪豹、小熊猫和企鹅。中央公园动物园的北部是蒂施儿童动物园，小孩可以观看和触摸家畜。

中央公园动物园的西部是乳品店，一栋建于1870年的维多利亚时代风格别墅。如画的建筑包含一个游客

are planned in Central Park. The Dairy is located at a former *pasture,* where cows *grazed* to provide fresh milk for the city's children, hence the name of the building.

The Mall, a wide *boulevard* lined with American *elm* trees, brings you from the Dairy to the Bethesda Terrace, one of Central Park's *architectural* highlights.

中心，可以得到地图、指南、礼品以及中央公园计划的活动信息。乳品店的所在地之前是一座牧场，那时牧场上的牛为城市的孩子提供新鲜牛奶，于是这栋建筑就叫乳品店。

购物中心的宽阔大道的两旁栽满了美国榆树，把你从乳品店带到毕士大平台，是中央公园的建筑亮点之一。

单词释义

monument 纪念碑	rugged 崎岖的	manicure 修剪
shrub 灌木	exhibit 展览	leopard 豹
picturesque 如画般的	pasture 草地	graze 放牧
boulevard 林荫大道	architectural 建筑上的	come across 偶遇

 美国特色文化

 特色表达One

不要以为在中央公园休闲就可以喝得烂醉了，千万不要drink like a fish，最后让人给拖出去。drink like a fish常指大口地喝着某东西，一般是指含酒精成分的饮料，就如我们常言的"牛饮"。所以这个短语的意思就是"狂喝滥饮"。

☆ **实景链接**

A：Tonight I have to accompany the customers for dinner. 今晚我需要陪客户出去吃饭。

B：Don't **drink like a fish**. I am a little worried about your health. 不要喝太多。我有点担心你的身体。

A：I have a sense of propriety. 我有分寸。

B：Every time you said those words, but you are drunk when coming back home. 你每次都这么说，但是你每次回家的时候都醉醺醺的。

特色表达Two

中央公园风景秀美，是个踏青休闲的好地方，但别过于疲劳而max out。max out可不是指搅和在一起，也不是一团糟的意思，这里是指"累惨了，累坏了"。另外，max out还可以用来表达钱花光了，你可以说I've maxed out my credit card.（我的信用卡刷爆了。）

☆ 实景链接

A: After a whole day walking in the Central Park yesterday **I'm totally maxed out.** 昨天在中央公园走了一天，累坏我了。

B: I remembered that you wore a pair of heels yesterday. 我记得你昨天穿的是双高跟鞋啊。

A: You are right. I did. 你说得对，我昨天确实穿了高跟鞋。

B: My god, I'd be dead if I walk that long with heels. 天啊，如果我穿高跟鞋走那么长时间，我一定累死了。

拓展特色句

1. Do you want to get some air at the Central Park? 你想去中央公园透透气吗？

2. I walked around the lake and enjoyed the beautiful scenery. 我沿湖走了一圈，欣赏了美丽的风景。

3. You can take a nap on the grass. 你可以在草地上小睡片刻。

"聊" 美国特色文化

A: Have you been to Central Park since you came to New York?

B: If you don't remind me, I may have forgotten about it.

A: It's Central Park that makes New York a great place to live. You must have regretted if you don't visit there.

B: Where is it located?

A: 你来纽约之后有去过中央公园吗？

B: 如果你不提醒我，我想我都会忘了那个地方。

A: 正是中央公园使纽约变成一个宜居的地方，如果你不去那里，你肯定会后悔的。

B: 它坐落在哪个地方呢？

A: 它坐落在曼哈顿的中心地带。离这

A：It is located in the center of Manhattan. Not far from here.

B：What can I do there?

A：It has several lakes, theaters, ice rinks, fountains, tennis courts, baseball fields, many playgrounds and other facilities. So you can exercise and relax there.

B：Wow, I can't help going there at once.

A：Central Park attracts millions of visitors each year.

里不远。

B：我去那里可以干什么呢？

A：那里拥有几处湖泊、剧院、冰场、喷泉、网球场、棒球场、许多游乐场及其他设施。你可以在那里锻炼和放松。

B：哇，我恨不得现在就去。

A：中央公园每年吸引着数百万游客前来参观。

美国特色文化

中央公园是美国房地产的传奇？

中央公园本来是一片近乎荒野的地方，到处是高低不平的土地、裸露的岩石、散布的低收入者的棚户，足以让任何一个房地产商望而却步。而当时的设计者奥姆斯特德及沃克斯二人却相信这片区域将来会成为让居民畅游自然风光的绝佳场所。他们的预料是有远见的，这里果然发展很快，1903年那年，纽约人口已达到400万，而很多摩天大楼已经拔地而起。

阅读笔记

第五大道

购物者的天堂在第五大道

New York's Fifth Avenue is best known as an unrivaled shopping street. Almost any upscale retailer has a prestigious store located at this street. However not all of Fifth Avenue is shopping-centric. Along Central Park Fifth Avenue becomes a more residential street with a large number of interesting museums.

Fifth Avenue starts just north of Washington Square and goes all the way north up to 143rd street in Harlem. It is one of the world's most expensive streets, especially the area between 49th and 59th street where some of the most prestigious stores can be found.

There are enough over-the-top shopping opportunities on Fifth Avenue to satisfy everyone's taste.

Women will love browsing and buying at stores like the famous Saks Fifth Avenue, Bergdorf-Goodman, Louis Vuitton, Prada, Emanuel Ungaro, Gucci, Ferragamo, and Versace. Men can check out Bergdorf Men, the NBA Store as well as the famous Apple Store.

Looking for something shiny or sparkly? Browse the displays at Harry Winston—jeweler to the stars,

纽约第五大道被称为无与伦比的购物街。几乎所有的高端零售商都会选择在这条街上开一家远近闻名的店铺。但第五大道并不全是购物中心，沿着中央公园的第五大道是住宅街，还有许多有趣的博物馆。

第五大道起于华盛顿广场以北，向北一直到达哈莱姆区第143大街。它是世界上最昂贵的街道之一，尤其是在第49和第59大街之间的区域，那里可以找到一些最负盛名的店铺。

第五大道上的购物机会非常多，可以满足不同人的需求。

女人们会喜爱在像著名的萨克斯第五大道精品百货店、波道夫·古德曼、路易威登、普拉达、伊曼纽尔·温加罗、古琦、菲拉格慕、范思哲这样的店铺闲逛和购物。男人们则可逛逛波道夫男装、NBA商店以及著名的苹果商店。

如果你想买一些璀璨耀眼的宝贝，可以逛逛"明星珠宝商"哈利·温

Bulgari, Cartier, Tiffany and Company, Van Cleef and Arpels, and Fortunoff.

斯顿、宝格丽、蒂芙尼、梵克雅宝、福图诺夫等著名珠宝店。

unrivaled 无与伦比的
residential 住宅的
sparkly 耀眼的

upscale 质优价高的
browse 浏览

prestigious 享有声望的
shiny 有光泽的

玩转博物馆

Fifth Avenue is not just a shopping street. Along Central Park, which **borders** Fifth Avenue, the street becomes more residential. Here you'll find palatial homes, grand churches and other historic buildings. You'll also come across numerous museums. In fact, there are so many of them that the area between 82nd and 104th Streets is known as the 'Museum Mile'.

During the 19th and early 20 century many wealthy industrials settled here along Fifth Avenue. They built *fabulous mansions* with views of Central Park. Many of these *magnificent* buildings are now home to museums.

There are many more museums for those interested such as the Cooper-Hewitt National Design Museum—housed in a mansion once owned by steel tycoon Andrew Carnegie, but the most famous of them all are the Metropolitan Museum of Art

第五大道不仅仅是购物街。第五大道沿着中央公园的区域更多是居民区。这里可以看到富丽堂皇的房子，宏伟的教堂以及其他的历史建筑，也会碰到众多的博物馆。事实上，在第82和第104大街之间有如此之多的博物馆，以至于这个地方被叫作"博物馆大道"。

到了19世纪末20世纪初，许多繁华的工业公司都坐落在第五大道边上。建造的大厦可以看到中央公园的风景。这些宏伟的建筑现在是博物馆的所在地。

对感兴趣的人来说，第五大道上还有更多的博物馆，例如库柏·海威特国家设计博物馆位于一栋曾经是钢铁

and the Guggenheim Museum.

The Metropolitan Museum, also known as 'the Met', is one of the world's largest museums. And the Guggenheim Museum is just as famous for the 20th century building in which it is housed as for the modern art that can be *admired* inside.

大亨安德鲁·卡内基财产的大厦里，但其中最著名的是大都会艺术博物馆和古根海姆博物馆。

大都会博物馆，也称为"大都会"，是世界上最大的博物馆之一。古根海姆博物馆也同样出名，因为这栋20世纪的建筑里藏有值得欣赏的现代艺术。

单词释义

border 与……接壤 　　　fabulous 难以置信的 　　　mansion 大厦

magnificent 雄伟的 　　　admire 称赞

 美国特色文化

特色表达One

在第五大道闲逛随时可邂逅baby dolls。可不是说常能见到婴儿玩偶，baby doll在俚语里常指"傻里傻气的女孩子"，或是"妙龄少女"等。如今用的最广的意思是"漂亮的女人"。

☆实景链接

A：Why do you always go to the fifth avenue? 你为什么总是跑去第五大道呢？

B：Just go for walk. 就是去散散步。

A：Don't say to me vaguely. I don't believe it's the true reason. 不要敷衍我。我不相信这是真实的原因。

B：Well, I just hunt for **baby dolls** there. 好吧，我只是去那里寻觅美女。

特色表达Two

行走在第五大道，入眼即是高档大气的名牌时装店或豪华的珠宝首饰店，但是这可不是一场high-street fashion show，high-street虽然是"商业街"的意思，但是high-street fashion并不指商业街的高档时装，而是平价时装。

☆ **实景链接**

A：The clothes here are so expensive for me. I don't think I will get what I want. 这里的衣服对我来说太贵了。我觉得我是买不到我想要的东西了。

B：Though it is Fifth Avenue, not all the clothes are high-class here. 尽管这里是第五大道，也不是所有的都是高档服装。

A：What do you mean by that? 你这么说是什么意思？

B：Just follow me; I'll show you some **high-street fashion**. 你就跟我走吧，我带你去看一些平价的衣服。

拓展特色句

1. We can park our car in the parking lot under the store. 我们可以把车停在商店的地下停车场。

2. Fifth Avenue is a tourism destination and shopping paradise. 第五大道是个旅游胜地也是购物天堂。

3. The Apple store on New York's Fifth Avenue is so big. 第五大道的苹果商店真大。

"聊" 美国特色文化

A：I am in search of a dress for a party. Let's go shopping.

B：No problem, I think Fifth Avenue is the best place to go.

B：(After arriving Fifth Avenue) I feel like watching a fashion show.

A：Yes, apart from these high-end designer brands, you can find some inexpensive brands like H&M.

B：First thing first, What do you think about this strapless dress?

A：Are you kidding? This dress costs me an arm and a leg.

A：我想买一件参加派对的裙子，我们去购物吧。

B：没问题，我觉得第五大道就是最佳去处。

B：（到达第五大道之后）我感觉自己像在看一场时装秀。

A：是啊，除了这些昂贵的名牌店，你还会发现平价的服装店，像H&M。

B：先办正事！这件无肩带的裙子怎么样？

A：你是在开玩笑嘛！这件裙子超级贵啊！

B：天啦，这里有NBA专卖店，我可以

B：My god. It's the NBA exclusive store. Can I go in and out, just a quickie?

进去看看就出来吗？马上！

A：No way, we can't afford anyone in it.

A：不行，里面的东西根本就买不起。

美国特色文化

第五大道是所有购物者心中的"圣地"吗？

在第五大道，随时都能感到上流社会奢靡华贵的气息，但不是所有美国人都喜爱来这购物的，除非你非富即贵，否则日常购物肯定吃不消。在纽约，也有一些廉价的商店颇受当地人民欢迎。比如说，纽约著名的跳蚤市场有Village(西村、东村、格林威治村)和Soho(苏活区)，那里是淘宝族的心之所系；而常见的二手服饰店(Vintage Shop)是流行男女喜欢光顾的地方。

阅读笔记

白宫

何为白宫

The White House has been the official residence of every President of the United States with the *exception* of George Washington.

The White House is located on a site near the Mall chosen in 1790 by president George Washington and Pierre l'Enfant, the *architect* who created the master plan for the new capital. Meanwhile the president resided in the President's House in the temporary *capital* Philadelphia.

Thomas Jefferson was the first president to allow public tours of the White House in 1805. Since September 11, 2001 they have been *suspended* but US residents can arrange group tours of ten or more people through their member of Congress.

The garden around the White House was first planted by John Adams. It was later redesigned by many presidents and first ladies. The most famous part of the garden was added in 1913 by Ellen Wilson, wife of president Woodrow Wilson. She created a Rose Garden, which would later be redesigned and used as a *venue* for official ceremonies by president Kennedy. It is located just outside the Oval Office.

白宫一直是美国总统的官邸，除了乔治·华盛顿。

白宫坐落于林荫大道旁边的地方，在1790年由乔治·华盛顿总统和皮埃尔·朗方选址，建筑师皮埃尔·朗方设计了新首都的总体规划。当时，总统居住在临时首都费城的总统官邸里。

1805年，托马斯·杰弗逊总统成了第一位允许公众参观白宫的总统。自从2001年9月11日后，公众参观已停止，但美国总统可以安排国会议员中的10个人或者更多的人来参观白宫。

白宫周围的花园最初是由约翰·亚当斯建造的。后来又被许多总统和第一夫人重新设计。花园最著名的部分是由伍德罗·威尔逊总统的妻子艾伦·威尔逊在1913年添加的玫瑰花园。玫瑰花园后来经过重新设计，成为了肯尼迪总统举行正式仪式的地方。它就坐落在椭圆形办公室的外边。

单词释义

exception 例外　　　　architect 建筑师　　　　capital 首都

suspend 延缓　　　　venue 地点

白宫开始并非为白色

Most people seem to think the building was first painted white after it was rebuilt in 1817, but already in 1798 it was made white by a *protective* lime-based whitewash. It wasn't named White House from the beginning though: it was originally named the 'President's Palace', 'President's House' or 'Executive Mansion'. It was soon nicknamed 'White House' and in 1901 president Theodore Roosevelt made it the official name.

The White House has been *extended* and *modified* many times. The most important *extensions* were the addition of the East Wing and the West Wing. The latter contains the famous 'Oval Office', the president's main office. The room was modeled on the 'Blue Room', an *oval* room at the center of the White House. The building contains a total of 132 rooms, some of them can be visited on a tour, including the Green Room, Blue Room, Red Room and State Dining Room.

大多数人会认为白宫在1817年重建后就粉刷成了白色，但是其实在1798年的时候它就已经涂上了保护性的石灰涂料。但是它不是一开始就叫白宫，最初叫作"总统府""总统住宅"或"总统官邸"，后来昵称为"白宫"，1901年西奥多·罗斯福总统将"白宫"定为官方名字。

白宫经过了多次的扩大和装修。最重要的扩展部分是东翼和西翼，后者包括著名的"总统椭圆形办公室"，是总统主要用来办公的地方。这个房间是在会客房"蓝厅"的基础上来进行模仿修建的，是白宫中央一个椭圆形的房间。这栋楼一共有132间房，有的可以在观光的时候进行参观，包括绿厅、蓝厅、红厅和国宴厅在内。

单词释义

protective 保护性的　　　　extend 拓展　　　　modify 修改

extension 延长　　　　oval 椭圆形

美国特色文化

特色表达One

什么人能在白宫工作呢？勤奋的人？聪明的人？当然最好能是all things to all men。这个短语的意思是"八面玲珑"，最早出现在《圣经·哥林多前书》第九章第二十三节，书中写道"和什么样的人打交道，就做什么样的人。"这个词组引申为"八面玲珑"。

☆ 实景链接

A：Why is your boss so successful? 你们老板怎么这么成功？

B：I think it is owing to his character. 我觉得这得益于他的性格。

A：Can you describe his character? 你能够描述一下他的性格吗？

B：He is **all things to all men**. 他是一个八面玲珑的人。

特色表达Two

去白宫参观时可千万别一时兴起留个"到此一游"，这个时候可能会遭人鄙视地说一句：That's a crying shame. It really is! 这是别人在告诫你真是太糟了。这里的a crying shame意思是极其令人羞耻的事情，叫人难以袖手旁观的太过分的事情，如It's a crying shame to waste all that food.（浪费那么多食物，真是太不像话了。）

☆ 实景链接

A：Wow, it was so splendid a building. 哇，建得真是太壮观了。

B：Of course. It is the place where the American Presidents live in. 当然了，这可是美国总统住的地方。

A：Hey, you see, there are some letters. "Brooks was here"… 嘿，你看，这边有几个字母。"布鲁克斯到此一游"……

B：Come on. **That's a crying shame** to scribble on the wall. It really is! 拜托，在这墙上涂鸦真是太丢脸了。太不像话了！

拓展特色句

1. President Obama welcomes President Hu to the White House. 美国总统奥巴马欢迎胡锦涛主席访问白宫。

2. Take a picture for me in front of the White House. 帮我在白宫前拍张照。

3. Most tourists would pay a visit to the White House when come to America. 大部分游客去美国游览的时候都会造访白宫。

 美国特色文化

A: John, how will you spend your summer vacation?

B: I plan to go to Washington and take a tour of the White House.

A: Wow! That sounds great!

B: Yes, it's the most famous historical building there.

A: Well, I heard that the Capitol building is very famous there.

B: Of course. I am itching to go there. So how about you? You wanna go there with me?

A: I'd love to, but I have to take care of my little brother.

B: What a pity! So are you planning to spend the summer sweating it out here?

A: I'm afraid so.

A: 约翰，你要怎么度过你的暑假呢？

B: 我打算去华盛顿参观一下白宫。

A: 哇！听起来真不错！

B: 是呀。白宫是那里最有名的历史建筑。

A: 嗯，我听说美国国会大厦也是非常有名的。

B: 当然了。我迫不及待要去那儿了。那你呢？你要和我一起去那吗？

A: 我很想去，但是我不得不照顾我的弟弟。

B: 真遗憾啊！那你的暑假就准备在这里苦熬喽？

A: 恐怕是的。

 美国特色文化

白宫的闹鬼传闻

　　大家很难猜到白宫是特别爱闹鬼的地方，名列全球十大闹鬼地之一。有传言，某些居住过白宫的人临死前不愿意放弃手中的权力，死后的鬼魂经常还要到这里逛一逛。约翰·亚当斯(John Adams)的妻子阿比盖尔·亚当斯(Abigail Adams)的鬼魂曾在东屋哗啦哗啦地洗衣服；多莉·麦迪逊(Dolley Madison)的鬼魂喜欢在玫瑰园里游荡；而林肯的卧室则可能是"诚实的亚伯"经常造访的地方。

阅读笔记

好莱坞：享誉世界的电影梦工厂

好莱坞：我为成功代言

Hollywood is a highly *diverse*, densely populated, mostly immigrant, low-income *residential neighborhood* in Central Los Angeles, California, as well as a *commercial* area and a name used to represent the motion picture industry of the United States. Since 1920, the Hollywood has been *dominating in* the world film industry and Hollywood films *are valued as* the most influential and attractive ones indicating high *box office* prices.

Whenever we mention Hollywood films, what comes to our mind first are usually words like super stars, blockbuster and special effects, which are just *prominent* features of Hollywood. Meanwhile, with shining stars and *elite* directors, the film producer never needs to worry about investments and there are many companies waiting in line to offer *sponsorships*. Apart from the above factors, another one *leading to* the prosperity of Hollywood films is the wide-spreading publicity, which is also on the premise of surplus money.

好莱坞位于加利福尼亚州洛杉矶市中心地带，这里具有高度多样化、人口稠密的特点，聚集着大量移民和低收入居民，这里还是商业中心，也是美国电影产业的代名词。自1920年，好莱坞一直在世界电影行业崭露头角，占据领先位置，好莱坞电影也被视为最具影响力和吸引力的影片，是高票房的保障。

一提到好莱坞，首先映入我们脑海的通常是超级巨星、大片和特效等词语。然而，即使拍片需要大牌明星和名导，电影制片人也从来无需担心资金问题，而且很多公司会排队等候提供赞助。除了上述的这些原因之外，另一个让好莱坞电影大获成功的因素是其铺天盖地的宣传，当然，这种宣传也是以富裕的资金为前提的。

diverse 不同的　　residential neighborhood 住宅区　prominent显著的
elite 精华；主力　sponsorship 赞助　　　　　commercial商业的
box office 票房　　dominate in 在……中占主导地位 be valued as 被……认为有价值
lead to 导致；形成

好莱坞电影很有"文化"

The public easily misunderstand Hollywood movies quite *commercial* and simply for *entertainment*. However, there is something about American culture *in common* in these films, which also attracts a large number of people seeing them out of appreciation of the culture values.

Independence and liberty has been the central American culture since the birth of US. Based on this, Hollywood created many classical films which talk about the *advocating* of values like free love, free marriage. Another culture element widely used in Hollywood films is people's *belief* that no one was born ordinary and anyone can become *extraordinary* with efforts.

However, the culture of Hollywood has dramatically changed over the years. For example, society's taste in movies has *radically* been *transformed*. In the old days, people preferred *classy* and high value movies, where as today, the common person prefers a movie with violence,

大众会很容易误解好莱坞电影只是追求娱乐的商业化作品。这些电影都蕴含着相同的美国文化，并因此吸引了大量欣赏美国文化的观众。

独立和自由是美国在成立之初就具备的核心文化。基于这种文化，好莱坞创作了很多提倡自由恋爱、自由婚姻的经典电影。另一个在好莱坞电影中经常出现的文化元素是每个人生来都绝不平凡，并且可以通过后天努力变得卓尔不凡的信仰。

然而，好莱坞文化在数年内已经发生了天翻地覆的变化。举例来说，整个社会对电影的品位已经发生了本质性的改变。以前，人们喜欢经典的、颂扬高尚品德的电影；然而现在，大众更喜欢充斥着暴力、裸露画面或其他具备这些性质的电影。好莱

nudity, or other things of that nature. Movies like Brokeback Mountain are rarely produced in the Hollywood "mainstream," and Hollywood will go on making socially relevant movies as long as they sell.

坞几乎不会制作《断背山》这类的电影，这不是他们的"主流"题材，相反，只要票房能够得到保障，好莱坞还是会一如既往地制作那些与社会密切相关的电影。

单词释义

commercial 商业的

advocate 倡导

radically 根本地

entertainment 娱乐

belief 信念

transform 变形

independence 独立

extraordinary 卓越的

classy 上等的

 美国特色文化

特色表达One

美国人在看电影《变脸》的时候，会说The movie is very woo. woo来源于吴宇森的姓氏woo，他最大的特点是解剖暴力，双手枪就是典型的吴氏标志。woo的意思是这个电影很英雄气概，后来吴宇森所拍的电影的特点命名为woo。类似地，如果说The movie is very Hitchcock.（就是意味着这个电影的悬疑做得很好。）

☆ 实景链接

A: I heard face off is directed by a Chinese. 我听说《变脸》是由一位中国导演拍的。

B: Yeah. John woo is a director of Hollywood action blockbusters. 是的，吴宇森拍摄了好莱坞的很多动作大片。

A: His shooting style is very unique. 他的拍摄风格非常独特。

B: Yeah, we call his movie very **woo.** 是啊，他拍的电影都很显英雄气概。

特色表达Two

如果我们观看的一部电影的预告片与真实的电影大相径庭，让我们觉得有种挂羊头卖狗肉的感觉，那么我们就是trailer fraud的受害者，trailer fraud就是指那些欺骗观众去看电影但是却与真实影片相差甚远的预告片。

☆ **实景链接**

A: Have you seen the blockbuster the Hollywood recently released? 你看了好莱坞最新出的大片没？

B: Not yet. I planned to go see it tonight. The trailer looked good! 还没有，我打算今晚去看看。预告片还不错！

A: **Trailer fraud!** The film sucked. 预告片都是骗人的。

B: My heart sinks. 太扫兴了。

拓展特色句

1. It's really a box office hit. 这部电影的票房很成功。

2. This star's taken his rise to stardom in stride. 这位明星星途顺畅。

3. This movie must be a huge box-office. 这个电影票房肯定很高。

"聊" 美国特色文化

A: Cindy, who is your favorite movie star?

B: Tom Hanks, who has played in **Forrest Gump**.

A: When mentioning this film, it comes to my mind that it embodies the American dream.

B: I couldn't agree more. It is a very typical Hollywood movie. Apart from this, Hanks has very good acting.

A: Its extraordinary story line and good cast are the main reasons that it gets huge box-office.

B: I can't figure out why Hollywood always can succeed.

A: Firstly, these films tell something about American culture. Secondly, the production team use the most

A: 辛迪，你最喜欢的影视明星是谁？

B: 汤姆·汉克斯，他曾经演过《阿甘正传》。

A: 一提到这部电影，我就想到这部戏里所体现的美国梦。

B: 我很同意。这是一部很具有好莱坞典型特色的电影，此外，汉克斯的演技也非常精湛。

A: 这部戏中精彩的故事框架以及强大的演员整容是这部戏获得大票房的主要原因。

B: 我不明白为什么好莱坞电影能如此成功。

A: 首先，这些电影都灌输了美国文化；第二，制作团队采用了先进的设备以及特效技能。最后，他们很擅长做宣传。

advanced equipments and the special effects. Lastly they are good at publicizing.

B: You can't know Holly wood worse.

A: I am flattered. I am just interested in Hollywood movies.

B: 你太了解好莱坞了。

 美国特色文化

多次在好莱坞大片中打酱油的好莱坞标牌到底为何方神圣?

曾出现在《怪物史莱克》《后天》《超人》《憨豆先生》等众多大片镜头里的好莱坞标牌已经成为洛杉矶乃至美国的世界性地标。那么这座标牌到底是何方神物呢? 最初, 这块标牌是房地产商于1923年为宣传其新项目而设的广告标牌, 当时标牌上饰有4000多个灯泡, 显

示着HOLLY WOODLAND字样, 每个字母高15米、宽9.1米, 这在90年前是相当壮观的。在后来翻修标牌时, 好莱坞商会决定去掉LAND, 只保留HOLLYWOOD。如今, 好莱坞标牌如同巴黎的埃菲尔铁塔、埃及的金字塔一样享誉全球。

阅读笔记

Part 9

音乐和体育

乡村音乐唱出美国文化

乡村音乐

Traditional music although first *marketed* in the early 1920s, did not rise to national *prominence* until the late '20s and early '30s when WLS's National Barn Dance and WSM's Grand Ole Opry were *broadcast* to a national audience and the barn-dance program became a recognized *format*. Initially *hillbilly* or old-time music was marketed to and consumed by *rural* and newly urban whites in the South and Midwest, but by the end of the '30s Country and Western music had attained a national, rather than a localized, identity.

On the flip side, growing immigrant populations were producing a more heterogeneous populace. This had two potential, if unclear, effects on the emerging genre of "country" music. In many areas, a nativist *backlash* grew in response to the new "un-America" groups. While this had *subsided* by the 1930s to some degree because of *immigration restrictions* imposed in the mid-'20s, country music's image as an *authentic* American (white) tradition may have contributed to its appeal. *Alternately*, as immigrants

传统音乐在20世纪20年代初被首次推向市场，到了20年代末和30年代初，全美国听众通过广播收听到了WLS的"民族谷仓舞"和WSM的"乡村大剧院"，于是谷仓舞节目成为了公众接受的风格，这时传统音乐才享誉全美。最初收听乡村音乐或古时音乐的是农村以及南部和中西部新型城市的白人，但是到了30年代末，乡村音乐和西部音乐已获得全美范围而不仅仅是区域性的认同。

另一方面，日益增长的移民人口使得大众趋向于多样化。这对新兴风格的"乡村"音乐产生了两方面潜在的影响，即使这种影响可能并不明显。在许多地方，对"非美国"群体的排外情绪快速增长。20世纪20年代中期对移民的限制在某种程度上使这种排外性在30年代有所平息，作为真正体现美国(白)人传统形象的乡村音乐更是增添了吸引力。或者说，随着移

sought ways to assimilate, "country" music may have provided a commodity that could allow one to buy into an American identity.

民者融入美国社会，"乡村"音乐可能就成了一件允许他们购买到"美国身份"的商品。

乡村音乐唱的是什么

Most American folk songs have *catchy melodies* that stick in a person's head. The subject matter of a lasting folk song is one that people can relate to down through the years. No matter what time period a person in, an American folk song can relate to their life in some way.

American folk songs pass down the culture and beliefs of the American people. *Amazing Grace* is an example of such a folk song. Actually, *Amazing Grace* is an English *hymn* was written by English poets and *composers* about slaver. It was so popular that Americans consider it to be an American folk hymn. The *tune* is simple enough for many people to sing. And many people can relate to the need of *forgiveness* and vast love of God that is expressed through the *lyrics* of this song. And because of America's history of *slavery* and

大部分美国民谣都有着朗朗上口的旋律，扣人心弦。一首岁月悠久的民谣的主题都是能够随着时光流逝，让人能够联想翩翩的。无论一个人在什么时候，一首美国民谣都能够或多或少让他联系其自己的生活。

美国民谣将美国人民的文化和信念传承下去。《奇异恩典》就是这样的一首民谣。实际上，《奇异恩典》是一首由英国诗人和作曲家撰写的英文圣歌，内容关于奴隶。这首歌传唱度很高，以至于美国人把它当作是美国民谣。这首歌曲的曲调足够简单，很多人都会唱。这首歌曲中的字里行间表达出了原谅的必要性以及上帝宽广的爱，许多人都可以联想到这一点。由于美国有一段关于

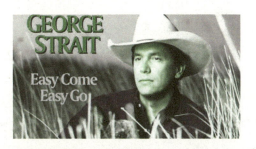

eventual fight over freeing slaves, ***Amazing Grace*** became a popular American folk hymn.

奴隶的历史，并且通过斗争，解放了奴隶，《奇异恩典》也就变成了一首流行的美国民谣。

单词释义

catchy 引人注意的　　　melody 旋律　　　hymn 圣歌

composer 作曲家　　　　tune 曲调　　　　forgiveness 原谅

lyric 歌词　　　　　　　slavery 奴隶制度　eventual 最终

 美国特色文化

特色表达One

在美国，乡村音乐常用吉他弹奏，那么"弹吉他"可以用pull some strings表示吗？其实pull some strings最早出自木偶艺术。当时的手工匠人将strings系在木偶上，操纵木偶摆动各种好笑的动作逗观众开心。后来pull some strings引申作运用关系或搞到关系，而弹吉他则直接用play guitar表示。

☆实景链接

A: **What do you know about that black singer?** 你对那名黑人歌手了解多少？

B: **He was a country music singer. That music style was not that popular at that time. So his first demo was refused for many times.** 他是一名乡村音乐歌手。那种音乐风格在那个时候并不很流行，所以他的第一张样本唱片被拒绝了很多次。

A: **What happened then?** 那后来呢？

B: **He had to pull some strings and finally got the chance to release his record.** 他不得已走了后门，终于得到了发布唱片的机会。

特色表达Two

在美国，不是每个玩乡村音乐的人都能玩出一番成就的，其中很多人都是打着玩音乐幌子的deadhead。你别被deadhead的字面意思吓到，它其实指的是"懒汉"。deadhead最早是蹭戏的人，因为早期戏院会让帮忙张贴海报的人免费看戏，所以有蹭戏一说。后来这个词开始指免费入场看戏的人，也出现了引申意义，表示没法为社会做贡献的懒汉。

☆ 实景链接

A：You know a lot about country music. Would you recommend me some great songs? 你非常了解乡村音乐。你能给我推荐几首乡村歌曲吗？

B：You can listen to Tim McGraw and Kenny Chesney's songs. I like them. 你可以听听蒂姆·麦格罗和肯尼·切斯尼的歌。我喜欢他们。

A：What about John's songs? 约翰的歌怎么样？

B：He was a totally **deadhead**. Don't listen to his junk music. 他完全是个懒汉，别听他的垃圾音乐。

拓展特色句

1. I am a big fun of country music. 我很喜欢乡村音乐。

2. This song brings back the good old days to me. 这首歌让我想起以前那些美好的日子。

3. Taylor Swift is a famous American country music singer. 泰勒·斯威夫特是一名美国著名的乡村音乐歌手。

"聊" 美国特色文化

A：Matt, what's your favorite kind of music?

B：My favorite kind of music is folk music, which can relate to my life in some way.

A：As you mention the folk music, I really can't figure out why only whites can sing it.

B：Initially folk music was marketed to and consumed by rural and newly urban whites in the South and Midwest. Those music reflected American culture.

A：When did folk music firstly appear in

A：马特，你最喜欢的音乐类型是哪种？

B：我最喜欢的音乐类型是乡村音乐，它可以让我在某种程度上联想起自己的生活。

A：你一提到乡村音乐，我就真的无法理解为什么只有白人可以唱。

B：最开始收听乡村音乐的是农村以及南部和中西部新型城市的白人。这些歌曲反映了美国文化。

A：乡村音乐是什么时候首次出现在市面上的？

B：很难估计出具体的日期，大概在20世纪20年代初。直到20世纪30年代

the market?

B: It's hard to calculate the specific date, but in the early 1920s. It didn't become popular until early 1930s.

A: Uhh, who is your favorite singer then?

B: Taylor Swift. She is so sweet and beautiful in appearance and her voice is lovely. I love her very much.

才逐渐变得流行。

A: 嗯，谁是你最喜欢的歌手？

B: 泰勒·斯威夫特。她在外形上很甜美，声音宛如天籁。我真的爱死她了。

 美国特色文化

乡村音乐是如何诞生的?

1920年，美国乡村音乐起源于美国南部与阿帕拉契山区，其融合了各种音乐，比如传统民谣音乐、凯尔特音乐及古时音乐。当时，阿马拉契亚山区少与外界有联系，没有受到美国城市化和工业化浪潮冲击，因此在文化上依旧相对独立，同时这里的村民继承祖先苏格兰、爱尔兰等族特有的民歌韵味，在此基础上创造了美国乡村音乐这样一种盛行几十年的音乐形式。

阅读笔记

蓝调音乐

美国黑人和蓝调音乐有何关系

In the late seventeenth century, the first groups of slaves were brought on a *tremendous* journey from their African *homeland* to America. To the white Americans of the time, the slaves were little more than strong arms and sturdy backs. They were meant to work and they were meant to *generate* money, but they were not meant to have a voice. Though many white Americans *appreciated* the slaves for their *exertion*, this appreciation typically did not *overstep* the *bounds* of their work relationship. Even after the slaves were freed, the *tide* of *oppression* did not pass immediately. Their newly *decreed* freedom could not command humanity for blacks in the eyes of whites. It did not give them a heart and soul. This is where blues comes in.

在17世纪晚期，第一批奴隶离开他们的非洲家园，踏上漫长的旅程，被带到美国。在当时的美国白人看来，奴隶不过是胳膊粗壮、后背结实罢了。他们生来就是为了工作，成为赚钱机器，但却不能有发言权。尽管许多美国白人对奴隶的辛勤很是赞赏，但这种赞赏通常不会逾越工作关系的界限。即使奴隶获得了自由，对他们的压迫也不会立刻终止。在白人的眼中黑人赢得了自由却不能享有人权。他们仍然没有心和灵魂。在这种情况下，蓝调音乐诞生了。

单词释义

tremendous 巨大的	homeland 家园	generate 生成
appreciate 欣赏	exertion 努力	overstep 逾越
bound 范围	tide 趋势	oppression 压迫
decreed 任命的		

蓝调音乐缓解"黑白关系"

The blues style of music *originated* in the work fields of the southern United States. Historians believe that blues began in *infancy* as a field holler whose "call and response" style developed into work songs that matured into the blues. *Minstrel* show music, *ragtime*, and *spirituals* were also *influential* in its evolution. In the nineteenth century, white Americans got their first taste of black music through blackface minstrel shows, which affected race relations in a positive and negative way. With the discovery and recording of blues in the twentieth century, this *familiarity* steadily *intensified*. Many historians *assert* that blues, the music created by blacks, has improved race relations in the United States since its recognition by whites. The music was a unique cultural offering that whites could not *deny*. It was something new and *intriguing* to whites that shed a new light on blacks and their place in American culture and society.

The entire *span* of the development and *popularization* of blues and its rock derivation have improved race relations in this country.

蓝调风格的音乐起源于美国南部的田野。历史学家认为，蓝调音乐最初源于田间吟唱，这种"唱与和"的风格发展成田间歌曲，最后就形成了蓝调音乐。黑人滑稽剧、拉格泰姆音乐和灵歌也对蓝调音乐的发展起到了影响。在19世纪，美国白人通过黑人滑稽剧第一次接触到了黑人音乐，这种给种族关系带来积极和消极影响的音乐。在20世纪，随着对蓝调音乐的发现和录制，人们对它也越来越熟悉。许多历史学家断言，黑人创造的蓝调音乐改善了种族关系，因为它获得了美国白人的认可。蓝调音乐对文化的独特奉献令白人也无法否认。它对白人来说是新鲜有趣的东西，同时也积极影响了黑人在美国文化和社会中的地位。

蓝调音乐发展与流行的整个过程以及其起源于摇滚的特点改善了美国的种族关系。

originate 创作　　　　infancy 初期　　　　minstrel 歌手

ragtime 繁音拍子　　　spiritual 圣歌　　　 influential 有影响力的

familiarity 熟悉　　　 intensify 增强　　　 assert 维护

deny 否认　　　　　　intriguing 有趣的　　 span 跨度

 美国特色文化

特色表达One

在19世纪之前，若提问美国白人何为蓝调音乐，说不定他们会回你一句 probably up in Annie's room behind the clock. 这句话的意思是"不知道"！其中up in Annie's room出自英国军营，指在女孩子Annie的房间里，可是军营里是不会有女孩的，所以up in Annie's room暗指某人去了说话人找不到的地方，别来烦他。之后随着时间推移演变成了up in Annie's room behind the clock.

☆ 实景链接

A: Kane, why are you a big fun of blues? 凯恩，你为什么那么喜欢蓝调音乐？

B: It is **up in Annie's room behind the clock.** I just like it. 不知道。我就是喜欢。

A: Well, when was blues created? 那蓝调音乐起源于什么时候呢？

B: It was in the late seventeenth century, after American civil war. 是在17世纪晚期，美国南北战争以后。

特色表达Two

蓝调音乐可以说是美国白人与黑人和解的重要文化因素，那"和解"一词在美国俚语中怎么说呢？美国人常说bring an olive branch，这句话字面意思是"带着橄榄枝"，大家都知道橄榄枝是象征和平的，所以这句话意思就引申为"抱着和解的愿望"。

☆ **实景链接**

A: I've come to you bringing an **olive branch**; I think we should stop quarrelling. 我抱着和好的愿望到你这儿来了。我觉得我们应当停止争吵。

B: It is my fault this time. Pardon me for my selfishness. 这次是我的错，请原谅我的自私。

A: I also apologize for my bad attitude. 我也为我的恶劣态度向你道歉。

B: It doesn't matter. Just let it go. We are good now. 没事的，就让它过去吧。我们和好了。

拓展特色句

1. Let's get some blue music going! 放点儿蓝调音乐来听吧！

2. This song has a pleasant melody. 这首歌旋律优美。

3. I am very into blue music. 我很喜欢蓝调音乐。

"聊" 美国特色文化

A: Every time I listen to blues, I unconsciously nod off.

B: The melody is always slow.

A: Where does the blues originate?

B: It's said to be originated in the work fields of the southern United States. At first, blues began with black slaves' work songs.

A: Then I know why those famous blues singers are black. Nowadays not only the black like blues, but also the white accepts it.

B: In some degree, the blues has improved race relations in the United States since its recognition by whites.

A: Then blues takes the important place in America.

A: 每次我听到蓝调音乐，我都会不知不觉想睡觉。

B: 节奏一般都很慢。

A: 蓝调音乐起源于哪里？

B: 蓝调音乐起源于美国南部的田野，最初源于黑人奴隶的田间吟唱。

A: 那我就知道为什么那些有名的蓝调歌手都是黑人了。现在不仅仅是黑人喜欢蓝调音乐，白人也接受了。

B: 在某些程度上，蓝调音乐增进了美国民族之间的关系，自从它被白人认可之后。

A: 那么蓝调音乐在美国占据很重要的地位。

B: 谁说不是呢？至少对我而言，我非常喜欢蓝调音乐。

B： Well no duh. At least for me, I like blues very much.

"问" 美国特色文化

蓝调音乐是"魔鬼的音乐"吗？

如同爵士乐、摇滚乐等文化一样，蓝调也有一段黑历史，因为有人说蓝调会导致暴力与犯罪，于是蓝调曾被冠上"魔鬼的音乐"一说。在20世纪初，蓝调吸引了很多美国白人，即便如此，蓝调还是被看作是不入流的音乐。后来，蓝调出来了一位非常出名的音乐家，他就是汉迪，他的蓝调令很多白人开始欣赏蓝调音乐。至今，蓝调已是美国黑人文化的重要一环，甚至是美国文化遗产的一个重要组成部分。

阅读笔记

嘻哈音乐为何

嘻哈音乐到底有何魔力

Hip-hop emerged from *rap* music. It is the term for urban-based creativity and expression of culture. It is the backing music for rap, which is often composed of a collage of "samples" from other songs. Hip-hop *sampling* is a way to revisit Black *musical* tradition. It may sound like *imitation*, but it is really just reworking earlier music. The sampling of rappers represents an *artistic continuity* and connection to Black cultural roots. Hip-hop proved its staying power by reaching into and affecting every corner of society. Rap's *exemption* to *geographic* and economic *boundaries* has made it rich. But with the strength that comes from diversity also comes *disunity*. The Hip-Hop Nation has become like its mother country: widespread with decision. Suddenly too complex to move as one, hip-hop is discovering the *dilemma* of power.

嘻哈音乐来源于说唱音乐。它主要来源于以城市为基础的创造力以及对文化的表达。它是说唱音乐的背景音乐，主要由其他歌曲的"采样"拼接而成。嘻哈音乐拼凑而成的音乐是一种重访黑人音乐习俗的方式。听起来好像是模仿抄袭，但是它其实却是将早期的音乐重整了一遍。说唱歌手所唱的这些拼凑歌曲展现出艺术上的连续性，以及跟黑人文化根源的关联。嘻哈音乐触及到了社会的方方面面，由此也证明了它持久的影响力。说唱音乐超越了地理和经济上的限制，让其内容形式变得丰富。但是多样性这些长处也引起了不统一。嘻哈民族变得跟它的母亲一样：断然地广泛流传。但是它突然之间太过复杂而不能作为一个整体地向前进，嘻哈音乐正陷入两难之地。

单词释义

rap 说唱	sampling 采样	musical 音乐的
imitation 模仿	artistic 艺术的	continuity 连续性
exemption 豁免	geographic 地理的	boundary 范围
disunity 不统一	dilemma 进退两难	

嘻哈音乐"真身"大还原

Hip Hop is a *movement* consisting of 4 main artistic elements: DJ'ing, Rapping, Breaking and Graffiti. But at its core, it is a *philosophy* based on the idea that self expression is an *integral* part of the pursuit of peace, love and unity. It was created by young *visionaries* who tapped into their greatest *potential* and *gave birth to* one of the most important cultural phenomenon the world has ever seen.

Shaped by the spirit of Africa, The Caribbean and Black America, it is a culture that binds us under the belief that we must *strive for* excellence through our *respective* art forms, as well as within our souls. It's a lifestyle that unites people from the U.S to Nigeria, France to Brazil, Japan to Mexico, often unable to speak each other's language but fully capable of understanding all that makes us who we are.

嘻哈是一项包含4个主要艺术元素的运动：打碟音乐、说唱、霹雳舞和涂鸦。但其核心是基于这样一个理念，即自我表达是追求和平、爱和团结不可分割的一部分。创作嘻哈的年轻梦想家们发挥着他们最大的潜力，创造出世界最重要的文化现象之一。

受到非洲、加勒比和美国黑人精神的影响，嘻哈这种文化让我们走到了一起，我们也相信我们可以通过各自的艺术形式以及我们的灵魂追求卓越。这种生活方式使来自美国、尼日利亚、法国、巴西、日本和墨西哥的人们团结起来，虽然他们大多不会讲对方的语言，但却能理解所有那些让我们之所以成为我们的东西(嘻哈精神)。

单词释义

movement 运动	philosophy 哲学	integral 完整的
visionary 梦幻的	potential 潜在的	respective 各自的
give birth to 产生；造成	strive for 争取	

 美国特色文化

特色表达One

美国人喜欢玩嘻哈音乐，而美国女孩称很多嘻哈音乐者为是mack daddy，这是为什么呢？mack daddy最初源自20世纪50年代的流行黑人歌曲"The great Mac Daddy"，其中mack的意思是"老弟，老兄"，而daddy泛指万人迷，mack daddy则经常用来形容有魅力以及具领导力的成熟男性。

实景链接

A: Why is hip hop music so widely appealing? Do you enjoy that kind of music? 为什么嘻哈音乐这么有吸引力呢？你喜欢那种音乐吗？

B: Yeah, I love it very much. And I am a big fun of Eminem. He is a **great Mac Daddy**. 喜欢啊，我超爱的，而且我是痞子阿姆的头号粉丝。他太有魅力了。

A: Recommend me a song of him. 给我推荐一首他的歌吧。

B: "Stan" is good which he sang with Dido. 《Stan》很好听，是他和蒂朵一起合唱的。

特色表达Two

美国乐坛不乏才华横溢的音乐才子，当然也不缺eye candy。在俚语中通常用eye candy指代在视觉上颇具吸引力的"养眼花瓶"，也可指金玉其外败絮其中的演员或艺术家。这一表达是在1983年，由INTERAC公司的界面设计师首先使用的，他们将文本、音频等元素融合一起做成非常吸引眼球的画面，就有了eye candy(炫目的视觉画面)。

实景链接

A: What a terrible voice of her! How can she become a singer? 她唱得太难听了，怎么能成为歌手呢？

B: Yeah, she was absolutely an **eye candy**. 是啊。她就是个养眼的花瓶而已。

A: I heard that she used to be a professional actress. 我听说她过去是名专业的演员。

B: Well, it was a big mistake of her to get in the world of pop music. 呃，那她踏足流行乐坛真是个巨大的错误。

拓展特色句

1. I used to love hip-hop music. 我以前喜欢嘻哈音乐。

2. Can you turn that hip hop music down? 能把那嘻哈音乐的声音调小一点吗？

3. The singer combined the hip-hop with Chinese opera. 这位歌手将京剧和嘻哈音乐进行了结合。

"聊" 美国特色文化

A: Can you recommend me some songs when running?

B: You can try to download some hip-hop songs. They made you energetic.

A: Many people think hip-hop music has negative influence.

B: Some of songs' themes are about poverty and dark sides of the society.

A: So I don't suggest kids to listen to this kind of music. Moreover it sounds very complicated or to say, noisy.

B: Hip Hop is a movement consisting of 4 main artistic elements: DJ'ing, Rapping, Breaking and Graffiti.

A: You are so professional. And somebody says hip hop just imitates other songs. Is that true?

B: You flatter me. Rather than imitation, it is really just reworking earlier music.

A：能推荐几首唱歌的时候听的歌吗？

B：你现在可以去下载一些嘻哈音乐。它们会让你精力充沛。

A：很多人会认为嘻哈音乐有消极的影响。

B：有些歌的主题确实是关于贫穷以及社会的黑暗面。

A：所以我不是很建议孩子们听这种音乐。并且，听起来很复杂，或者说很吵人。

B：嘻哈是一项包含4个主要艺术元素的运动：打碟音乐、说唱、霹雳舞和涂鸦。

A：你很专业嘛，但有人说嘻哈音乐只是模仿其他歌曲。是真的吗？

B：你抬举我了，与其说是模仿，还不如说是重温老歌。

美国特色文化

嘻哈为什么叫hip hop?

1961年5月15日出生于纽约布朗克斯区的梅勒·梅尔（Melle Mel）是第一个称自己是"MC"的说唱歌手，其他愤怒五人组（Furious Five）的成员还包括他的几个兄弟，其中牛仔（Cowboy）发明了"Hip Hop"这个词，因为他当时为了取笑一个刚入伍的朋友，唱"hip/hop/hip/hop"来形容他朋友以后的军队训练，他

戏言"练步伐的时候不就是屁股一颠一颠的嘛"，那不就是"Hip Hop"嘛。

阅读笔记

爵士音乐

爵士音乐如何"咸鱼大翻身"

Throughout the 1920s, jazz music evolved into an integral part of American popular culture. The "*primitive*" jazz sound that had originated in New Orleans diversified, and thus *appealed to* people from every echelon of society.

The effect of jazz music upon society can be *depicted* through a close *examination* of different aspects of popular culture. Jazz music had a profound effect on the literary world, which can be *illustrated* through the *genesis* of the *genre* of jazz poetry.

Fashion in the 1920s was another way in which jazz music influenced popular culture. The Women's Liberation Movement was *furthered* by jazz music, as it provided means of *rebellion* against set standards of society. The status of African Americans was *elevated*, due to the popularity of this *distinctly* African American music. For the first time in American history, what was previously considered "bottom culture" rose to the top and became a highly desired *commodity* in society.

经过了整个20世纪20年代，爵士乐已发展成为美国流行文化的一个组成部分。"原始的"爵士乐起源于新奥尔良，后来变得更加多样化，从此吸引着社会各阶层的人们。

从流行文化的不同方面仔细观察，可以看出爵士乐对社会的影响。爵士乐在文坛产生了深远的影响，追溯题材诗歌的起源就能证明这一点。

20世纪20年代时尚成为了爵士乐对流行文化的又一影响。爵士乐推动了妇女解放运动，因为它向人们提供了一种反抗约定俗成的社会标准的方式。非裔美国人社会地位的提高，同样得益于这种独特的美国黑人音乐的流行。曾经被视为"底层文化"的爵士乐最终脱颖而出，成为社会上不可缺少的一部分，这在美国历史上是绝无仅有的。

单词释义

primitive 原始的   depict 描述   examination 检查

illustrate 阐明   genesis 发生   genre 类型

further 促进   rebellion 叛乱   elevate 提升

distinctly 明显地   commodity 商品   appeal to 吸引

爵士乐引领新时尚

The influence of jazz upon popular culture is perhaps the most *apparent* when looking at the developments in the fashion industry during the 1920s. This whole industry *targeted* a society that *revolved* around a certain kind of music.

The flapper fashions *ostensibly* illustrate the importance of jazz to the consumer market of the Jazz Age. Because of the post-war economic *boom*, the consumer market was *enormous*, and the fashion industry followed the demands of the new and rising American youth culture. Jazz music was the *propelling* force of this new culture.

By 1925, the wild and primitive sound of jazz music filled the streets of every major city in the United States. The popularity of jazz music with the general populous was *unprecedented*. Part of the popularity of jazz music was due to the fact that it was *incredible* dance music. The Charleston quickly became the most popular dance in the dance

爵士乐对于流行文化影响最明显的时间段可能要数20世纪20年代时尚产业的发展了。当时整个社会都围绕着爵士音乐这种特定的音乐旋转，整个行业也朝着这个目标发展。

时髦少女这种时尚很大程度上表明了爵士音乐对于爵士年代的消费市场的重要性。由于战后经济繁荣，消费市场的潜力非常巨大，时尚产业紧跟新兴的美国年轻文化的潮流。爵士音乐是这种新型文化的推动力。

1925年以前，美国各大城市的角落都充斥着野性并且原生噪音的爵士音乐。爵士音乐在大众间受欢迎的程度是空前的。查尔斯顿摇摆舞很快就变成了美国各大舞厅里最受欢迎的舞

halls across the United States. The Victorian clothing of the pre-war era was clearly unsuitable jazz *apparel*.

蹈。战前的维多利亚式服装在这个爵士时代显而易见变得不大合适。

apparent 明显的　　target 以……为目标　　revolve 旋转
ostensibly 表面上　　boom 繁荣　　enormous 巨大的
propelling 推动的　　unprecedented 空前的　　incredible 不可思议的
apparel 服装

美国特色文化

特色表达One

　　早期爵士乐者总希望爵士乐能在美国众多流行音乐中脱颖而出，但被很多人嘲笑为pipe dream。18世纪、19世纪时，英国贵族阶层流行吸食鸦片，他们所用的pipe(烟斗)常被指代为鸦片，而pipe dream则指吸食鸦片后上瘾进入欲生欲死的状态。1895年后，pipe dream开始用来形容"白日梦，难以实现的空想"，不再是鸦片专用语了。

☆ 实景链接

A: Norah Jones was going to give a concert. Are you interested in? 诺拉·琼斯要举办演唱会。你有兴趣去看吗？

B: I know her. She is a jazz singer, right? Her songs are pretty special to me. 我知道她，她是个爵士乐歌手吧。我听她的歌觉得味道很特别。

A: Yeah, it must be a **pipe dream** for her 20 years ago to get where she is now. 是啊，20年前她一定想不到她会取得今天的成就。

B: I guess so. 我猜也是。

特色表达Two

　　一般看着Barbie Doll这个词就会想起芭比娃娃，然后回忆起小孩子常爱玩的各种高低胖瘦的娃娃，其实，在俚语里，Barbie Doll还指"没有头脑的人"的人，因为人们觉得芭比娃娃是空的，即使外表很漂亮，所以还可引申作"徒有其表的人"。

☆ **实景链接**

A： Lisa, I plan to express my feeling towards Beth. 丽萨，我打算向贝丝表达我的想法。

B： Are you kidding me? You like her? 你开玩笑吧？你喜欢她？

A： I think no man can resist her beautiful face. 我想没有男人能够抵挡住她那美丽的面孔。

B： She is just a Barbie Doll. I know her too much. 她就是一个徒有其表的人，我太了解她了。

拓展特色句

1. I prefer rock to jazz for it has a strong beats. 和爵士乐相比我更喜欢摇滚乐，因为摇滚乐节奏强烈。

2. The lively rhythm in this song makes me feel good. 这首歌节奏轻快，让我感觉很好。

3. You'll hear much jazz music here. 你会在这儿听到很多爵士音乐。

"聊" 美国特色文化

A： Hey, what are you listening to?

B： I am just listening casually.

A： Would you mind me seeing your iPod for a minute?

B： Not at all. I have got a ton of good stuff loaded up.

A： Let me see. You've got some great jazz standards here. Charlie Parker and Duke Ellington. You've got their greatest hits and some bootleg stuff, too. I never knew you were such a jazz buff.

B： Yeah, I love it from a very young age.

A： In most people's eyes, jazz is an American National Treasure.

A： 嘿，你在听什么呢？

B： 我只是随便听听。

A： 你介意让我看看你的ipod吗？

B： 不介意啊，我在里面下了无数的好东西。

A： 让我看看，你这还有一些很棒的爵士标准曲。查理·派克，杜克·艾灵顿。你还有最热门的歌曲及一些未正式出版音乐版本。我以前都不知道你是一个爵士乐迷呢。

B： 是啊，我从很小的时候就很喜欢了。

A： 在很多人眼里，爵士是美国的国宝。

B： 你不知道吗？爵士乐大师在华盛顿特区享有盛誉，并被印在邮票上。

B：Don't you know that? Jazz masters have been honored in Washington DC, appeared on postage stamps.

 美国特色文化

什么是爵士乐？

爵士乐(Jazz)，于19世纪末20世纪初源于美国，诞生于南部港口城市新奥尔良。爵士乐讲究即兴，以Shuffle节奏为基础，具有摇摆的特点，结合了非洲黑人文化和欧洲白人文化。最初爵士乐主要集中在新奥尔良发展，1917年后转向芝加哥、纽约，如今爵士乐风靡全球，其主要风格有：新奥尔良爵士、摇摆乐、比博普、冷爵士、自由爵士、拉丁爵士、融合爵士等。

阅读笔记

美式足球

足球和橄榄球

The game of American football (*hereafter* referred to just as "football") developed out of something like a cross between association football (or soccer) and rugby. Rugby itself grew out of the soccer tradition in England, so soccer is truly at the very core of this sport. However, as both games made their way across the Atlantic, they were both played at colleges and universities, and out of those two games, football was born.

The earliest history of the sport tells us that no single variety of the game was played; some schools played *essentially* soccer, others rugby, while still others played *various combinations* of the two (and certainly without any *formalized* rules). This first college game was essentially soccer, but *nevertheless* laid the *groundwork* for the modern game as we know it today. In order to do that, however, rules would have to be put in place to truly *differentiate* the sport.

美式足球(以下简称"足球")是由英式足球和橄榄球混合发展起来的一项运动。橄榄球本身源于英格兰的足球传统，所以英式足球才是这项运动的真正核心。然而，随着英式足球和橄榄球在美国的传播，二者成为了各类大学的运动项目；这两项运动混合发展，于是美式足球诞生了。

从足球早期的发展史来看，爱好者们并不仅仅局限于某一种球类；有的学校还是踢英式足球，其他的学校踢橄榄球，也有学校将两种球类混合起来(当然没有正式的规则)。足球依然是大学里的首选比赛，它奠定了我们今天所知道的足球运动的基础。然而，为了促成足球运动的发展，必须制定相应规则，把足球真正区分开来。

单词释义

hereafter 从此以后	essentially 本质上	various 各种各样的
combination 结合	formalize 使形式化	nevertheless 然而
groundwork 基础	differentiate 区别	

如何成为美国足球的冠军

While college football was played in the Midwest before the turn of the century, the earliest success in the sport *belonged to* schools from the East, specifically Ivy League universities. However, while most sports, be they college or professional, determined *champion*s based on a *playoff* system, or a single game or series, college football had, for its entire existence, the problem of failing to agree upon a method for determining a national champion.

In most cases, until recent history, the national champion was decided by *mathematical formula* or *poll*. In the oldest records, *numerous* teams were awarded national *championships* by different selectors. Around 1890, there began to be some agreement over the national champion, though there were still *dissenters*. However, no matter who did the choosing, the final decade of the 1800s belonged to the Ivies. From 1890 to 1900, Harvard, Yale, Penn and Princeton won all 11 national championship titles.

在世纪之交之前，即使都是美国中西部的大学在踢足球，但是运动方面所获得的最早成功的都是东部的学校，特别是常春藤大学。然而，大多数的运动，不管是校内比赛还是专业比赛，都是根据一套季后赛体系或者单一的一场比赛或者系列来决定冠军的，足球有它自身的一套体系，因而在决定国家冠军的问题上存在分歧。

在大多数情况下，直到最近，国家冠军是通过数学公式或者投票来决定。在最古老的记录中，无数的队伍都被不同的选择者予以国家冠军。在1890年左右，即使仍然对国家冠军的选择方法存在分歧，但是开始出现一些协定好的方法。无论是谁进行选择，19世纪最后的10年都属于常春藤大学。从1890年到1900年，哈佛大学、耶鲁大学、宾夕法尼亚大学以及普林斯顿大学将11项国家冠军的称号收入囊中。

单词释义

belong to 属于	champion 冠军	playoff 季后赛
mathematical 数学的	formula 公式	poll 投票
numerous 许多的	championship 冠军	dissenter 反对者

 **美国特色文化**

特色表达One

　　足球比赛中不到最后一刻谁也别太嚣张，因为某个球员会break one's duck也说不定呢！break one's duck这个表达和鸭子是没有任何关系的，它源自英国板球，完整的表达应该是to break one's duck's egg，duck's egg指的是"零蛋，零分"，所以该短语便指"突破零纪录"，之后常作to break one's duck，表示"打破失利局面，在最后时刻得分"，即大逆转。

☆ 实景链接

A: What is the result of the match? 比赛结果如何？

B: Joseph **broke his duck** and kicked a field goal before the clock was stopped which made the U.S. win the game. 约瑟夫来了个大逆转，就在比赛结束前踢进一球，所以美国赢了。

A: Awesome! We really should celebrate for that. 太棒了！我们真应该庆祝一下。

B: That's right. I'll call the others. 说得对，我来给其他人打电话。

特色表达Two

　　从古至今，足球比赛不只是单纯的体育竞技，很多球员都会被迫踢黑球，通常我们可以用Hobson's choice来形容这种情况。Hobson是英国的一位马匹出租生意的老板，他老是担忧顾客专挑那几匹好马，而造成了马儿过累，就定下规矩：每次只能选最外边的一匹马。这样，所有马匹都能有活干。之后人们就用"哈伯森提供的选择"来比喻"被迫做某事"，或者"根本没有选择"。

☆ 实景链接

A: Have you watched the football game last night? 你看昨晚的足球赛了吗？

B: No, the referees take bribes and players do match-fixing. It sucks. 没有，裁判受贿，球员踢假球。太没劲了。

A: Sometimes they were just caught in the **Hobson's choice**. If they don't do so they would be laid off. 有时候他们只是陷入了毫无选择的

境地，如果不那么做，就会被解雇。

B：All I can say is what a complicated world! 我只想说这世界太复杂了！

拓展特色句

1. Which team do you support? 你支持哪个队？
2. The referee called a foul. 裁判吹了犯规。
3. We'd better attempt a field goal before the clock is stopped. 我们最好在比赛结束前尝试射门。

"聊" 美国特色文化

A：Guys, are you ready for a pick-up game of touch football?

B：It sounds dangerous. It's ok for me to be a spectator.

A：Come on. It's really fun. If you don't try, you will be regretted.

B：I don't know the rules anyway.

A：We yesterday watched football game played on TV.

B：Uhh, yeah. I saw the players in pads tackled. We don't have pads.

A：Don't be worried. In touch football, people just tag you to stop the play.

B：Well, I want to have a try. But you'd better tag lightly.

A：伙计们，你们想要玩触身式美式足球吗？

B：听起来很危险，我当一名观众就可以了。

A：拜托，真的很有趣。如果你不试一下，你会后悔的。

B：但是我真的不知道规则。

A：我们昨天还在电视上看过足球比赛。

B：嗯，是啊，我昨天看到运动员穿着护具也被扑倒了。我们没有护具。

A：别担心，在触身式足球赛当中，人们很少会用到身体碰触。大家只会用手碰你，来阻止进攻。

B：好的，我想试试。但是你们最好碰轻一点。

 美国特色文化

何为美式足球?

美式橄榄球(American football)，又名美式足球，是橄榄球运动的一种，为北美四大职业体育之首。美式橄榄球最早来自英式橄榄球，传入美国后规则改变，改为采取攻防线进行回合制争球、没有跑位限制，并且可以向前抛掷传球。美式橄榄球是一种对抗竞争很强烈的体育运动，由于球赛中避免不了与对方球员激烈的身体冲撞，因此球员需穿戴头盔和护具出场。

阅读笔记

棒球

棒球简史

Baseball originated before the American Civil War (1861—1865) as rounders, a humble game played on sandlots. Early champions of the game fine-tuned it to include the kind of skills and mental judgment that made cricket respectable in England. In particular, scoring and record-keeping gave baseball gravity.

The first professional baseball league was established in 1871. By the beginning of the 20th century, most large cities in the eastern United States had a professional baseball team. Over the decades, every team has had its great players. Jackie Robinson (1919—1972) played for the Brooklyn Dodgers. A gifted and courageous athlete, he was the first African-American player in the major leagues in 1947. Prior to Robinson, black players had been restricted to the Negro League.

棒球在美国内战(1861—1865)前就出现了，那时还是在沙地上进行的类似圆场棒球的简单运动。早期的冠军们对棒球风格做了轻微改动，包括技巧和心理判断等方面，这些改动曾使板球在英国大受欢迎。尤其是评分和记录令棒球充满了吸引力。

第一个职业棒球联盟建于1871年。在20世纪初期，美国东部的大多数城市都有专业的棒球队。数十年来，每个球队都有自己有名的球员。布鲁克林道奇队的球员杰基·罗宾森（1912—1972），一位集天赋和胆量于一身的运动员，他是1947年第一位在职业性运动联盟中打球的黑人运动员。在罗宾森之前，黑人运动员只限于参加黑人联盟。

单词释义

humble 谦逊的   sandlot 沙地   respectable 可敬的
courageous 有胆量的   restrict to 局限于

棒球怎么比

Starting in the 1950s, baseball *expanded* its geographical *range*. Western cities got teams, either by *luring* them to move from eastern cities or by forming so-called expansion teams with players made available by established teams. Until the 1970s, because of strict contracts, the owners of baseball teams also *virtually* owned the players; since then, the rules have changed so that players are free, within certain limits, to sell their services to any team.

The major league baseball season lasts from April to October and includes the regular season, the playoffs, and the World Series. The teams were divided into two leagues, the National and American; during the regular season, a team played only against other teams within its league. The most victorious team in each league was said to have won the "*pennant*;" the two pennant winners met after the end of the regular season in the World Series. The winner of at least four games (out of a possible seven) was the champion for that year. This arrangement still holds today, although the leagues are now *subdivided* and pennants are decided in post-season playoff series between the winners of each division.

从20世纪50年代开始，棒球渐渐传到了许多地区。西部城市吸引东部球队西迁，或者建立所谓的扩编球队，球员从现有球队中挑选。到20世纪70年代，由于合同里的苛刻要求，棒球队的老板也几乎拥有了所有球员；从那时起，规则开始改变，球员在一定范围内可以自由效力任何球队。

主要职业棒球大联盟赛季从4月份持续到10月份，期间包括常规赛季、季后赛以及世界职业棒球大赛。球队被分成两个联盟，国家联盟和美国联盟；在常规赛季，一个球队只和它这个联盟里的其他球队进行比赛。每个联盟中获胜最多的球队则被认为赢得了"奖旗"；在常规赛季之后，两个联盟中的"奖旗"得主在世界职业棒球大赛再进行比赛。赢得至少四场比赛（如果比赛七场的话）的球队获得当年的冠军。这种安排直到今天还在实行，即使联盟现在更加细分了，奖旗得主仍是在每场比赛之后的季后赛决定的。

单词释义

expand 扩张	range 范围	lure 引诱
virtually 事实上	pennant 奖旗	subdivide 细分

 美国特色文化

特色表达One

在美国大选中常会用到ballpark estimate，这个表达是什么意思呢？在ballpark estimate这一短语中，ballpark指"棒球场"，estimate意思是"估计"，而通常每个棒球场都有大小尺寸一样的菱形内场，但是它们的外场面积大小不同，所以人们说到整个棒球场的大小往往会用大致估计的方法，即ballpark estimate。如今经常用在竞选当中，用来估计候选人的竞选概率。

☆ 实景链接

A：He's always been very popular here in this state. Do you think it is possible for him to win? 他在这个州一直很受欢迎。你认为他会赢吗？

B：I am not sure but I can give you a **ballpark estimate**. 我不确定，但我能给你一个他获胜的概率。

A：What ballpark? We are not talking baseball here. 什么棒球场？我们没在讨论棒球啊。

B：I mean I can estimate it roughly. 我的意思是我可以给你粗略地估计一下。

特色表达Two

美国人常用she really has lots on the ball赞美那些勤奋并有作为的政界女士，可是lots on the ball不是球上有很多东西的意思吗？其实，lots on the ball最初指棒球比赛中，投手投出特别有力的球，但是随着时日的推移，这个短语则用来指"工作勤奋、能力高强的人"，尤其用来形容政界人士。

☆ 实景链接

A：Hey, Cindy, come here. There is an expression that I am confused with. 嘿，辛迪，过来一下。这里有个说法我不太明白。

B：Which one? 哪个？

A：This sentence—**She really has lots on the ball**. This news was all about politics. It has nothing to do with balls. Why does the writer use this? 这句——She really has lots on the ball。这篇新闻都是跟政治相关的，跟球没有关系啊，为什么作者要这么写呢？

B： This expression is usually used to describe the woman who is diligent and capable in politics. 这个表达通常是用来形容政界勤奋又有能力的女士的。

拓展特色句

1. He is a baseball player. 他是一个棒球运动员。

2. I wish the baseball season would not be over soon. 我希望棒球赛季别那么快结束。

3. The pitcher hits a batter with the ball. 投球手击中了击球手。

"聊" 美国特色文化

A： Sorry, I'm late. What's the situation right now?

B： Sit down quickly. I helped save your seat. You've missed the most wonderful part.

A： What a pity. You haven't told me the score yet.

B： 7 to 5.

A： Which team is at advantage?

B： The Japanese team. I am afraid our team will lose.

A： It's still hard to say. The two teams are evenly matched. This is a close game. Look! The batter hit a flyball... Oh ,it's a foul ball.

B： He's got two strikes now.

A： I brought some beer with me. You want one?

B： That couldn't be better.

A： 对不起，我迟到了，现在局势怎么样？

B： 赶紧坐下来，我帮你保留了你的位子。你已经错过了最精彩的部分。

A： 真是遗憾啊！你还没有告诉我比分呢！

B： 7比5。

A： 哪支队占有优势？

B： 日本队，我觉得我们队会输。

A： 现在还很难说。这两支队势均力敌。这场比赛比分很接近。看！击球手打了一个高飞球……这是一个界外球。

B： 他投了两个好球了。

A： 我买了一些啤酒，你要一个吗？

B： 那太好了！

"问" 美国特色文化

对美国人而言，棒球意味着什么？

对美国人来说，棒球意味着生活，观看棒球比赛更是一种温馨的享受，就好像家庭小聚一样轻松。同时棒球还是一种世代的传承。在美国，祖父会告诉孙子，他曾经看过乔·迪马吉奥（Joe DiMaggio）比赛，父亲会告诉儿子，他曾看过汉克·阿伦（Hank Aaron）击出全垒打，而现在的孩子有一天则会告诉他们的孩子，他看过阿尔伯特·普侯斯（Albert Pujols）在大联盟的精彩纷呈。何为在美国会有这种传承呢？因为棒球不仅是一项全民性娱乐，还是可以统计的、能让人比较不同时代的球员的轻松好玩的活动。只要通过刻苦的练习，谁都可以有机会登上大联盟的殿堂，参加这样的运动何乐而不为？

阅读笔记

享誉世界的美国篮球

谁"发明"了篮球

Basketball is a *uniquely* American sport. It originated in 1891 when James Naismith, a young *physical* education teacher in Springfield, Massachusetts, was instructed by his boss to invent a new game that could be played indoors during the cold winter months to keep the students occupied and out of trouble.

Naismith thought back to his boyhood in Canada, where he and his friends had played "duck on a rock," which involved trying to knock a large rock off a boulder by throwing smaller rocks at it. He also *recalled* watching rugby players *toss* a ball into a box in a *gymnasium*. He had the idea of nailing up raised boxes into which players would attempt to throw a ball. Naismith had two bushel baskets, used for carrying peaches, nailed to the *balcony* at opposite ends of the school's gymnasium. He set up two nine-man teams, gave them a soccer ball, and told them the object was to toss it into the basket being *defended* by the opposing team. Most of the rules Naismith drew up still apply in some form today. He called the game Basket Ball, the modern version of which is

篮球是一项美国特有的运动。1891年，马萨诸塞州斯普林菲尔德年轻的体育老师詹姆斯·奈史密斯接到老板的指示，要他发明一项可以在寒冬的室内进行的新运动，以便让学生保持专注，少惹麻烦。

奈史密斯回想起他在加拿大的童年，在那里他和他的朋友们玩过"打石追"，通过投掷小石块把卵石上的大石头打掉。他还想起在体育馆看到橄榄球运动员将球扔进盒子里。于是他决定，钉起一个高挂的盒子，玩球的人试着把球投进盒子里去。奈史密斯把两个用于盛装桃子的蒲式篮子分别钉在学校体育馆两端的阳台上。他建立了两只分别由9人组成的球队，给他们一个足球，并告诉他们目标是把足球扔到对方防守的篮子里。奈史密斯起草的大部分规则今天在某种形式上依然适用。他把这项运动叫做篮

played by over 250 million people worldwide in an organized fashion, as well as by countless others in "pick-up" games.

球，目前全球范围内有超过2.5亿人以有组织的方式打现代篮球，不计其数的人参加临时的篮球比赛。

单词释义

uniquely 独一无二地
toss 投掷
defend 保卫

physical 生理上的
gymnasium 体育馆

recall 回忆
balcony 阳台

美职篮帮篮球涨"人气"

Basketball gained quickly *popularity* due to its simple equipment requirements, indoor play, *competitiveness*, and easily understood rules. The first professional basketball league was formed in 1898. Today, the National Basketball Association (NBA) is the major professional basketball league in the world, with teams in the United States and Canada. The NBA now has 29 teams competing in two conferences, the Eastern and Western, in four separate divisions.

Every year, in the second week of February, the NBA *interrupts* its season to celebrate the annual All-Star game, *featuring* the game's best players as selected by fans throughout the United States and Canada.

Superstar players like Michael "Air" Jordan increased the popularity of basketball *internationally*. In 1992, a so-

由于篮球对设备要求不高，又是室内运动，具有竞赛性，并且规则易于理解，篮球很快就获得了很高的人气。第一场专业篮球联盟组建于1898年。现今，国家篮球协会（NBA）是世界上主要的专业篮球联盟，球队来源于美国和加拿大。NBA现有29个球队，主要在东部和西部这两个赛区里面竞技，然后再细分为四个赛区。

每年二月的第二个星期，NBA都会中止比赛，来进行每年的全明星比赛，通过美国和加拿大球迷的投票来选择这场比赛中的参赛球员。

called Dream Team, made up of the top American professional basketball players, represented the United States in Olympic Games for the first time. Many teams in the National Basketball Association now have foreign players, who return home to represent their native countries during international competitions, such as the Olympic Games.

超级明星球员，像迈克尔·"飞人"乔丹提高了篮球在全球的名气。1922年，一个由美国顶级的专业球员组成的号称"梦之队"的篮球队第一次代表美国参加奥运会。NBA里的很多球队现在都有外籍球员，他们会在国际比赛的时候返回祖国参赛，比如奥运会。

单词释义

popularity 名气　　　　competitiveness 竞争力　　interrupt 打断
feature 特写　　　　　internationally 国际间地

美国特色文化

特色表达One

　　在美国，优秀的篮球明星炙手可热，但很多明星都只是一时风光无限，很快就over the hill了。over the hill最早源于军营俚语"当逃兵的"，在罗斯福新政时，人们常用这短语形容土木工人擅离职守的。后来，over the hill演变意义为某人风光不再，走下坡路，尤其用来形容成了过气的明星。

☆ 实景链接

A：My favorite basketball player is **over the hill** now. 我最喜欢的篮球明星现在走下坡路了。

B：Well, I still don't know who he is. 我还不知道你最喜欢谁呢？

A：It is Allen Iverson. 是阿伦·艾弗森。

B：Yeah, I know him, the one whose nickname is "the answer". 嗯，我知道他，就是那个绰号叫"答案"的人。

特色表达Two

　　美国NBA赛场上高手如云，有很多toss up，一不小心就满盘皆输。toss原是扔或者抛，toss up则是往上抛。Toss up源自古老的时候用抛硬币来做决定，以占卜前途。后来常用在运动场合与政界，指比赛双方势均力敌，难分胜负，所以引申作"难以预料的事情"。

☆ 实景链接

A：I bet Rocket will win this time. 我打赌火箭这次会赢。

B：I don't think so. Laker also has the possibility to win. 我觉得不一定，湖人队也有可能赢。

A：It's a toss-up. 真的很难预测。

B：So let's just enjoy the game. 所以让我们好好享受比赛吧！

拓展特色句

1. The basketball player bounced the ball pretty well. 该名篮球队员运球相当好。

2. Who will be playing against them in the final? 决赛是他们和哪个队比赛啊？

3. Our team is good at defense. 我们队擅长防守。

"聊" 美国特色文化

A：Who is that tall guy?

B：It's Kobe of course. Where are you on earth from? Nearly all girls know him.

A：Well. What position does he play?

B：Shooting guard. The same as Michael Jordan!

A：Kobe is really a good player, but I heard he is a womanizer.

B：It's just rumor. Don't believe it.

A：I don't care so much about it. My idol is Michael Air Jordan.

B：Jordan is a legend and no one can replace him.

A：那个很高的人是谁啊？

B：他是科比啊。你到底是哪里来的？几乎每个女孩都认识他。

A：好吧，他打哪个位置？

B：得分后卫。和迈克尔·乔丹是一样的位置。

A：科比打球打得好，但是我听说他很花心。

B：这只是传言。你不要相信。

A：我无所谓，我的偶像是迈克尔·飞人·乔丹。

B：乔丹是一个传说，没人能够取代他。

 美国特色文化

美国的篮球文化是什么？

在美国人看来，篮球不仅仅是一种竞技比赛还代表着一种特殊内涵，就像爵士乐和猫王一样在美国文化中占据着重要位置，是美国人生活中不可割舍的一部分；而篮球文化也正随着NBA在全球受到广泛关注，影响着世界体育文化。这里的篮球文化，是指观赏和参与篮球运动的人的思维方式和行为方式的制度化凝结，是篮球运动的知识、技能、习俗和制度的总称。

阅读笔记

Part 10

教育

美国竟然也有体罚现象

体罚还有性别歧视

Corporal punishment has been a *classic* method of *imparting* punishment since ancient civilizations. It had been reported that more than 200,000 U.S. children were subjected to corporal punishment. Corporal punishment is legal in 21 states in the U.S. and United States is the only country in the Western world that tolerates corporal punishment. Many American families also *resort to* corporal punishment to teach a child *discipline* and make him more *obedient*. Bans have been proposed in Massachusetts and California on all corporal punishment of children, but these moves were heavily defeated.

However, corporal punishment was forbidden from being used on girls and colored schools. It was believed that girls have a different kind of *mentality* and *flogging* would scar their minds for life. White boys were subjected to this *cruelty* as it was thought that it would make them manlier.

体罚自古以来就是常用的责罚。据报道，在美国有超过20万的孩子受过体罚。在美国的21个州，体罚是合法的，而且美国是唯一在西方国家里允许体罚的国家。很多美国家庭也都是用体罚教导孩子要守纪律，要更听话。虽然在马萨诸塞州和加利福尼亚州都有禁止体罚的议案，但是这些议案都受到了强烈地抵制。

但是，在有色人种学校和女孩子身上是不能动用体罚的。因为人们相信女孩的精神构造不同，体罚会给她们带来一生的伤害，而白人男孩接受体罚会使他们变得更像男人。

单词释义

corporal 肉体的	classic 经典的	impart 传授
discipline 纪律	obedient 顺从的	mentality 心态
flogging 鞭打	cruelty 残酷	resort to 诉诸

什么样的行为可以被称为"体罚"

What "corporal punishment" means: "Corporal punishment" is defined under human-rights law as any punishment in which physical force is used and intended to cause some degree of pain or *discomfort*. There is no *comprehensive* definition of corporal punishment under U.S. state or federal law.

The ACLU and Human Rights Watch documented cases of corporal punishment including hitting children with a belt, a ruler, a set of rulers taped together or a toy *hammer*; *pinching*, *slapping* or striking very young children in particular; grabbing children around the arm, the neck or elsewhere with enough force to *bruise*; throwing children to the floor; *slamming* a child into a wall; dragging children across floor.

"体罚"是什么意思呢？根据人权法对"体罚"的定义，体罚是指任何使用体力并且有意引起某些程度的不适和疼痛的惩罚。美国及其联邦法律都没有对体罚做出全面完整的定义。

美国公民自由联盟和人权观察组织用几个案子说明体罚包括用皮鞭、尺子或者是用胶水粘在一起的一套尺，或者玩具锤来打孩子，尤其是捏、拍打或者抽打那些非常幼小的孩子。用足够大的力气抓孩子的肩膀、脖子或者其他地方到瘀青；把孩子往地上摔；把孩子猛地往墙上扔；把孩子往地板上拖曳。

单词释义

discomfort 不适　　　　comprehensive 综合学校　　hammer 锤子
pinching 打尖　　　　　slap 掌击　　　　　　　bruise 瘀青
slam 猛击

 美国特色文化

 **特色表达One**

在美国，很多家长是up in arms体罚的。难道这里是说家长们拿着武器对付给孩子体罚的学校吗？其实虽然arm是"武器"，up in arms在战争年代指进行武

装斗争，但在日常生活中引申为"竭力反对"。

☆实景链接

A：What happened to your window? 你们家的窗户怎么啦？

B：It was broken by the naughty boy in the neighborhood. 被邻居家一个淘气的男孩给打破了。

A：You look so calm. Have you told it to his parents? 你看起来真淡定，你告诉孩子的父母了吗？

B：In fact, I **am up in arms** about this. I even don't know which boy he is. 事实上，我很生气。但是我都不知道这个男孩是谁。

💬 特色表达Two

若是老师体罚学生正好被学生家长逮个正着，那家长肯定会give sb fits。这里fit原意是"合适的"或者是"愤怒、失望"。因此，give sb fits的意思是"令某人恼怒"，这里是指家长肯定会生气。

☆实景链接

A：I really can't tolerate teacher's corporal punishment towards my child. It gives me fits. 我真的无法忍受老师对我孩子进行体罚。这让我很生气。

B：I can't imagine teachers are so cruel. 我都没想到老师会这么残忍。

A：I decided to sue the teacher. 我准备去控告那个老师。

B：It's not that serious. It could be ok to warn the teacher first. 也没有那么严重。先警告一下这位老师就行了。

拓展特色句

1. Stop passing notes in class. 不要在课堂上传递纸条。

2. He is very disruptive in class. 他在班上非常能捣乱。

3. Severe punishment may lead to child mental health problems. 严重的体罚可能会导致儿童的心理健康问题。

"聊" 美国特色文化

A: Can you accept the action of corporal punishment?

B: I totally disapprove this kind of action. It should be forbidden. It's kind of crime.

A: I couldn't agree more. But many teachers think physical punishment can help the students become obedient.

B: Lately I have read much news about it. A young teacher punished three pupils to stand naked in the class.

A: What? I even can't believe my ears? Has she received any punishment?

B: She isn't allowed to apply for any positions about teaching.

A: She really deserved it. I think the punishment is light.

B: Exactly.

A: 你能接受体罚这种行为吗?

B: 我完全不赞同这种行为,这应该被禁止。这简直就是犯罪。

A: 我非常同意,但是很多老师都觉得体罚能够让学生变得很听话。

B: 最近我读到很多关于这方面的新闻。一位年轻的老师惩罚三名学生在班上裸站。

A: 什么?我都不敢相信自己的耳朵。她受到什么惩罚了吗?

B: 她不能再从事任何有关教育的职务。

A: 这是她应得的。我觉得这种惩罚还算轻的。

B: 确实是。

"问" 美国特色文化

在美国也打学生屁股吗?

在美国有21个州都允许老师对学生进行合法体罚,而最常见的体罚方式就是打屁股。那些老师们将打学生屁股偷换概念成"拍一下",之后又用流行词替

换为"轻轻一舔"。一般来说,"犯错误"的学生最少也得挨三下,甚至十多下,多是由学校的校长亲自"执法"。而且打屁股的道具——那块硬板子可是专备的,有的校长一整天就拎个板子在走廊溜达,正所谓"杀鸡给猴看"。

家庭教育

立法前的家庭教育

Before *compulsory* laws requiring school *attendance* were introduced in 1852, a child's education took place at home. Through everyday life, young sons and daughters learned responsibilities necessary to manage a *homestead*. Tasks such as raising *livestock*, working the fields, making clothes, constructing homes, *forging* tools and so forth were primary sources of learning.

At the time, practical skills were more *essential* to *survival* than a person's ability to read or write. Although learning to read and write was available, children were usually taught just enough to handle basic affairs. However, when the fields demanded attention, the lessons were neglected.

The effectiveness of homeschooling was not in question during the eighteenth and nineteenth centuries. Some of the most well-known writers and inventors were homeschooled. Thomas Edison, who attended only three months of *elementary* school, was taught by his mother. Other famous homeschoolers include Benjamin Franklin, John Wesley,

在1852年推出义务教育法要求孩子去学校读书之前，孩子是在家里接受教育的。年轻的儿女们在每天的生活中要学会承担管理牧场的责任。比如放养牲畜、耕田种地、缝补衣服、建造房屋、锻造工具等，这些都是他们学习主要的资源。

在当时那个求生存的环境下，实际技能比读写的技能更加重要。即使那个时候可以教授孩子们读写的能力，但是孩子们却只被教授了那些足够处理基本事物的技能。然而，当田地需要人照管的时候，学业就被耽误忽视了。

家庭学校的可行性在18世纪、19世纪是毋庸置疑的。一些最著名的作家和发明家就是在家上学的。托马斯·爱迪生只上了3个的小学，他的母亲也是他的老师。其他家庭学校的名人包括本杰明·富兰克林、约翰·卫斯理、

Beatrix Potter, Charles Dickens and Alexander Graham Bell.

比阿特丽克斯·波特、查尔斯·狄更斯和亚历山大·格雷厄姆·贝尔。

现代家庭教育如何应运而生

The exact origin of modern homeschooling is difficult to *pinpoint*. It remained a *virtually underground* operation until the educational concerns of the 1970s unearthed it. The most *significant* turning point was when educational reformers and authors began to question both the techniques and the products of public schools.

现代家庭学校的确切起源很难确定。在20世纪70年代因教育问题而浮出水面以前，它都是以一种不公开的状态存在的。当教育改革者和专家开始质疑公立学校的技术和产品时，最重要的转折点出现了。

The new cost of *tuition* was beyond what average families could afford at the time, so smaller private schools across the nation closed their doors by the hundreds. This forced parents to decide between public school and home education. The choice wasn't really a choice for many of those families, and homeschooling numbers *soared* to record highs.

新学费超出了当时普通家庭可以承受的范围，全国有数百家小型私立学校只得关门。这迫使父母们在公立学校和家庭教育之间做出选择。许多家庭其实根本没得选择，家庭学校的数量迅速上升到历史新高。

Since the early 1980s, homeschool numbers have continued to rise at an *estimated* seven percent a year as more and more families are recognizing the long-forgotten value of home education. After its

自20世纪80年代初以来，家庭学校的数量预计以每年7%的增速持续增加，因为越来越多的家庭逐渐发现，

transition from commonplace to *countercultural*, homeschooling has now made a remarkable *comeback*.

家庭教育的价值已被人遗忘太久了。从司空见惯过渡为反传统文化，家庭学校的重新回归引人关注。

单词释义

pinpoint 查明	virtually 几乎	underground 地下的
significant 有重要意义的	tuition 学费	soar 高涨
estimate 预测	countercultural 反主流文化	comeback 恢复

美国特色文化

特色表达One

在美国，很多学生都觉得在家学习很好，尤其是那些nerd。美国学生常将一些词赋予另类含义，去形容那些不受欢迎的学生，例如nerd这个词的原意是"讨厌的人，卑微的人"，类似中国的"书呆子"。但其实被称为nerd的学生不呆，反而很聪明，都是学霸类型的。但由于他们太关注于学习而忽视了其他东西，尤其是同学间的人际关系，所以不讨人喜欢。

☆ 实景链接

A: Hey, the weather is great today. Why don't we go out and play football? 嘿，今天天气真好。咱们去踢足球吧？

B: I have to finish my report. And I have to preview the new lesson. 我得写完报告。然后我要预习功课。

A: Whenever I ask you to have fun, you are always studying! You are such a **nerd**! 我什么时候叫你去玩，你都在学习！你真是个书呆子！

B: Whenever I'm studying, you are always playing. I'm also wondering when you study. 我在学习的时候，你都在玩。我还好奇你什么时候学习呢。

特色表达Two

美国考试会有to be covered on the text吗？一般来说，即使有，老师也只是告诉你大概的。这里的to be covered on the text是指"考试的范围"。在询问考试范围时常可地道地来一句"What is going to be covered on the test?"

☆ **实景链接**

A: I think I am done for the examination. 我觉得我考试要完了。

B: The teacher had given us some hints. It won't be that bad. 老师已经给过我们暗示了，不会那么糟糕的。

A: Really? What is going to be covered on the test? 真的吗？你能告诉我考试范围吗？

B: Of course. You can just pay your attention to the underlined parts. 当然可以，你只用看有下画线的部分。

拓展特色句

1. I checked her homework every night. 我每天晚上都检查她的作业。

2. I got my daughter a tutor. 我给我的女儿请了一位家庭教师。

3. Do what the teacher tells you. 照老师说的做。

"聊" 美国特色文化

A: I feel exhausted that I should drop off or pick up my child from school every day.

B: You can try to homeschool your children. It's very prevailing recently.

A: I am afraid that he falls behind other peers in this way.

B: The effectiveness of homeschooling was not in question. Some of the most well-known writers and inventors were homeschooled.

A: Can you give me an example?

B: Thomas Edison, who attended only three months of elementary school, was taught by his mother.

A: Well, it seems homeschooling is a good choice.

A: 每天接送孩子上下学让我感到很疲惫。

B: 你可以尝试在家教育孩子。最近很流行啊。

A: 我担心用这种方式他会落后于其他的孩子。

B: 在家教育的效果是毋庸置疑的。很多著名的作家和发明家都是接受的家庭教育。

A: 你能给我举个例子吗？

B: 托马斯·爱迪生只上了3个月的小学，他的老师就是他母亲。

A: 看来在家教育也是一个不错的选择。

B: 在家教育的人越来越多，你真的可以好好考虑一下。

B：The homeschool population has grown large. You can really reconsider about it.

 美国特色文化

美国孩子在家上学是合法的吗?

如今在美国，"在家上学"已成合法的上学方式，被正式纳入法律保护渠道。这种学习模式不仅有可供选择的教材和教师指导手册，也允许自编教材，人手不够还可以找执业教师。"在家上学"与学校教育相通，孩子在家没法学习了随时可以回到学校继续教育。一般，都是父母学历很高或人生经历很丰富或多才多艺的父母才会选择让自己的孩子在家学习。

阅读笔记

家庭作业

每个学生都需要做家庭作业吗

Historically, homework was *frowned* upon in American culture. With few students interested in higher education, and due to the necessity to complete daily *chores*, homework was *discouraged* not only by parents, but also by school districts.

It is usually up to the teacher what *assignments* are to be completed, but the majority of grade school and high school students simply don't do homework.

In 1901, the California *legislature* passed an act that effectively *abolished* homework for those who attended kindergarten through the eighth grade. But, in the 1950s, with increasing pressure on the United States to stay ahead in the Cold War, homework made a *resurgence*, and children were encouraged to keep up with their Russian *counterparts*. By the end of the Cold War in the early 1990s, the *consensus* in American education was *overwhelmingly* in favor of issuing homework to students of all grade levels.

从历史上来看，家庭作业在美国文化中一直遭人反对。由于较少的学生对高等教育感兴趣，并且美国学生在学习之外还要做日常家务，所以家庭作业不仅受到家长的排斥，也让教职人员反对。

一般情况下，完成什么家庭作业是由老师决定的，但是大部分中小学生就是不会去做作业。

1901年，加利福尼亚立法机关通过了一项法案，有效地废除了那些从幼儿园到八年级学生的作业。但是，20世纪50年代，美国为了能够继续在冷战中占领先地位，压力递增，家庭作业在这样的情形下又"复活"了，鼓励孩子们赶上俄罗斯。20世纪90年代初，在冷战快要结束之际，针对美国教育达成共识，大家压倒性地支持每个年级的学生都要有作业。

单词释义

frown 不同意　　　　　chore 家庭杂物　　　　　discourage 阻止

assignment 任务　　　　legislature 立法　　　　　abolish 废除

resurgence 复兴　　　　counterpart 对应物　　　　consensus 一致

overwhelmingly 压倒性地

家庭作业做多少

Mason-Rice Elementary School in Newton, Massachusetts, has limited homework, keeping to the "10 minute rule." Raymond Park Middle School in Indianapolis has written a *policy* instructing teachers to "*assign* homework only when you feel the assignment is valuable." The policy also states, "A night off is better than homework which serves no *worthwhile* purpose." Others, such as Oak Knoll Elementary School in Menlo Park, California, have considered *eliminating* homework altogether. If these schools can do it, why can't everyone?

In American universities, the forms of homework are diverse. For example, a history teacher may ask students to write an *essay* about a historical event and a science teacher may ask students to conduct a physical experiment. Normally, there is no *standard* answer to the open ended questions. The grading is based on if the opinions are *logically* and clearly expressed in the homework.

位于马萨诸塞州牛顿的马森莱斯小学一直限制家庭作业量，始终遵守"10分钟规则"。印第安纳波利斯的雷蒙德公园中学定下规定，要求老师"只有当你觉得这项家庭作业非常有价值的时候，你才能布置"。这条规则还表明"休息一晚上总比完成那些毫无价值的家庭作业要好"。还有其他的学校，比如加利福尼亚州门洛帕克的橡树山丘小学，一直考虑要废除家庭作业，如果这些学校能够这样做，为什么其他的学校不能呢？

在美国高校，家庭作业的形式非常多样化。比方说，历史老师也许会要求学生就某个历史事件写篇论文，科学老师则可能让学生做一个物理实验。通常，这些问题都没有标准答案，老师根据作业中的观点是否符合逻辑，表述是否清晰来评分。

单词释义

policy 政策　　　　assign 布置　　　　worthwhile 有价值的

eliminate 消除　　　essay 论文　　　　standard 标准

logically 逻辑上

 ## "品" 美国特色文化

特色表达One

美国学生常常叫嚷I'm up to my neck in work right now. 意思是"我现在忙得不可开交"。想象一下繁重的工作把人埋没，一直埋到了脖子的位置，因此up to one's neck就是"很忙，没法应付其他事情"的意思，这个说法十分形象。

☆ 实景链接

A：Do you have a minute? 你有时间吗？

B：Well, what's up? 嗯，怎么了？

A：I have a problem in my work and I don't know how to deal with it. Could you help me? 我在工作中遇到一个问题，不知道该怎么解决。你能帮我一下吗？

B：Can you wait for a while? I'm **up to my neck** now. 你能等一会吗？我现在忙得不可开交。

特色表达Two

与中国学生一样，美国学生每天也要做很多的家庭作业，可他们考试时却不像中国学生可以回去找old exam。这里的old exam直译是"老试卷"，其实指"真题"，说的是老师们不用费心思随便想出的考题。

☆ 实景链接

A：Do you have the confidence to pass the examination? 你有信心能够通过这次考试吗？

B：Sort of. I had made full preparations for it. 算有吧。我已经做足充分的准备了。

A：I even don't know how to review. Can you give me some tips? 我甚至都不知道如何复习，你能给我些建议吗？

B: The best way is to review the **old exam** papers from my experience. 从我的经验看，最好的方法就是复习真题。

拓展特色句

1. Does everybody understand the assignment? 大家都清楚作业内容了吗？

2. Have you got your homework done for today? 今天的作业做完了吗？

3. Work will not be accepted for credit after the due dates. 规定日期之后上交的作业不能获得学分。

"聊" 美国特色文化

A: Tom, what's our homework today?

B: Review Chapter 5 and summarize the main content, then finish the exercise in this chapter.

A: I get fed up with this kind of homework. I really can't understand why we should review it. I have digested it during classes.

B: Mr. Smith says it can consolidate what we have learnt in class.

A: When did you finish your homework yesterday?

B: Around eight o'clock. I spent half of an hour doing the homework. What about you?

A: I nearly spent one hour. Why did you finish so quickly?

B: Because I have the reference book.

A: 汤姆，今天的家庭作业是什么？

B: 复习第五章，然后总结主要内容，还要完成这一章的练习。

A: 我已经厌烦这种家庭作业了，我真的搞不懂为什么我们要复习。我已经在上课的时候消化它了。

B: 老师说这个可以帮助我们巩固在课堂上学到的知识。

A: 你昨天什么时候写完作业？

B: 8点左右。做作业我花了半个小时。

A: 我做了快一个小时。你为什么完成得这么快？

B: 因为我有参考书。

 **美国特色文化**

美国的家庭作业好做吗?

中国，一般高中生的作业都有标准答案，学生只需得出与标准答案一致的结果。而美国高中生的作业不仅内容多，形式灵活，难度也高，美国小学生需要数小时，甚至数天来完成作业。美国的家庭作业最突出的特点是阅读量大，且几乎没有标准答案，尤其是文科类作业，老师只出题目，剩下的部分都要靠学生们互相合作发挥，比如写报告、做项目、演讲等。

阅读笔记

美国人如何养孩子

自主式教育法

To Americans, the goal of parents is to help children stand on their own two feet. From *infancy*, each child may get his or her own room. As children grow, they gain more freedom to make their own choices. Teenagers choose their own forms of *entertainment*, as well as the friends to share them with. When they reach young *adulthood*, they choose their own careers and marriage partners. Of course, many young adults still seek their parents' advice and *approval* for the choices they make. But once they "leave the nest" at around 18 to 21 years old, they want to be on their own, not "tied to their mother's *apron* strings."

The relationship between parents and children in America is very informal. American parents try to treat their children as individuals-not as extensions of themselves. They allow them to *fulfill* their own dreams. Americans praise and encourage their children to give them the confidence to succeed. When children become adults, their relationship with their parents becomes more like a friendship among *equals*.

对美国人而言，教养的目标在于帮助孩子们自力更生。从婴幼儿期开始，每一个孩子都可能拥有自己的房间；随着孩子的成长，他们有更多机会自己作决定；青少年们选择自己喜欢的娱乐方式，以及跟什么样的朋友一起玩；当他们进入了青年期之后，他们选择自己的事业和结婚伴侣。当然，很多的年轻人在作选择时，还是会寻求父母的忠告和赞同，但是当他们一旦在18岁到21岁左右"离巢"之后，就希望能够独立，不再是个离不开妈妈的孩子了。

在美国，亲子之间的关系不是那么严肃，美国父母们试着将孩子视为个体，而不是他们自我的延伸，他们允许孩子去实现自己的梦想。美国人会赞美并鼓励孩子以给予他们成功的信心。当孩子长大成人之后，亲子之间的关系会更像地位平等的朋友。

infancy 婴儿　　　　entertainment 娱乐　　　adulthood 成年人
approval 同意　　　apron 围裙　　　　　　fulfill 完成
equal 平等

训诫孩子

Most young couples with children struggle with the issue of *childcare*. Mothers have traditionally stayed home with their children. In recent years, though, a growing trend is to put preschoolers in a day care center so Mom can work. Many Americans have strong feelings about which type of arrangement is best. Some argue that attending a day care center can be a positive experience for children. Others insist that mothers are the best *caregivers* for children. A number of women are now leaving the work force to become full-time *homemakers*.

Disciplining children is another area that American parents have differing opinions about. Many parents feel that an old-fashioned *spanking* helps youngsters learn what "No!" means. Others prefer *alternate* forms of discipline. For example, "time outs" have become popular in recent years. Children in "time out" have to sit in a corner or by a wall. They can get up only when they are ready to act nicely. Older children and teenagers who break

大部分有孩子的年轻夫妻们都为了养育孩子的问题而大伤脑筋。传统上，母亲们会和孩子待在家里，但是近几年来，把孩子放在幼儿园好让妈妈去工作的趋势渐长。对于哪一种安排才是最好的，许多美国人都有自己强烈的主张，有些人认为进幼儿园对孩子而言是很正向的经历，另一群人则坚持母亲是照顾孩子的最佳人选，许多的妇女现在也离开职场成为全职的家庭主妇。

训诫孩子是另一项引起美国父母们争议的议题。许多父母觉得老式的责打能够帮助年幼的孩子明白父母说"不"的意思，然而有些人则较赞同其他形式的训诫方式。例如："隔离法"即是近年来颇被接受的方式，被隔离的孩子必须坐在墙角或是墙边，除非他们肯乖一点才可以起来；年纪稍大的孩子或是青

the rules may be grounded, or not allowed to go out with friends. Some of their *privileges* at home-like TV or telephone use—may also be taken away for a while. Although discipline isn't fun for parents or children, it's a necessary part of training.

少年若是违反规定，则可能受到被迫停止某项权益或是不准和朋友出去的处罚，而他们在家中的某些特权，像是看电视或是打电话，也会被取消一段时间。虽然处罚对于亲子双方都不是什么有趣的事，但是它仍是训诫孩子时必要的一部分。

单词释义

childcare 儿童照管　　　caregiver 护理者　　　homemaker 主妇

spank 拍掌　　　　　　　alternate 交替　　　　privilege 特权

"品" 美国特色文化

特色表达One

　　美国崇尚自由轻松的教学环境，但这与混日子不同，学生们要想完成课业，还是得fight tooth and nail。通常用复数形式fight teeth and nails，其中fight是打斗，teeth是牙齿，nails是指甲，那么这个短语的意思是把牙齿、指甲都派上用场来打架吗？其实在日常生活中，美国人多用其引申义"用力搏斗、全力以赴"。

☆ 实景链接

A：Have you prepared for the exam? 你为考试做好准备了吗？

B：Although I've prepared since last month, I have no confidence to pass it. 尽管我从上个月就开始准备，但我还是没有信心能通过。

A：Take it easy. You have **fought teeth and nails**. 放轻松。你已经全力以赴了。

B：Thanks for your encouragement. 谢谢你的鼓励。

特色表达Two

　　在美国，很多宝宝还没出生时，父母们就step up to the plate，准备了很多的备用名。step up to the plate来自棒球运动，plate就是本垒板。棒球比赛中，当球员用击球时，先得踏上本垒板，也就是step up to the plate。所以，这个短语的意思就是开始着手做某事了。

☆**实景链接**

A：Are you ready for being a mother? 你做好当母亲的准备了吗？

B：Lately I read so many book and videos about child rearing. 最近我读了很多以及看了很多关于育儿的书。

A：I can't believe it. You have just **stepped up to the plate**. 我无法相信，你竟然已经做了这么多准备。

B：That's essential. 那是必须的。

拓展特色句

1. As his parents you should bring up him to be polite. 作为孩子的父母，你们应该教养孩子懂礼貌。

2. They spend too much money on educating their children. 他们花了很多钱教育孩子。

3. I hope my children get well-rounded education. 我希望我的孩子能受到全方位的教育。

"聊" 美国特色文化

A：Yesterday I talked with one of my colleagues. He is the native here. I was shocked by his educational methods towards his children.

B：Can you illustrate it?

A：He put emphasis on his children's independence. They have their own rooms after infancy.

B：Aren't he worried about dangers his children could fall into?

A：I had the same concern. But he said it's their culture.

B：I just thought the relationship between children and parents is informal. They are more like friends.

A：昨天，我和我的一位同事聊天，他是当地人。我被他教育孩子的方式震住了。

B：你能说得更细点吗？

A：他非常注重自己孩子的独立性。孩子们在婴儿期过后就拥有自己的房间了。

B：他不担心自己的孩子出危险吗？

A：我也有同样的忧虑，但是他说这是他们的文化。

B：以前我只以为孩子跟家长的关系非常随意，他们更加像朋友。

A：这个依情况而定。很多家长会打他们孩子的屁股，让他们知道什么不

A: It depends. Many parents spank their kids to help them learn what "No!" means. Others prefer alternate forms of discipline.

B: It seems their ways of raising children is far away from us.

能做；其他的家长会选择不同形式的教育方式。

B: 看来他们教育孩子的方式跟我们大有不同。

 美国特色文化

美国家长竟然与学校关系如此密切？

美国学校很多地方都值得中国借鉴，尤其是家长对于学校事务的参与。与中国一样，所有的学校几乎都有家长委员会，也就是PTA(Parent-Teacher Association)。美国的家长委员会时常与学校联系，会参与学校的建设和发展、筹款以及参加学校的大型活动等。除了PTA，还有固定的课堂家  长会帮助班主任处理很多杂事。平时家长通过电子邮件与老师和学校联系。另外，每学期开始时有返校之夜，提供家长与老师面对面交流的机会。

阅读笔记

美国人的名字

美国人如何给孩子取名字

Americans choose names for their children with care. Parents usually think about the impression a name gives, not its meaning. Most Americans would consider a "Jennifer" more attractive than a "Bertha," for example. The last name, or *surname*, must also be considered when choosing a first and middle name. A name like Lester Chester Hester would sound *poetic*, but *odd*.

Parents may avoid names that remind them of people they don't like. On the other hand, people might name their children after a *respected* older relative or even a famous person. The popularity of certain names can change with each new generation. Names that were once common, like Fanny or Elmer, sound old-fashioned today. But other names—like John and David, Mary and Sarah—have stood the test of time and continue to be favorites.

美国人会很小心地为孩子取名，父母们通常会考量名字给人的印象，而不是名字本身的意义。比如说大部分的美国人会觉得"詹妮弗"这个名字比"贝莎"更吸引人。在取名字和中间名的时候，也要将姓氏考虑进去。像莱斯特·切斯特·海斯特这样的名字或许听起来很诗意，而且押韵，但这是个很奇怪的名字。

父母们会避免选择能让自己想起不喜欢的人的名字。另一方面，人们会以一位他们敬佩的年长亲戚或是名人的名字来给孩子命名。特定名字的受欢迎程度在每个时代都不尽相同。像是范妮或埃尔默这种曾经相当普遍的名字如今听起来都有些过时，不过像是约翰、大卫、玛丽和莎拉这样名字历久不衰，仍是大家的最爱。

单词释义

surname 绰号　　　　　poetic 诗的　　　　　odd 奇怪的
respected 受尊敬的

如何称呼他人的名字

People in America don't always call their friends and relatives by their given names. Instead, they often use nicknames. Sometimes nicknames are short forms of a longer name. For instance, a girl named Elizabeth may be called Lisa, Beth or Betsy.

In informal settings, people are normally on a first-name basis. Sometimes older *folks* even allow young people to call them by their first name. But in most formal situations, people use an appropriate title—such as Mr., Ms., Dr. or Prof.—with a person's last name. After an introduction, the person may say, for example, "Please call me Tom."

Americans still use a few very formal titles which reflect their Old World heritage. The British address their king and queen as Your Majesty; Americans address the judge in a court as Your Honor. Americans speaking to their nation's leader *respectfully* call him Mr. President. And many churches refer to their leader as Reverend. In everyday situations, the polite forms sir and madam show a measure of respect. But Americans don't generally use the names of *occupations* or positions as formal *titles*. Students might address their teacher as Mr. (or Ms.) Hudson, but not Teacher Hudson.

美国人通常不会直呼亲戚或朋友的名字，而是喊他们的昵称，有时候昵称就是较长名字的简称。例如名为伊丽莎白的女孩可能被叫做丽莎、贝丝或是贝兹。

在非正式的场合，人们通常都是直呼其名。有时候年长的人甚至会让年轻人直呼其名。但是在大多数正式场合，人们会用合适的头衔来称呼他人——比如在姓氏前面加上先生、女士、博士、教授等表示尊称。在自我介绍的时候，可能会有人说，比如，"请叫我汤姆。"

美国人仍然在使用少数非常正式的头衔，反映了他们旧世界的文化遗产。英国人在称呼他们的国王或者王后的时候，会用国王陛下；美国人在法庭上称呼他们的法官时会用法官阁下。美国人在称呼他们国家的领导人的时候，会尊称其为总统先生。很多教堂称呼他们的领导为尊敬的牧师。日常情况下，尊称形式的先生和女士表现了一定程度的尊敬。但是美国人并不会把他们职业的名称或者职位来作为正式场合下的称呼。学生称呼他们的老师为哈德逊先生(或女士)，而并非哈德逊老师。

单词释义

folk 老人　　　　　　respectfully 尊敬地　　occupation 职业
title 头衔

 美国特色文化

特色表达One

　　同中国父母一样，美国人也希望给孩子取个好名字来交好运。此外，knock on wood也可以带来好运。这个说法来自爱尔兰神话，传说在爱尔兰生活着一种善良的小精灵，他们住在树上，当你敲木头时，他们就会赐予你好的运气。所以，当你听见有人说knock on wood时，就表示他在祈祷，希望厄运不要降临。

☆ 实景链接

A：I feel anxious about the result of the exam. 想到考试结果我很紧张。

B：You can **knock on wood**. 你可以敲敲木头带来好运。

A：But I'm still nervous. 但我还是紧张。

B：What you should do is to calm down. 你只需要淡定下来。

特色表达Two

　　父母在给孩子取名的时候，通常需要和亲戚们touch base。Base指垒，一般指棒球比赛中球员用球棒击出球后，立即飞奔前往一垒。美国人常在政坛上使用这个短语，表示与关键人物进行沟通，在日常生活中则用touch all the bases表示跟有关各方作必要的联系。

☆ 实景链接

A：Have you given name to your baby? 你给你们的孩子取好名字了吗？

B：Not yet, I have to touch all the bases. 还没有，我需要和所有亲戚沟通。

A：That's exaggerated. 太夸张了。

B：I had the thought, too. But my relatives like to give me all kinds of suggestions. 我也是这么想，但是我的亲戚喜欢给我各种意见。

拓展特色句

1. Pick a name for our baby. 给我们的孩子取个名字吧。

2. Windy is named after her grandmother. 温蒂这个名字是根据她祖母的名字来取的。

3. The last name is the family name. The first and the middle name is the given name. 最后一个字是姓，第一个和第二个是名字。

聊 美国特色文化

A: Have you given your baby name?

B: I don't have any mentality. Did you have any suggestions?

A: Not really. I have too many names for you to choose from.

B: Then what's your favorite name?

A: I like the name of Coco. It sounds really amiable.

B: In my opinion, that name is much like nicknames. It seems very informal.

A: Then how about Michael?

B: I want a unique name for my son.

A: 你给孩子取名了吗？

B: 我没有任何思路。你有任何建议吗？

A: 也不算是。我有很多名字供你选择。

B: 你最喜欢的名字是哪个？

A: 我喜欢可可这个名字。听起来很亲切。

B: 在我看来，这个名字很像昵称。听起来非常不正式。

A: 你觉得麦克尔这个名字怎么样？

B: 我想给我儿子取一个比较独特的名字。

问 美国特色文化

在美国流行的名字有哪些？

美国的一些常见名字都有其含义，比如"尼古拉斯(Nicholas)"，源自希腊语，表示群众的胜利；"凯文(Kelvin)"来源于爱尔兰，代表繁华的小岛；"艾米(Amy)"来源于拉丁语，是受喜爱的意思。美国人还喜欢给孩子取神话里的名字。另外，在不同时代美国人取名字也有不同趋势。曾经Samantha(萨曼莎)是美国人最喜欢的女孩名字，据说在美国操场大吼一声Samantha，会有一群女生答应。

Part 11

穿越回去看看美国历史

哥伦布身世大揭秘

Christopher Columbus was born in Genoa, Italy, in 1451. His origins were very *humble*—his father was a tavern-keeper and a *weaver*—and so it was due to hard work and *endeavor* alone that he would achieve the riches and *distinctions* of later life. Genoa was a great Italian port, and Columbus grew up surrounded by the sea, ships, and sailors.

Columbus settled in Lisbon, Portugal, in 1477 and married Felipa Perestrello Monizin in 1479. By now he considered himself to be a *veteran* of the seas and had *formulated* his great plan to sail to the Indies by crossing the Atlantic Ocean. He initially met with *frustration* and his plans were rejected several times by the Portuguese, but he finally received royal approval for the *voyages* from Spain in 1492—not before the death of his wife.

克里斯托弗·哥伦布于1451年出生在意大利的热那亚。他出身寒门——他的父亲是一位酒馆掌柜和织布者——所以他晚年所取得的财富和名望都仅仅只是因为他的努力。热那亚是意大利一个很大的港口城市，哥伦布就是在这样一个周遭都是海洋、轮船和水手的环境下长大。

哥伦布1477年定居于葡萄牙的里斯本，1479年和菲丽帕·佩瑞斯特莉罗·莫尼斯结婚。在那之前，他都觉得自己是一个熟悉大海的老手，并构建了穿越大西洋航行到印度群岛的伟大规划。在开始的时候，他不断受挫，他的计划几次遭到葡萄牙人的拒绝，但是最终在1492年的时候，他受到了西班牙航海队的支持——那时他的妻子还没有去世。

单词释义

humble 谦卑的	weaver 织布者	endeavor 努力
distinction 荣誉	veteran 老兵	formulate 规划
frustration 丧气	voyage 航行	

到底有没有发现

Christopher Columbus is famous the world over as the man who "discovered" America. In America, he is widely *revered* as the man responsible for founding the country that exists today. This *assessment* of Columbus does not sit well with many *historians*, however. Modern scholarship questions how it is possible to "discover" a place that is already *inhabited*, and instead speaks of Columbus' "*encounter*," for example. This is a far more apt term, since it *emphasizes* how the "discovery" was *mutual*. The American natives were meeting the Europeans for the first time too, and the term "encounter" better recognizes this.

Secondly, it seems odd to give Columbus such *prominence* in American history when he never set as much as one foot on North American soil. Further, his role in the *exploitation* and *enslavement* of the native population causes many modern *commentators* to *squirm* uneasily. So, does the place of Christopher Columbus in American history need to be re-evaluated?

In order to answer this question it is necessary to look at how Columbus has been perceived by Americans since he first sailed to the New World in the late fifteenth

克里斯托弗·哥伦布因"发现"美洲而世界闻名。在美国，他备受推崇，被尊为建立这个国家的人。但是，许多历史学家对此评价并不认同。现代学者质疑，找到已经有人居住的地方根本不能称之为"发现"，举例来说，其实这可以叫作哥伦布的"偶遇"。这个表达要更为恰当一些，因为它强调了这场"发现"过程中的相互性。美国原住居民也是首次遇到欧洲人，"偶遇"这个词语很好地诠释了这一点。

其次，哥伦布本人从未踏上过北美洲的土地，却在美国历史上享有这样的声誉，真有点不可思议。而且，他还积极地参与剥削和奴役土著居民，这使得许多现代的评论家感到羞愧不安。那么，克里斯托弗·哥伦布在美国历史上的地位是否需要进行重新评估？

要回答这个问题，有必要先看看

| and early sixteenth centuries. Even at the time, there was no consensus on who had been responsible for "discovering" America. | 哥伦布在15世纪末和16世纪初第一次到达新大陆时美洲人对他的看法。即便是在当时，人们也没有一致认为是他"发现"了美洲大陆。 |

单词释义

revere 敬畏	assessment 评估	historian 历史学家
inhabit 栖息	encounter 相遇	emphasize 强调
mutual 互相的	prominence 显著	exploitation 开采
enslavement 奴役	commentator 评论员	squirm 蠕动

 美国特色文化

特色表达One

当初来到美国的欧洲白人，包括很多非洲黑人在内都想shoot for the stars。这里shoot for the stars可不是射击星星，而是用其比喻意义"有远大抱负"。其中stars是星星，shoot for有争取成功的意思，那么shoot for the stars直译为"朝着像距离星星那么远的射程来发射"，即指"发射非常远"，这是一种远大抱负。

☆ 实景链接

A: The first permanent English colony in America was founded in 1607. 英国在美国的第一个永久性殖民地是在1607年建立的。

B: At Jamestown, in the old dominion of Virginia, exactly. 嗯，具体是在弗吉尼亚州旧自治领的詹姆斯敦。

A: When the English came to the American continent they must want to **shoot for the stars.** 当初在英国人踏上美洲大陆的时候，他们一定是想大干一场的。

B: And France, Germany, Holland as well. 还有法国、德国、荷兰。

特色表达Two

当年，发现新大陆的哥伦布，可谓在各方面都成了a stand-out。a stand-out这个短语可不是说一个站出来的人，而是指一个杰出的优秀的人。所以这里的意思是哥伦布发现了新大陆，人们觉得他是一个优秀的人才。

☆ **实景链接**

A：How do you think of Columbus? 你觉得哥伦布这个人怎么样？

B：In my eyes, he is totally **a stand-out**. 在我眼里，他是一位非常优秀的人才。

A：He can achieve such riches and distinctions from a humble background. 他出身贫寒却可以获得这样的财富和声望。

B：His courage to conquer all kinds of challenges is also impressive. 他勇于战胜各种挑战的勇气也令人印象深刻。

拓展特色句

1. The second Monday in October is celebrated as a national holiday, Columbus Day, to honor the European explorer. 10月的第二个星期一是一个举国同庆的日子，哥伦布日，用以纪念这位欧洲探险家。

2. A few settlements were built after Columbus's explorations. 哥伦布的探险之后，建立了几个殖民地。

3. When Columbus returned home, he brought with them some new and useful products. 当哥伦布回家时，他带回去了一些新鲜有用的东西。

"聊" 美国特色文化

A：What is your view of Christopher Columbus?

B：He is a brave voyager who discovered America.

A：Some people said that there were people in America, so we can't say that he "discovered" it.

B：But it requires courage to sail across the ocean.

A：At this point, I agree with you.

B：What's more, he connected America

A：你如何看待克里斯托弗·哥伦布？

B：他是发现了美洲的勇敢的航海家。

A：一些人说美洲本来就有人生活，所以我们不能说是他"发现"的。

B：但漂洋过海需要勇气。

A：在这一点上我同意你的说法。

B：更重要的是，他让美洲与世界上的其他地方联系起来。

A：这是他的伟大功绩，对吗？

B：正是如此。

with other places of the world.

A: That is a great feat of him, right?

B: Exactly.

 美国特色文化

哥伦布发现新大陆是好事吗?

自从哥伦布发现新大陆之后，美国印第安人的文明也遭受了某些程度的毁灭。从长远来看，西半球还为此出现了一些新的国家，他们的行为习惯与曾在该地区定居的各个印第安部落截然不同，这对旧大陆的各个国家都产生了极大的影响。自发现新大陆之后，海外贸易的路线也由地中海转移到了大西洋沿岸。西方也从此终于走出了中世纪的黑暗，开始以不可阻挡之势崛起于世界，并在之后的几个世纪中，成就海上霸业。一种全新的工业文明成为世界经济发展的主流。

阅读笔记

美国移民热

The nineteenth century was a time of *massive* population growth for the United States. In 1800, *slightly* over five million people called America home. By 1900, that number *skyrocketed* to seventy-five million.

A large portion of this *extraordinary* growth can be attributed to European immigrants. Europeans hit America's shores in two different waves: "old" and "new." "Old" immigrants were those who migrated to the United States between the 1820's and 1870's. It was during this time that many Britons, Germans, and those of Scandinavian *descent* crossed the Atlantic and landed in America. These immigrants were typically English speaking, literate, Protestant or Jewish—except for the Irish Catholics—and could *blend* fairly easily into American society. "New" immigrants, however, did not merge into American culture as easily. Instead, they faced a variety of struggles.

19世纪是美国的一个人口急剧增长的时期。1800年，美国有人口略超过500万。到1900年，美国人口飙升到7500万。

美国增长的大部分人口来源于欧洲移民。欧洲人分成"旧"和"新"两波到达美国。"旧"移民者在1820年和1870年间移民到美国。许多英国人、德国人和北欧人就是在此期间横跨大西洋，到达美国的。这批移民通常都说英语，有文化，信仰新教或犹太教，但不信仰爱尔兰天主教，并能轻松地融入美国社会。但是，"新"移民者却并没有那么轻松就融入美国文化，而是面临各种挣扎。

单词释义

massive 大量的　　　　slightly 稍微　　　　skyrocket 飞涨
extraordinary 非凡的　descent 后代　　　　blend 混合

为何会有大波移民者

For "old" Irish immigrants, America was the land of opportunity. Especially in *rural* communities, Irish immigrants were generally welcomed and easily found work. An 1870's book by an Irish-Catholic priest encouraged Irish immigration by explaining to Irish immigrants the ease of obtaining land and traveling in the United States:

German immigrants were similarly encouraged to immigrate to the United States. In his Report on a Journey to the Western States of North America, Prussian lawyer Gottfried Duden detailed the advantages of life in America and described how American life avoided many of the *societal* and political problems that were present in nineteenth century German society. Duden *preached* that America was a *bastion* of cheap and available land, especially in the western states and *territories*. He encouraged Germans to escape the political *chaos* and limited economic opportunities of Germany to start a new, freer life on the American prairie.

对于老一批的爱尔兰移民者，美国对他们来说是一方充满机会的土地。尤其是在农村，爱尔兰移民者普遍都受到欢迎并且轻易能找到工作。1879年，一本由爱尔兰天主教的神父写的书向爱尔兰移民者解释了在美国获得土地的容易以及在美国能够到处旅行，以此来鼓励爱尔兰人移民到美国。

德国的移民者也是这样类似地被劝说移民到了美国。在一份到北美西部各州旅行的游记中，普鲁士的律师戈特弗里·德杜仔细地描述了在美国生活的益处以及美国是如何避免那些在19世纪出现在德国的社会和政治问题的。德杜到处说教，把美国说成是一个充满便宜土地的堡垒，尤其是在西部地区。他鼓励德国人逃离乱政以及工作机遇缺乏的德国，去美国大草原上开始更加自由全新的生活。

单词释义

rural 乡下的　　　　　　societal 社会的　　　　　　preach 说教

bastion 堡垒　　　　　　territory 土地　　　　　　chaos 混乱

"品" 美国特色文化

特色表达One

最早移民来美国的人都成了富翁了吗？其实当时有很多人整天from pillar to post。from pillar to post源于最早的real tennis(室内网球)，当时室内网球馆的四周都立着墙柱子，网球一撞到柱子上就会四处弹跳，网球手为捡球就会在柱子间奔来跑去，由此，from pillar to post常用来形容一个人为寻找某物四处奔波，后引申作为谋生而各地奔跑。

⭐ 实景链接

A：I was just on the phone with Henry and Amy. 我刚刚在和亨利和艾米通电话。

B：They have immigrated to America for ten years and still lead a pretty hard life. Why didn't they come back home? 他们移民到美国已经有10年了，生活还是很艰苦。为什么不回国呢？

A：Maybe they enjoy that kind of life, drifting **from pillar to post**. 可能他们喜欢那种到处漂荡奔波的生活吧。

B：I really can't understand what they think. 真不明白他们是怎么想的。

特色表达Two

最早移民美国的人们肯定想不到如今的美国总统是选出来的，而且有很多的wild cards对大选结果至关重要。这里的card是扑克牌，a wild card是庄家在发牌前认定的百搭牌。所谓"百搭牌"就是可以由持牌人随意决定牌值、代替任何其他的牌。人们用这个wild cards形容事先难以预测、但是却对局势发展至关重要的决定性因素。

⭐ 实景链接

A：It's really hard for the independent to win in the general election. 独立候选人在大选中获胜的机会非常渺茫。

B：But if he can raise money for a big campaign, the chances will be greater. 但是如果他能筹集可观的捐款，那机会就大多了。

A：In that case, he is **a wild card**. 那这样的话，他就有可能获胜了。

B：That's it. 就是这样的。

拓展特色句

1. When did the first immigration wave come to America? 美国的第一批移民潮是什么时候？

2. Most of immigrants seek job opportunities and living place in foreign countries. 很多移民者是在异国寻找工作机会和住的地方。

3. Generally generations after the first wave of immigrants adapted to local culture. 通常第一波移民者的后代都能适应当地的文化。

"聊" 美国特色文化

A: Is America a country of immigrants?

B: Yes. A large portion of the population of America is European immigrants.

A: Do you think it is good to live in America?

B: Sure. I'm yearning for the democratic atmosphere.

A: Have you considered immigrating to America?

B: No. I don't want to leave my hometown.

A: And it is difficult to get a green card.

B: You are absolutely right.

A: 美国是一个移民国家吗？

B: 是的。美国人口的很大一部分都是欧洲移民。

A: 你认为生活在美国好吗？

B: 当然。我很向往民主的氛围。

A: 那你考虑过移民吗？

B: 没有。我不想离开家乡。

A: 而且绿卡也很难拿到。

B: 你说得太对了。

"问" 美国特色文化

为什么大批人移民美国？

美国为了吸引欧洲人移民来促进自己的发展，因此颁布了许多优惠政策，恰巧这个时候正处于第一个世界移民热潮，当时黑奴贸易开始盛行，大量黑人奴隶来到了美洲地区。第二次移民浪潮发生在第二次世界大战期间，当时美国国内的环境比较安定，经济实力也日益增强，这也是吸引欧洲移民的主要原因。第二次世界大战后，美国是唯一的资本主义超级大国。欧洲国家开始唯美马首是瞻，此后美国开始逐渐限制移民，也相应地抬高了移民门槛。

殖民时代

殖民概况

European nations came to the Americas to increase their wealth and *broaden* their influence over world affairs. The Spanish were among the first Europeans to explore the New World and the first to settle in what is now the United States.

By 1650, however, England had established a *dominant* presence on the Atlantic *coast*. The first colony was founded at Jamestown, Virginia, in 1607. The *Pilgrims*, founders of Plymouth, Massachusetts, arrived in 1620. In both Virginia and Massachusetts, the colonists *flourished* with some *assistance* from Native Americans. New World grains such as corn kept the colonists from starving while, in Virginia, *tobacco* provided a valuable cash crop. By the early 1700s *enslaved* Africans made up a growing percentage of the colonial population. By 1770, more than 2 million people lived and worked in Great Britain's 13 North American colonies.

欧洲国家的人到达美洲，力图增加财富和扩大对国际事务的影响力。西班牙人就是第一批探索新世界并在今天的美国定居的殖民者。

但是，到1650年，英国已经统治了美洲大西洋沿岸地带。1607年，第一个殖民地在弗吉尼亚的詹姆斯敦成立。马萨诸塞的普利茅斯殖民地的创建者是英国清教徒，他们于1620年到达美洲。在土著印第安人的帮助下，弗吉尼亚和马萨诸塞的殖民地开始繁荣起来。新世界的玉米等谷物使殖民者们获得食物，尤其弗吉尼亚的烟草具有很高的经济价值。到18世纪初，非洲黑奴在殖民地人口中所占的比例越来越大。到1770年，英国在北美的13个殖民地生活和工作的人口已超过200万人。

单词释义

broaden 扩展	dominant 主导的	coast 海岸
pilgrim 朝圣者	flourish 兴旺	assistance 援助
tobacco 烟草	enslave 束缚	

多个殖民地的建立

By royal charter in 1691, Plymouth Colony and Massachusetts Bay Colony were joined together to form the Massachusetts Colony. Plymouth had created its own form of government through the Mayflower Compact. Massachusetts Bay was created a by a *charter* from King Charles I which accidentally allowed the *colony* to set up their own government. John Winthrop became the *governor* of the colony.

The origins of Virginia began in 1607 with the founding of Jamestown. The Virginia Company, which had been given the charter to found the colony, set up a General Assembly. In 1624, Virginia became a royal colony when the Virginia Company's charter was *revoked*. However, the General Assembly stayed in place which helped set a *model* for *representative* government in this and other colonies.

New Hampshire was created as a *proprietary* colony. The Council for New England gave the charter to Captain John Mason. Puritans from Massachusetts Bay also helped settle the colony. The government included a governor, his advisers, and a representative assembly.

1691年，根据皇家宪章，普利茅斯殖民地和马萨诸塞湾殖民地合并为马萨诸塞殖民地。普利茅斯殖民地当时已通过《五月花号公约》建立了政府。马萨诸塞湾殖民地根据英王查理一世的特许状成立，并碰巧获得了自行建立政府的授权，约翰·温思罗普成为殖民地总督。

弗吉尼亚州源于1607年建立的詹姆斯敦。弗吉尼亚公司根据特许状成立了殖民地，并建立了最高议会。1624年，弗吉尼亚殖民地的特许状遭吊销，于是成为王家殖民地。然而，最高议会依然存在，对弗吉尼亚和其他殖民地代议政府的建立起到了促进作用。

新罕布什尔州建立时只是业主殖民地。新英格兰理事会将特许状授予约翰·梅森上校，马萨诸塞湾殖民地的清教徒也在帮助建立殖民地的过程中发挥了作用。政府机构包括州长、州长顾问及代表大会。

charter 特许   colony 殖民地   governor 省长

revoke 取消   model 模型   representative 代表

proprietary 所有权

"品" 美国特色文化

特色表达One

殖民时代，美国有来自世界各地的商人，他们一遇到英美冲突，基本都会选择站在英国的立场上，而美国自然就被went by the board。这个短语中的board一般指帆船的船舷侧边，所以go by the board原意是把什么从船侧抛到船外去，后来常引申作彻底抛弃某事物。

☆ 实景链接

A： You must feel excited to travel. 要去旅行，你肯定很激动吧！

B： All my careful arrangements **went by the board**. 我的精心安排全部泡汤了。

A： What happened? 发生了什么事情？

B： The trip was cancelled at the last minute by company. 这趟旅程最后一刻被公司取消。

特色表达Two

殖民时代，很多美国人生活艰苦，很多人shoot the works也要反抗英国殖民者。shoot the works源自1920年前后，当时用来指赌博时押上全部赌注，后来引申为某人为做某事不惜一切代价。

☆ 实景链接

A： I am eager to enjoy a big feast, but I am running out money. 我很想吃一顿大餐，但是我的钱不多了。

B： Don't worry. Let's go out to dinner and **shoot the works**. 别担心，不要管太多，我们去吃饭吧。

A： Save some for a cab back. 留下回来的车费。

B： You are so humorous. 你真幽默。

拓展特色句

1. Where and when was the first colony founded? 第一个殖民地是在什么时候什么地方建立的？

2. How many colonies does this nation have? 这个国家一共有多少殖民地？

3. What do you mean by proprietary colony? 业主殖民地是什么意思？

"聊" 美国特色文化

A：Who were the first to settle the America?

B：The Spanish.

A：Is the first colony founded by them?

B：No. The first colony was founded by England in Virginia in 1607. And the Pilgrims founded colony in Massachusetts in 1620.

A：What was the reaction of the Native people?

B：The Native people assisted the Pilgrims and the colonists flourished.

A：How were the developments of the colonies?

B：By 1770, there were 13 Great Britain colonies and more than 2 million people lived there.

A：谁是最早在美国定居的一批人？

B：西班牙人。

A：他们是第一个殖民地的建立者吗？

B：不是。第一个殖民地是英格兰于1607年在弗吉尼亚建立的。而清教徒则于1620年在马萨诸塞州建立了殖民地。

A：土著居民的反应如何？

B：土著居民帮助清教徒，殖民地开始繁荣起来。

A：殖民地的发展情况如何？

B：到1770年已经有13个英国殖民地，并且有超过200万人生活在那里。

"问" 美国特色文化

殖民地时期的美国各地经济发展如何？

在18世纪中期，在英国资本及技术的输入下，属于英国殖民地的北美地区迅速发展。在北部，主要是工商业蓬勃发达；美国中部地广水资源丰富，因此盛产小麦；而南部主要是黑人奴隶打点的种植园，也是一派繁荣。这些都导致了英属北美殖民地生产的很多产品能够在美国当地甚至国际上媲美英国。

独立战争解放黑奴

战争概况

The American Revolution began in 1775 as open *conflict* between the united thirteen *colonies* and Great Britain. By the Treaty of Paris that ended the war in 1783, the colonies had won their independence. While no one event can be pointed to as the actual cause of the *revolution*, the war began as a *disagreement* over the way in which Great Britain treated the colonies *versus* the way the colonies felt they should be treated. Americans felt they deserved all the rights of Englishmen.

The British, on the other hand, felt that the colonies were created to be used in the way that best suited the *crown* and *parliament*. This conflict is *embodied* in one of the *rallying* cries of the American Revolution: No Taxation without Representation.

1775年，美国13个殖民地联合起来与英国公开发生冲突，美国独立战争开始了。根据1783年签署的《美英巴黎条约》，殖民地赢得了独立。尽管美国独立战争不是起源于某一具体的事件，战争的爆发的确是源于英国对待殖民地的态度并没有达到殖民地认为应该获得的对待态度。美国人认为他们理应享有英国人的所有权利。

另一方面，英国觉得建立殖民地就是为了最大程度地满足国王和议会的利益。这种冲突的表现之一就是美国革命的口号：没有代表权就不纳税。

单词释义

conflict 冲突
disagreement 争论
crown 王冠
colony 殖民地
versus 与……相抗
embody 体现
revolution 革命
parliament 议会
rally 集会

战争原因

And many events fed the growing desire of the thirteen colonies for independence. Following are the major events that led to the Revolution.

The French and Indian War (1754—1763) between Britain and France ended with the **victorious** British deeply **in debt** and demanding more **revenue** from the colonies. With the defeat of the French, the colonies became less dependent on Britain for protection.

The Stamp Act (1765) required tax stamps on many items and documents including playing cards, newspapers, and marriage licenses. Prime Minister George Grenville stated that this direct tax was intended for the colonies to pay for defense. Previous taxes **imposed** by Britain had been indirect, or hidden.

To assist the failing British East India Company, the Company was given a **monopoly** to trade tea in America. (The Tea Act—1773)

A group of colonists **disguised** as Indians **dumped** tea overboard from three ships in Boston Harbor. (Boston Tea Party—1773)

British troops were ordered to Lexington and Concord to seize stores of **colonial** gunpowder and to capture Samuel Adams and John

许多事件导致了13个殖民地独立的愿望越来越强烈，以下是引发战争的主要事件。

英国与法国之间的法国印第安人战争（1754—1763）的结果是，英国获胜但深陷债务危机，需要从殖民地获得更多收入；法国战败，殖民地对英国保护的依赖减弱了。

《印花税法案》（1765）规定很多物品和文件包括纸牌、报纸和结婚证都要印花纳税。乔治·格伦维尔首相表示，印花税属于直接税，用于对殖民地的防护。英国以前征收的税为间接税和隐蔽税。

救济已日益衰落的英国东印度公司，允许该公司在美国垄断茶贸易（茶法案，1773）。

一群殖民者居民伪装成印第安人，将三艘船上的茶叶倾倒在波士顿港（波士顿倾茶事件，1773）。

英国军队奉命前往列克星敦和康科德占领殖民地火药库，同时抓捕塞

Hancock. At Lexington, open conflict occurred and eight Americans were killed. At Concord, the British troops were forced to retreat with the loss of 70 men. This was the first instance of open warfare. (Lexington and Concord—1775)

缪尔·亚当斯和约翰·汉考克。在列克星敦，双方爆发公开冲突，8名美国人遇难。在康科德，英国军队损失了70人后，被迫撤退。这是双方第一次公开交火（列克星敦和康科德，1775）。

单词释义

victorious 胜利的　　　　revenue 税收　　　　　impose 强加

monopoly 垄断　　　　　disguise 伪装　　　　　dump 倾倒

colonial 殖民地的　　　　in debt 负债

 ## 美国特色文化

 ### 特色表达One

没有大陆军的toe the line，就没有美国独立战争的胜利。这句话中的toe the line是什么意思？难道要靠大陆军踮起脚尖走在一条线上才能胜利？Toe the line最初源自18世纪。line是指在船的甲板上或阅兵场上画的一条直线，每年新兵集合的时候都必须在直线上列队，这样一来toe the line就有了"服从命令"的含义。

☆ 实景链接

A: Which year the American Revolutionary War ended in? 美国独立战争是在哪一年结束的？

B: In 1783, the *Treaty of Paris* ended the war. 1783年，《巴黎和约》的签订结束了战争。

A: Well, what do you think is the most important factor for their victory? 那你认为他们能取胜的最重要的因素是什么？

B: It relies much on the American soldiers who **toed the line** and fought to their death during the war, I think. 我认为很大程度上是靠美国士兵的严守军纪和拼死作战。

特色表达Two

独立战争时期，英美双方不停地on the warpath。据说这个短语最早来自印第安人的战斗方式，即印第安人踏着warpath怒吼着冲向对面的敌人，而warpath是他们常年行走的小道。后来，on the warpath用来泛指相互争斗，常用在商界与政坛。

☆ 实景链接

A：How will your company solve this case? 你们公司打算如何解决这个案子？

B：We are **on the warpath**, trying to bring an end to the illegal copying. 我们非常生气，打算终止非法的拷贝。

A：You really should star to bring an action against them. 你们确实应该开始给他们点颜色看看了。

B：I quite agree with you. 我非常同意。

拓展特色句

1. The war of American independence could be described as a civil war. 美国独立战争可以被描述为内战。

2. The American independence war was the first case in which colonies successfully won independence through fighting. 美国独立战争是第一例殖民地通过自己的斗争赢得了独立。

3. The American independence war was the war between America and Great Britain. 美国独立战争是美国和英国之间的战争。

"聊" 美国特色文化

A：When did the American Revolution begin?

B：It began in 1775.

A：What led to the outbreak of the war?

B：The Americans are not satisfied with the way the Great Britain treated them.

A：美国独立战争是什么时候发生的？

B：独立战争是1775年开始的。

A：是什么导致了战争的爆发？

B：美国人不满英国人对待他们的方式。

A：他们采取了何种行动？

B：殖民地寻求独立，他们的口号是

A：What actions did they take?

B：The colonies were seeking independence and "No Taxation without Representation" is their slogan.

A：What is the result of the war?

B：The British were deeply in debt and the colonies became dependent.

"没有代表权就不纳税"。

A：战争的结果怎么样?

B：英国人的债务加重了，而殖民地得到了独立。

 **美国特色文化**

美国独立战争有什么意义?

　　美国独立战争是世界历史上第一次大规模的殖民地争取民族独立的战争，它的胜利，给大英帝国的殖民体系打开了一个缺口，为殖民地民族解放战争树立了范例。独立战争又是一次资产阶级革命，它推翻了英国的殖民统治，创造了世界上第一个总统制共和制国家：美利坚合众国，从而解放了生产力，为美国资本主义的发展开辟了宽广的道路。正如列宁所说："现代的文明的美国的历史，是由一次伟大的、真正解放的、真正革命的战争开始的。"

阅读笔记

经济危机

危机概况

Great Depression, in U.S. history, the severe economic crisis generally considered to have been *precipitated* by the U.S. stock-market *crash* of 1929. Although it shared the basic characteristics of other such crises, the Great Depression was *unprecedented* in its length and in the wholesale poverty and tragedy it *inflicted* on society. Economists have disagreed over its causes, but certain *causative* factors are generally accepted.

The *prosperity* of the 1920s was unevenly *distributed* among the various parts of the American economy—farmers and unskilled workers were notably *excluded*—with the result that the nation's productive *capacity* was greater than its capacity to consume. In addition, the *tariff* and war-debt policies of the Republican *administrations* of the 1920s had cut down the foreign market for American goods. Finally, easy-money policies led to an *inordinate* expansion of credit and installment buying and fantastic speculation in the stock market.

美国历史上的大萧条是一次严重的经济危机，起因通常认为是1929年的美国股市崩盘。尽管此次大萧条具有其他此类经济危机的基本特征，但大萧条在持续时间和大面积地造成贫困和不幸方面，是史无前例的。经济学家对大萧条的起因尚有争议，但是某些诱发因素是普遍认可的。

20世纪20年代的经济繁荣在美国社会中的分配不均匀——农民和非技术类工人不能享受繁荣的果实——造成的后果是国家的生产能力大于其消费能力。加之，20世纪20年代共和党政府关税及战债政策减少了美国商品的海外市场。最后，宽松的货币政策造成了过度的信贷扩张和分期购买以及股票市场不可思议的投机行为。

单词释义

precipitated 沉淀的	crash 破产	unprecedented 空前的
inflict 使遭受	causative 成为原因的	prosperity 繁荣
distribute 分布	exclude 排除	capacity 能力
tariff 关税	administration 管理	inordinate 过度的

危机的影响及原因

The American depression produced *severe* effects abroad, especially in Europe, where many countries had not fully recovered from the aftermath of World War I.

In Germany, the economic disaster and resulting social *dislocation* contributed to the rise of Adolf Hitler.

In the United States, at the depth (1932—1933) of the depression, there were 16 million unemployed—about one third of the available labor force. The *gross* national product declined from the 1929 figure of $103,828,000,000 to $55,760,000,000 in 1933, and in two years more than 5,000 banks failed.

As a social *consequence* of the depression, the birthrate fell *precipitously*, for the first time in American history falling below the *replacement* rate. The economic, agricultural, and relief policies of the New Deal administration under President Franklin Delano Roosevelt did a great deal to *mitigate* the effects of the *depression* and, most

美国的大萧条在国外产生了严重的影响，特别是在欧洲，许多国家甚至都没有从第一次世界大战的创伤中完全恢复过来。

在德国，经济灾难带来了社会的混乱，最终导致了阿道夫·希特勒的崛起。

在美国，在大萧条最严重的时候（1932—1933），1600万人（约可用劳动力的1/3）失业。国民生产总值从1929年的1038亿2800万美元下降到1933年的557亿6000万美元，两年内有5000多家银行破产。

大萧条带来的社会后果是，人口出生率急剧下降到低于人口替换率，这在美国历史上还是首次。富兰克林·德拉

importantly, to *restore* a sense of confidence to the American people. Yet it is generally agreed that complete business recovery was not achieved and unemployment ended until the early 1940s, when as a result of World War II the government began to spend heavily for defense.

诺·罗斯福总统的新政采取的经济、农业以及救助政策大大减轻了大萧条的负面影响，最重要的是，它让美国人民恢复了信心。然而，普遍认为，商业完全回复和失业的结束直到20世纪40年代才实现，因为第二次世界大战使政府开始急剧加大国防预算。

单词释义

severe 严重的	dislocation 混乱	gross 总额
consequence 结果	precipitously 陡峭地	replacement 替换
mitigate 缓和	depression 萧条	restore 恢复

 美国特色文化

 特色表达One

美国经济危机期间，工厂不景气，很多老板都期待着员工out of the picture，他们甚至会感谢上帝道"Thank God the old man is out of the picture at last！"这句话的意思是谢天谢地，这个老头终于走了。out of the picture原指某人不在相片里，在俚语里指某人不再参与某行动了。

☆ 实景链接

A：Have you seen foreman today? 你今天看见工头了吗？

B：You don't know that he has been transferred to another department? 你不知道他已经被调到其他部门了吗？

A：Really?! Thank God the old man is **out of the picture** at last! 真的吗？！谢天谢地，那个老头终于走了！

B：Yeah, we are going to hold a little party to celebrate tonight. Come and join us. 是啊，我们今晚打算开个小聚会庆祝一下，你也跟我们一起吧。

 **特色表达Two**

经济危机时期，仅靠罗斯福一人就能想出好办法吗？当然还得倚仗那些Kitchen Cabinet。Kitchen Cabinet源于1832年，据说当时厨房是整个房子里布置最随意的地方，所以主人家常赏同熟人在厨房聊天。据传说，总统会边打扑克边和他的私人顾问们聚会商议。Kitchen Cabinet就是总统的私人顾问团。

☆ **实景链接**

A: I always wonder how president can think out of the strategies to solve so many complicated problems. 我经常好奇总统是如何想出那么多解决复杂问题的方案的。

B: It's not all his efforts. He has his **kitchen cabinet.** 这并非全是他的功劳，他有自己的智囊团。

A: Are they an official group? 他们是官方的团体吗？

B: Not yet, they are unofficial. 不是的，他们是非官方的。

拓展特色句

1. The economic crisis engulfed the entire capitalist world. 经济危机席卷了整个资本主义世界。

2. How did the economic crisis break out? 经济危机是如何爆发的？

3. How much losses did this financial crisis suffer? 这场经济危机遭受了多少损失？

"聊" **美国特色文化**

A: What is the cause of the Great Depression?

B: It is said to be the U.S. stock-market crash of 1929.

A: What was the financial situation at that time?

B: The prosperity of the 1920s was unevenly distributed. And the

A: 大萧条的起因是什么？

B: 据说是因为美国股市1929年的崩溃。

A: 当时的财政状况如何？

B: 20世纪20年代的经济繁荣没有得到平均的分配。且国家的消费水平无法跟上生产水平。

A: 大萧条是否产生了严重的影响？

B: 它的严重影响甚至波及了其他国

nation's capacity to consume legged behind its productive capacity.

A: Did the Great Depression produce severe influence?

B: Its severe influence even effected abroad, especially in Europe.

A: What about its social consequence?

B: The birthrate fell below the replacement rate for the first time.

家，尤其是在欧洲。

A: 在社会方面造成了何种后果?

B: 出生率首次下降到低于人口更替率。

 美国特色文化

爆发经济危机的原因?

资本主义经济危机的根本原因在于资本主义制度本身，是生产的社会化与资本主义私人占有形式之间的矛盾。经济危机早在简单商品生产中就已经存在，这同货币作为流通手段和支付手段之间是相互联系的。但是，只有在资本主义生产方式占统治地位以后，危机的可能性才具有现实性。随着简单商品经济的矛盾——私人劳动与社会劳动之间的矛盾发展成为资本主义的基本矛盾，就使经济危机的发生不可避免的了。

阅读笔记

罗斯福新政帮"脱困"

新政到来

The Great Depression was the largest and most significant economic depression to affect not only America but also the world. The Stock Market Crash on October 29, 1929 is cited as the beginning of the Great Depression. Herbert Hoover was president when the Crash occurred but felt that the government should not become *overly* involved in helping *individuals* dealing with economic troubles. However, this changed with the *election* of Franklin Roosevelt. He worked to create numerous programs through his New Deal to help those affected worst by the Depression.

The New Deal, introduced by F D Roosevelt was to *transform* America's economy which had been *shattered* by the Wall Street Crash. The economic *downturn* that followed the Wall Street Crash also had a major *psychological* impact on America.

大萧条是最大和影响最深远的经济危机，不仅危及了美国而且影响到了世界。1929年10月29日的股市崩盘被认为大萧条的开端。当时的美国是总统赫伯特·胡佛，但他认为政府不应过分参与个人对经济问题的处理。然而，富兰克林·罗斯福当选为总统后，政府的态度改变了。他通过新政努力创造了很多项目，来帮助那些受大萧条影响最严重的人。

富兰克林·德拉诺·罗斯福采取新政的目的是扭转已被华尔街崩盘破坏的美国经济。华尔街崩盘后的经济衰退也给美国带来了巨大的心理创伤。

单词释义

overly 过度地　　　　individual 个人　　　　election 选举
transform 变形　　　　shatter 碎片　　　　downturn 衰退
psychological 心理的

总统的那些年

Franklin Roosevelt grew up in a wealthy family and often traveled *overseas* with his parents. His *privileged upbringing* included meeting Grover Cleveland at the White House when he was five. He was cousins with Theodore Roosevelt. He grew up with private tutors before attending Groton (1896—1900). He attended Harvard (1900—1904) where he was an average student. He then went to Columbia Law School (1904—1907), passed the bar, and decided not to stay on to graduate.

Franklin Roosevelt was admitted to the bar in 1907 and practiced law before running for the New York State Senate. In 1913, he was appointed Assistant Secretary of the Navy. He then ran for Vice President with James M. Cox in 1920 against Warren Harding. When defeated he went back to practicing law. He was elected Governor of New York from 1929—1933.

Roosevelt spent 12 years in office and had an *enormous* impact on America. He *took office* in the depths of the Great Depression. He immediately called Congress to special session and *declared* a four-day banking holiday. The first "Hundred Days" of Roosevelt's term were marked by the passage of 15 major laws.

富兰克林·罗斯福在富裕的家庭里长大，经常和父母去往海外。他成长的背景优越，5岁时曾在白宫见到了当时的美国总统格罗弗·克利夫兰，与第26任美国总统西奥多·罗斯福是堂兄弟。私人导师陪伴他长大，从1896年到1900年，罗斯福在格罗顿中学上学。他大学在哈佛大学（1900—1904），但只是个普通的学生。后来他又去哥伦比亚大学法学院（1904—1907），通过了司法考试，于是决定不等毕业，直接离开。

1907年，富兰克林·罗斯福进入司法系统，担任律师直到后来竞选纽约州参议员。1913年，他被任命为海军助理部长。1920年，他作为副总统和詹姆斯·M·考克斯搭档与沃伦·哈定竞选。竞选失败后他继续回去当律师。他后来当选为纽约州州长，任期从1929年到1933年。

罗斯福执政12年，对美国产生了巨大影响。他在大萧条最严重的背景下就任总统，立即召集国会召开特别会议，给银行放假4天。罗斯福政府的前100天主要通过了15部法律。

单词释义

overseas 在海外

privileged 享有特权的

upbringing 教养

enormous 巨大的

declare 宣布

take office 就职

"品"美国特色文化

特色表达One

经济危机期间，很多人一夜倾家荡产，不得不搬去the wrong side of the tracks。可是身无分文与铁路的另一边有什么联系呢？据说，在美国最早选定在城市中心修建铁路，于是修好的铁路就将城市分成两半，一半是富人区，另一半则是贫民窟了。所以the wrong side of the tracks就是贫民窟。

☆ 实景链接

A：Who's the guy over there? 那边那个家伙是谁？

B：His name is Chris and comes from the **wrong side of the tracks**. 他叫克里斯，来自贫民窟。

A：But he doesn't look like that way. 但看着不像啊。

B：He was born in a rich family but his father's company bankrupted during the financial crisis. So... 他原本出生在一个富裕家庭，但他父亲的公司在经济危机期间破产了，所以……

特色表达Two

在罗斯福新政开始时，很多人都不看好这个改革，但还是有人与他fall into line，希望罗斯福拯救当时的美国。fall into line有点像是军官喊立正时战士们都站好，其实在日常生活中，美国人常使用这个短语的引申意义，即立场一致，步调一致。

☆ 实景链接

A：Are you for or against the manager's idea? 你是否同意经理的想法？

B：I totally **fell in line** with him. What about you? 我完全同意。你呢？

A：I have divergence of views. He doesn't take the climate changes into consideration. 我的意见有分歧。他没有把季节变化这个因素考虑进去。

B: But these factors have little influence on the effects. 但是我觉得这些因素对效果没有什么影响。

拓展特色句

1. President Franklin Roosevelt implemented the so called "New Deal" to pull the United States out of the great depression. 罗斯福总统实行所谓的"新政"是为了将美国从大萧条中拯救出来。

2. The New Deal produced the social-security system and created jobs for struggling workers. 新政实行了社会保障以及为工人创造了工作。

3. The government sold off the property to individuals and investors. 政府把财产卖给个人和投资者。

"聊" 美国特色文化

A: How do people speak of the President Franklin Roosevelt?

B: People advocated him when he took up the post of the 32nd President of America.

A: Why did people advocate him?

B: Because he put forward the New Deal.

A: What is the significance of the New Deal?

B: It was helpful to those who were affected by the Great Depression.

A: Did it help the recovery of America's economy?

B: Yes. It relieved the Economic crisis and the social contradictions caused by the Great Depression.

A: 人们如何看待富兰克林·罗斯福总统?

B: 当他出任美国第32任总统时，受到了人们的拥护。

A: 人们为什么拥护他?

B: 因为他提出了新政。

A: 新政的意义是什么?

B: 新政帮助了那些受到大萧条严重影响的人们。

A: 它帮助了美国经济的复苏吗?

B: 是的。它大缓解了大萧条带来的经济危机与社会矛盾。

美国特色文化

罗斯福新政的社会影响是什么？

罗斯福新政在一定程度上调整了资本主义生产关系，缓和了社会矛盾，使美国从经济危机中走了出来，并对其他国家也产生了示范效应。此后，国家开始干预和调控经济，美国经济逐渐走出低谷，这一点缓和了美国的社会矛盾，避免在危机形势下走上法西斯道路。开创了国家干预经

济发展的新模式，使资本主义告别"自由放任"政策占统治地位的时代，迎来国家垄断资本主义时期。

阅读笔记

图书在版编目（CIP）数据

每天聊点美国文化：一本书读懂美国／金利主
编.北京：化学工业出版社，2014.5（2024.5重印）
ISBN 978-7-122-20211-6

Ⅰ.①每… Ⅱ.①金… Ⅲ.①文化-美国-通俗读物
Ⅳ.①G171.2-49

中国版本国书馆CIP数据核字（2014）第063063号

责任编辑：马　骄　　　　　　　　　　　　责任校对：战河红
装帧设计：尹琳琳

出版发行：化学工业出版社（北京市东城区青年湖南街13号　邮政编码100011）
印　　装：涿州市殷润文化传播有限公司
710mm×1000mm　1/16　印张25　字数400千字
2024年5月北京第1版第9次印刷

购书咨询：010-64518888
售后服务：010-64518899
网　　址：http://www.cip.com.cn
凡购买本书，如有缺损质量问题，本社销售中心负责调换。

定　　价：58.00元　　　　　　　　　　　　版权所有　　违者必究